ALSO BY ROBERT P. BROADWATER
AND FROM McFARLAND

American Generals of the Revolutionary War:
A Biographical Dictionary (2007)

Civil War Medal of Honor Recipients:
A Complete Illustrated Record (2007)

Chickamauga, Andersonville, Fort Sumter and
Guard Duty at Home: Four Civil War Diaries
by Pennsylvania Soldiers (2006)

The Battle of Olustee, 1864:
The Final Union Attempt to Seize Florida (2006)

The Battle of Perryville, 1862:
Culmination of the Failed Kentucky Campaign (2005)

Did Lincoln and the Republican Party Create the Civil War?

An Argument

ROBERT P. BROADWATER

McFarland & Company, Inc., Publishers
Jefferson, North Carolina, and London

LIBRARY OF CONGRESS CATALOGUING-IN-PUBLICATION DATA

Broadwater, Robert P., 1958–
 Did Lincoln and the Republican Party create the Civil War? :
an argument / Robert P. Broadwater.
  p. cm.
 Includes bibliographical references and index.

 ISBN 978-0-7864-3361-2
 softcover : 50# alkaline paper

 1. United States— History— Civil War, 1861–1865 — Causes.
 2. Lincoln, Abraham, 1809–1865 — Political and social views.
 3. Republican Party (U.S. : 1854–)— History —19th century.
 4. United States— Politics and government —1845–1861.
 5. United States— Politics and government —1861–1865.
 6. United States— Politics and government —1865–1883. I. Title.
 E459.B79   2008
 973.7'1—dc22   2008022972

British Library cataloguing data are available

On the cover: Abraham Lincoln and Fort Sumter (Library of Congress)

Manufactured in the United States of America

McFarland & Company, Inc., Publishers
 Box 611, Jefferson, North Carolina 28640
 www.mcfarlandpub.com

To Lyssa
with appreciation,
admiration, and affection

Table of Contents

Preface

Most historians and buffs of the American Civil War, when asked to state the cause of the conflict, will readily respond that the conflagration was fought for one of three reasons: slavery, to save the Union, or states' rights. Indeed, these have been the overriding issues that have come to define the four years of sectional strife that cost the nation more than 600,000 lives, while bringing one portion of the country under the military rule of another.

History is more than subjective, it is emotional, and it serves as the tie that binds peoples and nations to a common heritage. For the true historian, however, it is important to separate the emotion from the facts in order to achieve an accurate interpretation of the events which have carried us to the place in time where we all now exist. Every so often, we must reevaluate our own history to cull the legend and myth from the reality. In order to do this, we must question what we have learned, and what we have been told, refusing to accept history at face value. Many years ago, I had an experience that happens to historians all too frequently that exemplifies this principle. I had written a book titled *Of Men and Muskets* which was a collection of stories about various leaders of the war. In collecting these stories, I had come across one that dealt with Confederate General Patrick Cleburne. As the story went, Cleburne, at the Battle of Franklin, had witnessed one of his men leaving bloody footprints in the snow because he lacked shoes. Moved by the scene, the general had given the soldier his boots, remounted his horse, and led the fateful charge that cost him his life shoeless. This story was to be found in a number of soldier histories written in the decades immediately following the war, and, in fact, was so often encountered that its accuracy was little questioned by the author. During the editing process, all of the stories included in the book were checked and double-checked to ensure they were correct, and it was found that the story about Cleburne was a complete fabrication. The general was wearing his boots at the time of his death, and they were among the possessions of the Carter House Museum at Franklin. The story had been started, obviously by an admirer, and had been repeated over and over again until it had become "fact" to men who were then writing their recollections of the war. Regrettably, this is an all too

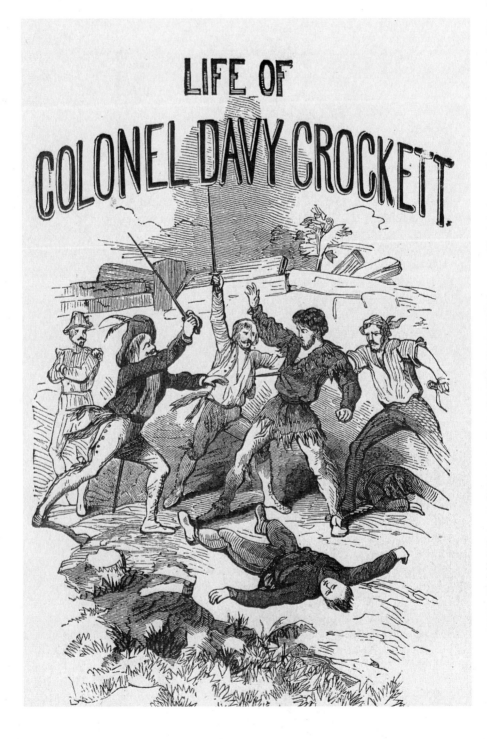

common occurrence in history. Generations of Americans have grown up with the legend of the Alamo and Davy Crockett, and have been told about the gallant last stand made by the Tennessee hero during the final phases of the battle. We have seen him depicted on the big screen, in several movies, mounting the last gasp of resistance to the onslaught of General Santa Anna's relentless horde. In more recent times, many historians have come to question the manner of Crockett's demise, due to the appearance of archival and other sources that refute the standard tale of his last moments. Evidence strongly suggests that Davy Crockett survived the assault on the Alamo and was captured by the Mexicans, to be executed after the fall of the mission. The image of John Wayne as Crockett blowing up the powder room and taking a number of the enemy with him is likely about as accurate as any other representation of Crockett's death popularized for more than one hundred years after the event — that is to say, not at all.

A few years ago, while on a trip to the Perryville battlefield, I stopped to visit a Civil War museum in Bardstown, Kentucky. Among an impressive collection of displays, I found one about Johnny Clem, or "Johnny Shiloh," as he was referred to. Most of us are very familiar with this boy-hero of the Civil War, and remember the stories of his heroism on the fields of Shiloh and Chickamauga. Walt Disney even made a feature-length movie about him back in the 1960s that showed how, after having his drum shattered by enemy fire, he picked up a musket and fought the rest of the Battle of Shiloh as a soldier. The truth is that John Lincoln Clem was never at Shiloh, and never claimed to have been there. He was a member of the 22nd Michigan Infantry, a unit that was not mustered into the service until August of 1862, four months after the Battle of Shiloh. Johnny did not join the unit himself until May of 1863, over a year after Shiloh had been fought. How could a historical discrepancy like this go unnoticed? Clem had become a national hero due to his boyhood heroics on the field of Chickamauga, and in 1872, a Baltimore newspaper writer by the name of W.W. Carter wrote a glamorized article about him for his paper. Carter later forwarded a copy of the article to President Ulysses S. Grant, asking that it be included in Clem's military file at the War Department. Carter had exaggerated Clem's service and contributions, but Grant forwarded the document, with his endorsement, and the article became a part of Clem's official

Opposite: Artist's depiction of the death of Davy Crockett at the Alamo. Most historians now credit archival information that asserts that Crockett was not killed during the battle, but was captured and later executed. (From *Life of David Crockett, the Original Humorist and Irrepressible Backwoodsman Comprising His Early History; His Bear Hunting and Other Adventures, His Services in the Creek War; His Electioneering Speeches and Career in Congress; with His Triumphal Tour Through the Northern States, and Services in the Texan War, to Which Is Added an Account of His Glorious Death at the Alamo While Fighting in Defense of Texan Independence*, John E Potter and Company, Philadelphia, Pa., n.d.).

record, without anyone ever checking the validity of the information it contained. Many decades later, when Disney was doing research for his movie, Clem's official record was examined, and due to the fact that it was an official military file, all of the information contained was assumed to be correct, when it was, in fact, largely a collection of fallacies and exaggerations.

The three preceding examples are but a sampling of myths and legends that have crept into our history books, our national heritage, and our popular culture, and have become accepted as truth. They are presented here to give the reader a foundation, a starting point, if you will, from which we can begin our discussion with an open and questioning mind. The single most cited cause given for the Civil War is that of slavery. To be sure, the question of slavery had been a moral, social, and political division between the two sections of the country for decades preceding the outbreak of the war. The issue had led to open violence in Kansas and Missouri, and had been the basis for John Brown's abortive raid on Harpers Ferry, Virginia, and his dream of establishing a new republic in the Appalachian Mountains. Slavery had polarized public opinion, both North and South, and had become the line of demarcation between the two regions. But if, as many historians allege, slavery was the driving reason for the war, I would submit the following questions: 1. Why did the Emancipation Proclamation free no one? 2. Why was slavery allowed to continue in the District of Columbia until 1863? 3. Why was slavery allowed to exist in border states until is was abolished by Constitutional amendment after the war? 4. Why were slaves in portions of Southern states under Federal control forced to continue in the slave labor system, with the crops they raised being seized by the Federal government? 5. Why did enlistments in the North fall to critical levels, necessitating the ever-increasing bounty system, following the Emancipation Proclamation's going into effect in January of 1863? 6. Why were there more slaveholding officers in the Northern army than there were in the Southern army? 7. Why would men opposed to the institution, such as Robert E. Lee and Thomas "Stonewall" Jackson, fight a war if it was founded on the principle of perpetuating that institution?

How can historians dismiss these facts and continue to cling to the supposition that the Civil War was fought solely over slavery? In light of the historical record, it would seem absurd to do so, yet this doctrine has been forwarded by many in the Civil War community for decades. In the pages of this book, these questions, and many more, will be examined, in an effort to dispel the myths and determine the true historic foundations of the causes and prosecution of the Civil War. We will view the role played by Abraham Lincoln, and the Republican Party, in furthering the hostilities that led to open warfare. We will also address how the war, and its aftermath, benefited the Republicans, and raise questions as to the political motivations the party had in implementing its wartime policies and strategies. In the end, I think the reader will walk away with an entirely different conception of the Civil War,

Abraham Lincoln, and the Republican Party. At the very least, it should cause readers to question information they have previously accepted, and if this objective is realized, then the purpose of the book will be considered a success.

Over the course of decades of reading and researching, I frequently came across information concerning the war that did not conform to that found in most of the popular, conventional histories. Though easy enough to find if one takes the time to dig for it, information contradictory to the mainstream, widely accepted versions of the war, and of the Republican Party, were to be found primarily in magazines and periodicals. Books like *A Review of the Political Conflict in America from the Commencement of Anti-Slavery Agitation to the Close of Reconstruction* (1876) and *The Unwritten South: Cause Progress and Result of the Civil War–Relics of Hidden Truth After Forty Years* (1903) were somewhat rare offerings in the book market. Herndon's Lincoln was an exception among the hundreds of books that eulogized Abraham Lincoln, altering the facts, when necessary, to create the image of the 16th President as the perfect leader, Christian, and man. As such, Herndon's biography was largely dismissed by the public, and was almost a complete marketing failure. Much has been written about the Lost Cause propaganda that defined the South in the decades after the war, but I noticed that no one stopped to consider that the same sort of posturing had been taking place in the historical accounts of the war that emanated from Northern writers and publishing houses. Books such as those previously mentioned sparked my interest in seeking out similar information, and to question some of the commonly held beliefs concerning the causes of the war, and the way in which it was pursued by the Federal government. Over the past decade, it would seem that a number of other historians have come forward to dispute the credibility of some of the history we have all been indoctrinated with since before the turn of the twentieth century. As we approach the milestone 200th anniversary of Abraham Lincoln's birth, there seems to be an effort to get the story right, to correct many of the inaccuracies that have become a part of our national heritage. Articles like "Uncovering the Real Abe Lincoln," appearing in *Time Magazine* in 2005, and "Martyr Under the Microscope," which ran in *America's Civil War* in 2006, display a no-nonsense approach to Lincoln and the Republican Party that would not have been well received in previous decades. Historians are going beyond Herndon and questioning much of what they thought they knew, and the resulting shift in the historical record is one that I feel will be continued for decades to come. In compiling this work, I have utilized the perspectives of a number of Lincoln contemporaries and historians, from Colonel Alexander McClure and Orville Browning to Carl Sandberg and J.G. Randall. The end result presents a different portrayal of Lincoln and the party he represented than the general public is accustomed to reading, but it is one that I hope gives a more balanced history of the man, the party, and the period. For many people much of the material in this book would be something of a revelation. Even those tidbits that may be familiar to readers often surface as isolated pieces of trivia, and have never been brought together in one place to tell the other side of the story and to give readers an opportunity to make up their own minds after being given all of the facts.

Introduction

The American Civil War has traditionally been felt to be the result of sectional differences arising out of the institution of slavery in the South. In fact, if you ask people, they will usually state slavery as being the primary cause of the war. This reasoning is, and always was, far too simplistic an explanation, but it came to be the umbrella which encompassed all of the other differences between the two sections of the country, and has been handed down in popular literature about the war for generations, until it has become ingrained in society's perception of the war. There is an old saying among historians that if you repeat a fallacy three times, it becomes a fact. Such is the case with the umbrella treatment of slavery as the root cause of the Civil War. It has been repeated time and time again, until it became virtually etched in stone, as it were, and was taken for granted as a matter of fact. To state otherwise, especially among Civil War enthusiasts, would be controversial to the majority, and heresy to a large number. But such is indeed the case. The Civil War was not fought over the institution of slavery. It was not a holy war to set men free, to eliminate the bondage of slavery from this nation. I would ask the reader, if this were the case, why then did slavery still exist in Washington, D.C., for over a year after the start of the war? Why did slavery continue to be practiced in all of the border states that remained in the Union until after the war was ended? Why did the Emancipation Proclamation, that vaunted and revered document of liberty, actually free no one? Why were freed slaves, in Southern states, forced to continue to labor as slaves, with the fruit of their toil being confiscated as contraband by the Federal government? The reason for these, and a number of other troubling questions, is that the war never was fought over the issue of slavery. It was not the cause or the root of the conflagration. It was used, in a veiled attempt to attach honor and legitimacy, by the Republican Party to evoke patriotic ardor at home, and to dissuade foreign intervention from abroad.

The true cause of the war is one that is as old as civilization itself: the power to rule. The Republican Party, a relative newcomer to national politics, had, by a twist of fate, secured the election of Abraham Lincoln to the presidency, in only its second presidential election. The Democratic Party had become split, and had divided into three factions, each nominating its own candidate for the election. Lincoln won the executive office with a decided minority of the popular vote, and his presidency promised to be one of limited power or influence. The Republicans had won the White House, but they could not exert control over the national government so long as the Democratic Party maintained a majority of the voters in the land. The Republican Party had made all of its inroads in the North, where the platforms of the various components of the party appealed to Northern factory workers and small farmers. The South remained overwhelmingly Democratic in its politics, adherents to the old Jeffersonian ideals of state's rights and self-determination. It became apparent to the Republicans, right from the beginning, that even with the presidency, they could exert no great influence over national politics unless the hold of the Democrats was broken. The most expeditious manner to accomplish this was to eliminate the solid Democratic bloc that was the South. The sectional crisis that erupted with the election of Lincoln, and the secession of South Carolina, could have been avoided through mediation and diplomacy, but the Administration opted against such a course. Vowing to "save the Union," the Republicans did everything in their power to dissolve the confederation and split the nation. When Stephen Douglas offered his name and influence to the Lincoln administration in an effort to quell Southern fears, he was summarily dismissed and informed that his assistance was neither needed nor desired. When Senator Crittendon of Kentucky proposed a compromise that would have averted a division of the country, he was shouted down in the halls of Congress. His compromise was not even allowed to be brought to a vote. When the senator attempted to take his compromise to the people, to allow the voters to decide for themselves, the rallies became the scenes of violence, as Republican thugs disrupted them in the same bullying manner used by union busters half a century later. No efforts of conciliation were allowed to be undertaken by the Republican Party, and to the Democrats of the South, this constituted proof that they had much to fear from this new and radical party.

The South was manipulated by the Republicans into firing on the flag of the United States, in an effort to gain the support of the masses in the North. Most people, North or South, had agreed with the Constitutional right of the Southern states to leave the Union. The prevailing sentiment in the North was to let the Southern dissenters go in peace. The firing on Fort Sumter changed all that. Northerners, who were previously willing to let the South go its own way, were outraged by the perceived insult of armed aggression against their nation's flag. Just as with Pearl Harbor nearly a century later, a nation that had previously been opposed to war mobilized overnight to defend its national honor.

Once the conflict had begun, the most pressing business of the Lincoln administration was to raise a sufficient army, and to secure the border states.

The administration dispensed generals' commissions liberally to regional leaders in order to receive the support of their constituents, regardless of the individuals' abilities to command. In this way, large numbers of Irish and German immigrants were mustered into the army. More importantly, large numbers of Northern Democrats were enlisted into the fold. Northern Democratic politicians such as Benjamin Butler and John McClernand were commissioned to be generals, and Democratic officers like George B. McClellan experienced a meteoric rise in rank and responsibility. For a period of time, the designations of Republican and Democrat even ceased to be used, as Northerners were bound together in what was referred to as the Union Party. The Republican moves made it unpatriotic not to support the war against the South, and the presence of so many prominent Northern Democrats in positions of high stature in the army ensured that the rank and file of the Northern citizenry would flock to the Union banner. The Republicans now had the military might they would need to wage a war against the South. They would later deal with the Democratic leaders who had helped to make that army possible.

The situation in the border states proved to be more complicated, especially in Kentucky, where the citizens proclaimed neutrality, unwilling to choose sides in the impending struggle. In Maryland and Missouri, the administration settled the issue by the use of military force. Ben Butler, the newly commissioned brigadier general, was sent to Maryland to secure the state for the Union, and to ensure that its duly elected state legislature did not vote for secession. In a bold move, the military arrested all members of the Maryland legislature who were thought to be Southern sympathizers. These representatives were imprisoned at Fort McHenry, the Old Capitol Prison, and other locations, for periods up to two years, without being tried or even accused of a particular crime. Butler's actions were taken under the direction of the administration, and President Lincoln promptly proclaimed that the writ of habeas corpus, one of the foundations of American freedom, was being suspended in all of these political cases as a necessary war measure. The administration continued to use this suspension, in cases of political intrigue, throughout the early days of the war, despite the fact that the Supreme Court of the United States found the practice to be unconstitutional.

In the case of Missouri, General John Frémont, the Republican Party's first presidential candidate in 1856, was sent to maintain order and keep the state for the Union. Frémont took the liberty of declaring martial law in the state and used strong-arm tactics to disarm potential enemies and force Southern supporters out of the state government. Frémont, assisted by Nathaniel Lyons and Franz Sigel, enlisted the support of the vast German population of St. Louis to raise his army and ride roughshod over the majority of the citizens, who favored alliance with the Confederacy. In the end, Frémont was able to force the Southern sympathizers out of the major metropolitan areas, to a region in the southwest portion of the state. The fate of Missouri would be a bone of contention for the next few years, but the military regime Frémont had established there in 1861 made it possible for the state to be held in the Union by the administration, against the will of the majority of its people.

The seizure of Kentucky proved to be a more difficult proposition. The people of the state, though largely Southern in their sympathies, were rigidly adhering to their declared neutrality, and being watchful lest either side encroach upon it. Both contending governments realized that a wrong step on their part would drive the state into the arms of the enemy. The struggle to seize Kentucky was fought in the shadows of politics, as the Confederates were maneuvered into violating Kentucky's neutrality, giving the North the premise of sending an army into the state to protect it from Southern encroachment. By sheer force, or by political maneuvering, the Lincoln administration accomplished its goal of keeping a tight grip on the border states, without which it could not have hoped to win the war.

During the first year of the war, the Union armies experienced a shortage of success in the field, leading to discontent among the voters at home. Indeed, the Union armies had been thrashed on numerous occasions, particularly in the East, where media coverage was at its most thorough. In the summer of 1862, popular sentiment in the North was running strongly against Lincoln's war policies, and a cry for change was beginning to take hold. Democrats who had aligned themselves with the Union Party now broke free to campaign against the current administration, and the Democratic Party in the North threatened to sweep the fall Congressional elections and end the war, with or without victory in the field. Democratic efforts to take back the national government were thwarted by several actions taken by Lincoln and his supporters, as well as some plain old luck for the Republicans. The Battle of Antietam, a draw that resulted in the withdrawal of the Confederate army back to Virginia, was hailed as a stunning victory, proof that Northern arms could prevail in the struggle. Pennsylvania Governor Andrew Curtin called for a conference of the loyal Northern governors at Altoona, Pennsylvania, during which he and his allies maneuvered those in attendance into public support of Lincoln and his war policies, making it political suicide for any of them to later turn against the president. Lastly, Lincoln issued the Emancipation Proclamation, in an effort to dissuade foreign intervention and to polarize opinion at home. The effect of these three events served to take some of the steam out of the Northern Democrats, but they were still a force to be reckoned with in the November elections. Not willing to leave anything to chance, Northern Republicans endeavored to ensure that their balance of power in the Federal government would not be weakened. Charges of election tampering were leveled at the administration, and there are recorded instances in several states where elections were canceled when a Democrat was winning. There are even charges that some of those Democratic candidates were then banished to Confederate lines.

With the government now securely in the hands of the Republicans, the time had come to rid the army of its Democratic leadership. Over the course of the last few years of the war, a large number of high-ranking Union officers with a prominent affiliation to the Democratic Party found themselves disgraced and out of the army. Most of these men had been used to induce their Democratic constituents to enlist in the army. Now, they were expendable. In fact, they had become a liability. For a political party, seeking to gain control of the national government, it would not do to have military heroes and potential political opponents arising from the high command of the Union army. From George B. McClellan to Don Carlos Buell, Fitz Porter, John McClernand, Ben Butler, and many more, the Union army was systematically purged of the Democratic influence that had served to create it in the first place. But removing the high-ranking Democrats was not enough. The government went a step further to assure that these men could not rise from the ashes to gain political prominence by performing character assassinations on all of them, publicly citing their alleged incompetence to command in the Republican-run newspapers of the North. In the end, a few of these officers were able to clear their names and set the record straight, but for most, their reputations and contributions were besmirched for future generations. An examination of the historical record will quickly show that the majority of these prejudices still exist today among historians of the period.

Prominent members of the U.S. Congress also did their part to strengthen the Republican grip on the government. The Committee on the Conduct of the War became one of the most feared bureaus of sanction in all of American history, on a scale not to be seen again until almost a century later in the days of the McCarthy "Red Scare." The Committee on the Conduct of the War furthered the platforms of the Republican Party through a system of political witch-hunting that was quite effective in securing the compliance of even its political foes. The power of the Committee was such that even being called before that body could damage an officer's reputation, and a rebuke from the Committee could end a career. With radical Republicans like Ben Wade at the helm, the Committee on the Conduct of the War became a Republican terror weapon the like of which had rarely, if ever, been seen before in America.

Disillusion over the success of the war, combined with outrage over the Federal government's draft policy, led to open conflict in the Northern home front as citizens attempted to express their dissatisfaction with an unpopular war and an unpopular government. In the streets of New York City, the coalfields of eastern Pennsylvania, and numerous other places, open revolt became the order of the day. In most cases, Union troops were necessary to put down the protests. The strong-armed tactics of the government led to many of the movements going underground, as was the case for the Knights of the Golden Circle, a Northern organization pledged to bring about the overthrow of the existing Federal government.

During this time, Clement Vallandigham stepped forward to become the leading spokesman for the opposition and the Democratic Party. Democrats, as well as members of other parties, who had become disillusioned with the Republican leadership were quick to support Vallandigham, and he soon became a threat to the stability of the Republican status quo. The government proclaimed Vallandigham to be a traitor, and derisively attached the name of Copperhead to the opposition movement. The threat posed by Vallandigham and his followers was finally eliminated when the leader was arrested by Federal authorities and banished to Confederate-held territory.

Military intervention, and the banishment of Vallandigham, served to thwart those in opposition to Lincoln and the Republicans in their efforts to become organized. It did not, however, stop them from voicing their displeasure, or calling for change. In many cases, those of the opposition relied on the most basic of American principles to mount their attack upon the Republicans: the freedom of speech. Democratic newspapers across the North lashed out with discordant editorials in an effort to effect change. The administration responded by undertaking a campaign to purge the North of dissenters and quiet their voice in national politics. All across the North, offices of newspapers that showed themselves to be in opposition to the Republicans were destroyed, and their editors arrested. Midnight raids by both civil and military authorities became the norm, as the administration mounted a campaign of terror designed to eliminate its opponents. Private citizens were imprisoned for no other reason than that they openly and honestly disagreed with the government. Lincoln had reverted to the practice he used when the legislatures of the Maryland Assembly were arrested by suspending the writ of habeas corpus, and most were incarcerated without the benefit of any formal charges against them. Lincoln had avowed that the sacred duty of his government was to protect the Union and the Constitution, but he openly trampled upon that document anytime it interfered with the political agenda of the Republican Party.

The 1864 presidential election was the most closely contested in the nation's history. George B. McClellan, the former commander of the Army of the Potomac, and one of the recipients of the Republicans' wrath when they purged the army of high-ranking Democrats, was very popular with vast numbers of the Northern electorate. In fact, political polls showed that he was leading Lincoln and would probably defeat the incumbent president at the ballot box. In most popular histories of the war, it is widely acknowledged that the soldier vote made the difference in the election, securing victory for Lincoln and the Republicans. What is not commonly written in the popular histories is that the Republicans found a way to manipulate the ballot box with those same soldier votes. The 1864 election caused Democrats, in and out of the army, to cry foul at the manner in which the election was conducted. Many Democrats charged that soldiers who were permitted to go home and vote were carefully chosen men from districts known to be heavily Republican in their affiliations. Those from Democratic strongholds were reported to be denied the opportunity of casting their ballots for their party's candidate, and were forced to remain at the front. The charge of election fraud was made in all parts of the nation, but no investigation was ever mounted.

The end of the war brought a whole new set of problems for the Republicans to consider. With the Southern states now part of the Union again, Republicans were once more facing a minority status that could have excluded them from prominence in national affairs. This threat was met by different means. Disenfranchisement of ex–Confederate officials and officers not only prevented them from voting, it also precluded them from holding any public office, decimating Southern leadership. The North then established a balance of power through the Freedman's Bureau, by giving Southern blacks the vote and assimilating them into Republican politics. The newly freed slaves were enticed with the promises of "forty acres and a mule" which were to be given to all, and were then reminded that it was the Republicans who were responsible not only for giving them a new life, but for destroying slavery in the first place. Blacks were quickly mobilized into a voting bloc that ensured Republican dominance in the reconstructed Southern states, the effects of which led to a period of Republican control of the government that was to last for over thirty years. Democrats were not able to mount any serious opposition to the Republicans until they began to woo black voters away from that party, breaking the voting bloc the Republicans had established.

The story of the Civil War is one of gallantry, devotion to cause and country, and personal sacrifice on a level never before seen in this nation. It is also the story of political intrigue and manipulation in the name of power and control on a scale that has also never before been seen in this country. Both snapshots of the war are correct, but only the former has received the attention of most historians of the period. It is the purpose of this book to explore and expose the latter, so that students of the period may have a better understanding of all of the events that combined to create the most critical period of the history of the United States: the Civil War.

All of the information contained in this work is to be found in the public record of the war. There are no new and earth-shaking discoveries contained here in that are being examined for the first time. Indeed, the material presented in this book has been largely ignored by historians for almost a century and a half. Certainly, it has never been brought together in one work to present a case for political intrigue in the instigation and prosecution of the war. The reader may ponder how this could be so. Why, with the thousands and thousands of books written about the Civil War, would this topic never be undertaken? The answer to that question is possibly the last remaining vestige of the campaign for power levied by the Republican Party in the 1860s: One of the spoils of war is that the victor gets to write the histories. The North won. The Republican Party was in charge of the government at the time of the victory. Lincoln was assassinated, immediately becoming a martyr, above the reach of critics or detractors. The South experienced a period of military occupation and reconstruction for twelve years following the end of the war, during which time Northern, or Republican, versions of the war were promulgated and those of a Southern bent were repressed. A legacy was created, passed from generation to generation, and became accepted as fact. This book will attempt to cut through the legend and legacy to uncover the truth, to set the record straight, and to open new avenues of discussion about the most studied and written-about period of our nation's history.

This book will focus but little on the military aspects of the war, as the prime intention of this work is to show the political maneuvering that both brought about the conflict and furthered its prosecution through to final victory. The military actions of the war will be examined only so far as they pertain to the civil and political actions that were taking place behind the scenes of the battlefields.

I hope that you will enjoy this book. May it give you a new perspective of the period, and of the major actors in a defining chapter of America.

CHAPTER ONE

Birth of the Republican Party

The Republican Party was a relative newcomer to the American political landscape when it ran its second presidential candidate, Abraham Lincoln, in the election of 1860. Indeed, the party had been formed only six years before, in the Northwest, as part of a grassroots effort to oppose the spread of slavery into the new territories. During the decades that preceded the war, a delicate balance had been maintained in the Federal government between the Democratic and Whig Parties, as each attempted to prevent the other from securing dominance for its particular section of the country. American politics had become a series of compromises, with conciliation being the prime tactic employed in affairs of state. The disintegration of the Whig Party had left the Democrats in control of Federal affairs, and threatened to shift the balance of power in favor of the Democrats' strongest base, the South. The Kansas-Nebraska Act of 1850 served to polarize the nation, North and South, over the question of the expansion of slavery into the western territories. A number of opposition parties arose or strengthened in response to this circumstance, including the American (or Know-Nothing) Party, the Free-Soilers, and the Republicans. The exact date of the formation of the Republican Party is open to debate. It is certain that its formation took place during the summer of 1854 in the Old Northwest, with Ripon, Wisconsin, and Jackson, Michigan, both claiming the honor of being its birthplace. The political agenda of the new party was, at first, extremely limited: to prevent the western expansion of slavery. It was the belief of these founders that the capitalistic society of the North could not survive if it had to compete with the institution of slavery, and the unfair advantages this labor resource afforded to the South. For the most part, the first members of the Republican Party were the displaced and disaffected members of the disappearing Whig Party.[1]

In order to understand the Republicans and the Republican Party, it is important to trace its heritage beyond the Whig Party. The Whigs had been in existence for only a few decades at the time of their demise. The party had been formed following the dissolution of the Federalist Party in the early 1820s, and its members championed many of the same causes and ideals as had its pred-

Birthplace of the Republican Party, in Ripon, Wisconsin (during a later-years celebration). Many members claim the party was officially begun in this structure in 1854 (Military History Institute, United States Army War College).

ecessor. The Federalist Party had been formed by politicians strongly supporting the ratification of the newly penned Constitution. Their name was adopted from the title of the book written by Alexander Hamilton, James Madison, and John Jay, *The Federalist Papers*, which was intended to sway popular opinion in favor of ratification of the Constitution. Hamilton became a leading force within the Federalists, who supported a strong centralized government, expansion of industry, and attention to the needs of the merchant class. Its membership was made up of Northern large landowners, wealthy merchants, and captains of industry, the aristocracy of the North. The Federalists sought to establish a well-ordered society within the new nation.

This last statement of a "well-ordered" society bears further examination. In foreign policy, Federalists aligned themselves with Great Britain. Though they had just fought a war for their independence, many favored a monarchy to a democratic form of government. The leader of the party, Alexander Hamilton, had, following the end of the Revolution, attempted to convince George Washington to become the first king of America. Hamilton had little faith in the ability of the common masses to govern themselves. He felt the people needed a strong ruler, chosen from among the educated and enlightened wealthy aristocracy of the nation.

The Democratic Party had been formed in opposition to the Federalists and their quest for a stronger central government. At first, they were called the Anti-Federalists. The name was then changed to the Democratic Republicans, and finally they became known simply as Democrats. Thomas Jefferson became the standard bearer for the Democrats, as the party fought for the right of self-government for the common man.

To the Federalists, the South had an unfair advantage in the affairs of the national government, as men like Jefferson, Madison, and Monroe, all Virginians, rose to the presidency. Feeling their influence in national politics threatened by what they perceived to be a Southern bloc, and in protest of the war of 1812, leading members of the party called the Hartford Convention in 1814 to discuss the proposal that the New England states leave the Union. From December 15, 1814, to January 4, 1815, the delegates from the various New England states met in secret deliberations to discuss severing ties with the Union. In the end, moderates within the party prevailed, and the possibility of disunion was averted. Instead, the assemblage drafted a number of governmental reforms to be forwarded to Washington. The Treaty of Ghent, which ended the war, combined with Andrew Jackson's victory at New Orleans, served to make the demands of the convention a moot point, and signaled the beginning of the end for the Federalist Party. It is indeed curious that a party founded in the belief of strong central government would be the leading proponent of states' rights, but such was the case with the Federalists at the Hartford Convention, as the leaders of New England sought to redress their grievances with the Union by invoking their right to separate from that Union.

When the Whig Party arose as the primary opposition to the Democrats, its ranks were filled with disaffected Federalists. The passion for a strong centralized government, and the abiding suspicion that the masses were not capable of governing themselves, were therefore passed from the Federalist Party to the Whigs. Upon the dissolution of the Whig Party, the majority of its former members aligned themselves with the new Republican Party, taking their sentiments of strong central control with them.[2]

In order to understand the division and distrust between the Democrats and the Federalists/Whigs/Republicans, it is necessary to examine some of the history between them that led to each faction believing that the other was out to break up the Union and destroy the compact that the thirteen original states had entered into for mutual benefit. The parties in opposition to the Democrats feared their perceived control over national affairs, which, by policy, hurt the merchant and manufacturing classes of the North. Northern business interests felt continually under siege from a government that did little to protect their enterprises, and even less to help them grow and flourish. To many in the North, the Jeffersonian Democrats were subjugating them to a political system that was not in their best interests, and they viewed the current situation to be little better than it had been when they were colonies of the Crown.

In fact, many Northeasterners wondered if they had not made a mistake in breaking with England. In 1809, dissatisfaction with the Federal government led some New England Federalists to open talks with the British government.

In February of that year, Governor Craig, the royal governor of Canada, sent an emissary to Boston with the instructions: "I request you to proceed with the earliest convenience to Boston. The known intelligence and ability of several of its leading men must give it considerable influence over the other States and will probably lead them in the part they are to take. It had been supposed that if the Federalists of the Eastern States should be successful and obtain the decided influence which may enable them to direct public opinion, it is not impossible that rather than submit they will exert their influence to bring about a separation from the general Union. I enclose a credential, but you must not use it unless you are satisfied it will lead to more confidential communication."

The scheme was uncovered, leading James Madison to take the matter before Congress. "I lay before you copies of certain documents which remain in the Department of the State. They prove that at a recent period, on the part of the British Government through its public minister here, a secret agent of that government was employed in certain States in fomenting disaffection to the constitutional authorities of the country; and intrigued with the disaffected for the purpose of bringing about resistance to the laws, and eventually in concert with a British force of destroying the Union and forming the eastern part thereof into a political connection with Great Britain."

The British agent reported that he found the Federalist leaders quite agreeable to severing with the Union. The sentiment of the masses was another story, as the majority of the commoners of the Northeast strongly supported the Constitution and the Federal government. The agent further stated that it would be an impossibility to further the scheme unless some sectional domestic issue could be raised that could serve to drive a wedge between the two parts of the country. He suggested that slavery become the sectional difference that the Federalists target in order to create this rift and stir the passions of the people. This policy was adopted, and its first opportunity for national implementation came in 1820 with the Missouri Compromise, slavery being its issue of contention.

In a letter to the Marquis de Lafayette, Thomas Jefferson stated his opinion of what was going on in Washington: "On the eclipse of Federation with us, but not its extinction, its leaders have set up the false front of lessening the measure of slavery by the Missouri question, but with the real view of producing a geographical division of parties which might insure them the next President." The Federalists knew they could not alter the Constitution to manage the matter of citizenship, through the Alien and Sedition Acts, but showed their disposition to break the solemn compact contained in the Constitution. As the two parties existed at the time of the framing of the Constitution, and were honorably bound to defend it as construed at the time, any attempt to distort it to their sectional advantage meant treason and false dealing. The Alien and Sedition Acts, the Hartford Convention, secret dealings with the British government, and the dividing of the country into sections over the issue of slavery caused Democrats to hold the opposing party with apprehension and disdain.

Over the next three decades, the divisive issue of slavery was raised in a series of compromises, culminating with the Kansas-Nebraska Act of 1850, which led to open hostilities and bloodshed. The Democratic Party viewed the Federalists and their heirs, the Whigs and Republicans, as a threat to their very freedom as well as to the national government, and fought to maintain a balance in national affairs. The Republicans saw the Democrats as an obstacle to establishing the form of government that favored Northern interests and economics. It was in this inflamed environment and with this heritage of political ideology that the Republican Party was formed.[3]

Hatred of the Kansas-Nebraska Act, and the open hostilities in Kansas, had been stoked by the writing of a Maine woman, who sought to relate the evils of slavery to the nation in her book, *Uncle Tom's Cabin, or Life Among the Lowly*. Harriet Beecher Stowe wrote the novel in 1852, depicting the cruel and dehumanized existence of slaves in the South. Stowe had only spent one weekend in a slave state, and had not personally witnessed any of the atrocities she wrote about. Her novel was an exaggerated and inflamed look at life in the

South, but it met with immediate acceptance all over the North, selling more than 300,000 copies in the first year after its release. More than one and one half million were sold worldwide during that same period. For many Northerners, it was their first introduction to the "peculiar institution," and the effects were staggering. Almost overnight, the North was filled with abolitionists. They overlooked the fact that the main villain in the book, Simon Legree, was a New Englander, and focused only upon the piteous plight of the slaves as written in the pages of the novel. Southerners were aghast at what they felt to be a slanderous representation of their way of life, and Southern writers responded by writing some thirty novels to refute Stowe's book. But the die was cast. Northerners had already made up their minds, and the Southern offerings found little market outside of their own section of the country. Always a point of contention, slavery became a symbol of division following the publication of

Harriet Beecher Stowe. Her book, *Uncle Tom's Cabin*, became one of the most widely read books of the 19th cetury, and though she had barely ever been in the South, her depiction of slavery helped to mold public opinion in the North against the institution (Military History Institute, United States Army War College).

UNCLE
TOM'S CABIN.

BY

HARRIET BEECHER STOWE.

WITH

Twenty-seven Illustrations on Wood

BY

GEORGE CRUIKSHANK, ESQ.

EVA AND TOPSY.

LONDON:
JOHN CASSELL, LUDGATE HILL.

1852.

Uncle Tom's Cabin. Bloody Kansas only served to convince many Northerners that Southerners were a barbaric race intent on spreading their vile form of life throughout the nation.[4]

During the early days its existence, the Know-Nothing Party was the main Northern competitor with the Republicans for anti–Democratic voters. The Know-Nothings, or American Party, began as a secret fraternal society, and acquired their popular name because of the tendency of its members to refuse to answer any probing questions about the organization by stating that they didn't know the answers. The main political focus of the Know-Nothings was not slavery. Instead, the party was a nativist group, pledged to restrict the impact and rights of the immigrants who were constantly flooding into the ports of Boston, Philadelphia, and New York. As the majority of the immigrants were Irish Catholics, the secondary goal of the Know-Nothings was to stem the growth and influence of the Catholic Church in America.[5] An anonymous party member wrote in 1855, "That the dangers to which our nation is exposed are not visionary, is manifest from acknowledged corruptions in our political system, and also from the efforts of foreign governments to fill our land with their paupers and criminals." He went on to describe the bulk of Irish immigrants as "British Criminals," stating that the British government was encouraging them to emigrate to America, in the process ridding itself of the unwanted malcontents of its shores. The writer avowed that "criminals from Botany Bay would be more valuable and more welcome visitors than the shoals of Irish who are annually turned out upon those [American] shores." He also deals with the struggle for religious supremacy, pronouncing "veiled efforts made, to create a train of influences which might gradually weaken and ultimately destroy the Protestant element in our country. This could only be accomplished by a variety of means, and these used clandestinely. Our nation being a complete amalgam of the leading nations of the earth, the Jesuitical maxim, 'divide and conquer,' could play with more hope of success than where such circumstances did not favor. One great object was therefore to adopt such a line of policy as to create of the Catholics, an 'imperium in imperio,' and to sow as much dissension as possible among the remainder of the citizens."[6] The Know-Nothing Party was founded on the principle of "America for Americans," and sought to consolidate political power in the hands of native-born, Protestant citizens. As such, it was among the most bigoted and narrow-minded of any political party ever formed in the country.

To the Free-Soilers, the driving issue of the day was the western expansion of the territories, and the free distribution of western lands to settlement and development. Free-Soilers sought to expand the social and economic ben-

Opposite: Title page from Uncle Tom's Cabin, by Harret Beecher Stowe. A worldwide bestseller, this book brought the sectional differences of the North and South to the forefront and became the Bible of the abolitionist movement.

efits of a capitalistic culture, and the settlement of free western lands seemed the most viable political option to accomplish this agenda.

While the main focus of the contending opposition parties was widely divergent, each group contained among its membership an antislavery element. In 1856, John Brown helped to bring the antislavery factions in each party to the forefront, and to sound the destruction of both the Know-Nothings and the Free-Soilers. During that year, the struggle for the control of Kansas took center stage in national politics. The territory, inhabited largely by antislavery adherents, was attempting to request admittance to the Union as a free state. Proslavery Democrats, trying to maintain a balance of power in the Federal government, sought to alter the vote concerning the status of Kansas as a free state or slave state by flooding the territory with thousands of proslavery constituents from nearby Missouri, in an effort to have them illegally vote in the election. Violence broke out almost immediately between the two factions as both sides poured men and arms into the territory.

John Brown was among those who rushed to the territory in support of the antislavery faction. Brown saw himself as fighting a holy crusade, and he and his small band of followers dispensed their own brand of justice in dealing with the proslavery supporters. By 1856, Brown had settled in Osawatomie, Kansas, with his four sons and had become a captain in the emergency force organized by the local free-state citizens for the defense of Lawrence. Up to the time of Brown's arrival, there had been few killings in Kansas, but on the night of May 24–25, 1856, that would change. In retaliation for a proslavery raid on Lawrence, Brown and his followers attacked the cabins of proslavery families along Pottawatomie Creek. Five men, all connected with the proslavery district court at Dutch Henry's Crossing, were similarly executed, and their gashed and mutilated bodies left as a warning to all slave-state men. Professor James C. Malin, a leading student of Brown's life, contends that the Pottawatomie massacre was "political assassination, not merely private murder." In any event, Republican newspapers repressed the story of the massacre, Congress glossed over the incident during its investigation, and neither Brown nor any member of his party was ever arrested for or charged with the crime.

Brown's actions touched off a wave of bloodshed known as "Bloody Kansas." Within a short time of his attack at Pottawatomie Creek, proslavery supporters responded by attacking Brown's settlement at Osawatomie. Both sides sustained losses, including the death of Brown's son, Frederick. Brown and his supporters were forced to abandon Osawatomie, which was burned to the ground by the proslavery men. Shortly after this, John Brown left Kansas for the East, leaving behind a state already engrossed in civil war.[7]

Sectional violence was not confined to the territory of Kansas. It found expression even in the hallowed halls of Congress. Over the course of May 19 and 20, 1856, Senator Charles Sumner of Massachusetts delivered a scathing speech, titled "The Crime Against Kansas," in which Sumner decried the violence in the territory. He also took the opportunity to launch personal attacks against South Carolina and Andrew Pickens Butler, an absent senator from that state. One Michigan member of the Senate stated that Sumner's speech was "unpatriotic" and "un–American" and hoped he would "never hear again" such a diatribe. Congressman James S. Brooks, a fellow South Carolinian and relative of Butler, took upon himself the matter of calling Sumner to task for the statements he had made concerning Butler and his native state. On May 22, Brooks walked into the Senate chamber following the adjournment of that body, walked up to Sumner, and announced that he had come to punish him for the slanders he had committed against an aged and absent relative. He then proceeded to strike Sumner on the head repeatedly with his cane. Though Brooks stated that he only intended to whip Sumner, not to hurt him, it was more than three years before Sumner was able to return to his seat in the Senate. The incident inflamed many in the North as it was widely reported in Republican newspapers. It also served to sway many undecided Northerners against the Southern Democrats and the proslavery faction, both of whom were portrayed as barbarians.[8]

Violence in Kansas and in the halls of Congress served to overshadow the platforms and agendas of all of the opposition parties in the North. Through the extension of slavery into the territories, the South was seen as trying to seize complete control of the national government. Since the South was solidly Democratic in its politics, the Democratic Party became viewed by many in the North as a usurper, heightening the sectional differences that already existed. The violence in Kansas forced many in the North to choose sides, even if that choice meant that they would have to become submissive in the prosecution of their own political agendas. Defectors from the Know-Nothing and Free-Soiler Parties began to align themselves with the Republicans. Over the course of the next four years, the Republican Party would absorb the vast majority of the membership of the other two parties, as the Republicans became the leading antagonist to the Democratic Party.

The year 1856 also witnessed the Republican Party nominate its first candidate for the presidency, John C. "Pathfinder" Frémont. In Frémont, the party seems to have found a perfect candidate to bind together its various factions. A renowned army officer and frontiersman, Frémont was an acknowledged American hero, and possessed of a well-known name. The party next attempted to portray him as a man of the people, a commoner who had risen above adversity to become a leader of men. This would be the first such marketing of a Republican presidential candidate. It would be refined and perfected four years later, when Abraham Lincoln rode his log-cabin, rail-splitting image to the White House. A political biography of Frémont, written in 1856 to influence the election, portrayed the candidate thus:

John Charles Frémont was the heir of poverty. His inheritance, however, was the richest of all legacies—"a sound mind in a sound body." The love and care of a widowed mother, and the responsibility, as the eldest of the group, attendant upon the protection and maintenance of an orphaned brother and sister, were the chief means of his early discipline. Though destitute of the adventitious aide of wealth or influential connections, his own sterling qualities were more than compensation. He possessed, in an eminent degree, what alone constitutes the basis of true greatness, and of certain and continuous success—vigorous powers of mind and body, entire self-reliance, and persevering application to wisely chosen pursuits.

That he should have risen from a position so humble, by the unaided influence of his own powers, to one so conspicuous as that which he now occupies, is at once a gratifying tribute to his genius and worth, and an example full of encouragement to American youth.

In the first great civil contest between freedom and slavery, he has been selected as the standard-bearer of the former. From among the scores of experienced, talented, and noble men, he, the youngest, and in some respects the least experienced of them all, has been selected, not rashly and in haste, not by excited and inconsiderate men, but by one of the largest, most talented, august, and deliberate political bodies that ever convened in this country.[9]

Major General John C. Frémont. The first presidential candidate of the Republican Party in the 1856 election, Frémont would also be the first to issue an emancipation proclamation for the slaves, though it was rescinded by the Lincon administration (Military History Institute, United States Army War College).

To even the casual reader, the comparisons between Frémont and Lincoln are readily evident. Frémont's humble beginnings, the early loss of a parent, the responsibility for younger siblings, the self-made success, and the wise and intelligent bearing are all qualities that would surface again in the person of Abraham Lincoln in the

1860 election. With this marketing campaign, the party sought to distance itself from the polished, professional political aristocracy that many in the North considered to be the perpetrators of the current national difficulties. Incumbents were portrayed as being members of the privileged portion of society — wealthy and aristocratic, and out of touch with the issues affecting the common man. Republicans sought to harness the common masses of the North into a voting bloc by convincing the labor class of the North's farms and factories that they could only be represented by one of their own. Hence the birth of the hardscrabble candidate, the self-made leader, in Republican politics. It was a theme that would be repeated over and over again in presidential campaigns for the next three decades. Ulysses S. Grant's inability to earn a living before the war actually became an attribute in the story of how he fulfilled his destiny of leadership during the war. James A. Garfield's log-cabin heritage, and the early loss of his father, also became a foundation of his election campaign.

Frémont was but the first of the many man-of-the-people candidates offered up by the Republican Party. His primary opposition came from the Democratic candidate, James Buchanan of Pennsylvania. Buchanan had defeated incumbent President Franklin Pierce's bid for reelection, acquiring his party's nomination. John C. Breckinridge of Kentucky was selected to be Buchanan's running mate. The Know-Nothing Party selected ex–President Millard Fillmore of New York to carry its banner. Andrew J. Donelson of Tennessee was chosen as the vice presidential candidate. Officially hailing from California, Frémont was at an immediate disadvantage. The West did not yet wield the political clout that it would in later generations, and California was not yet a "must-win" state in national elections. In an effort to tether East to West, William L. Dayton of New Jersey was selected as Frémont's running mate.

The issues of the campaign on the Republican side came down to a simple desire to curtail the further expansion of slavery into the new territories. Democrats labeled the Republicans to be radicals, and warned that the election of a Republican president

James Buchanan. The Democratic president from Pennsylvania who was in office during the period when the states of the deep South seceded and formed the Confederacy (Military History Institute, United States Army War College).

would lead to civil war. They proposed to leave the question of slave or free to the individual states, citing that it was the right of the residents of any territory to decide for themselves what course to follow when they applied for statehood. The Know-Nothing Party completely ignored the issue, choosing instead to concentrate its efforts on restricting the flow of immigrants into the country, and limiting the influence of those who had already come. The Know-Nothings proved to be a powerful third-party force, winning almost twenty-five percent of the popular vote, and effectively deciding the election in favor of the Democrats by cutting into the voter base that otherwise might have voted for the Republican ticket. The Democrats were responsible, in large measure, for the impressive showing of the Know-Nothings. They had spread a false rumor that Frémont was a Catholic, which caused many people who otherwise might have voted for Frémont to vote for Fillmore. None of the candidates did any "stump" campaigning, or made many personal appearances to meet the voters. Instead, the electorate was introduced to the candidates through the use of print media. One example of this is *The Life of Col. John Charles Frémont, and His Narrative of Explorations and Adventures in Kansas, Nebraska, Oregon and California*, a book written to extol Frémont's virtues and give voters the party platforms upon which he was running. With a slogan of "Free Speech, Free Press, Free Soil, Free Men, Frémont and Victory!," the Republicans portrayed the campaign as being a struggle to reestablish the republican values upon which the nation had been founded. It was largely an election of contending ideologies, rather than a contest of personal charisma or polish. Predictably, the Republican Party did well in the North and Old Northwest, where it had established its roots. Just as predictably, Republicans garnered little support in the South. In fact, Frémont received fewer than 600 total votes from all the slave states combined, and the vast majority of those came from Maryland and Delaware.

In the end, Frémont came up short, capturing only 32 percent of the popular vote, and 114 electoral votes. He was able to carry eleven states: Maine, Vermont, New Hampshire, Massachusetts, Rhode Island, Connecticut, New York, Ohio, Michigan, Wisconsin, and Iowa. Though they received over 20 percent of the popular vote, Fillmore and the Know-Nothings secured only eight electoral votes by winning Maryland. Buchanan carried the rest of the country, nineteen states, and won 174 electoral votes in the process. The Democrats did well in the North, largely because of voter fear that a Republican victory would result in the Democrats' making good on their threat to secede. Though unsuccessful in its bid for the presidency, the Republican Party had made a good showing in its first great struggle on the national stage. The Democrats had won the White House, but Republicans had managed to get a large number of members elected to Congress. Over the next four years the fight for control of the national government would begin in earnest.

Between 1856 and 1860, the Republican Party began to show the effects of the various components from which it was formed, as it broke into three different and distinct segments: the conservatives, the moderates, and the radicals. Conservatives favored gradual emancipation, combined with colonization, or exportation abroad, of the free blacks. Moderates favored emancipation, but with reservations. The radicals were for immediate and unconditional emancipation. Antislavery Democrats usually fell under the category of conservatives. Former Whigs, Free-Soilers, and Know-Nothings tended to align themselves with the moderates. Abolitionists were the driving force of the radical faction. Though they were by far the smallest group in the party, the radicals made up for their small numbers by being the most active and vocal of the three groups. The radicals were also able to secure a number of important positions in the government, which served to accentuate their importance. Among their most prominent members were Galusha Grow, Thaddeus Stevens, Owen Lovejoy, Joshua Giddings, George Julian, Charles Sumner, Henry Wilson, John Hale, Zachariah Chandler, Salmon Chase, and Benjamin Wade.

As the party grew in numbers and influence, its leaders struggled to maintain a coalition between its three divergent parts. Many in the party felt the radicals to be too extreme in their convictions. For their part, the radicals thought the conservatives to be too vacillating in supporting the cause. If the party was to be bound together, leadership would have to come from the moderate segment, a group that was acceptable to the two extremes. As the election of 1860 neared, a dark-horse candidate began to emerge from the state of Illinois: Abraham Lincoln. A known moderate in his politics, Lincoln would come to be the man who would bind together the different factions of the party.

With this historic foundation for the formation and early history of the Republican Party, we are now ready to examine the presidential election of 1860, the Republican victory in the campaign and capture of the White House, and the ensuing events that led to the Civil War.

CHAPTER TWO

The White House by Default

The sectional tensions that had defined the 1856 presidential election continued to fester and grow in the four years leading up to the 1860 election. Buchanan's presidency had failed to defuse the contentions of the competing parties, and passions were brought to the boiling point during the course of his term in office. On March 6, 1857, just two days after Buchanan had been sworn in as president, the Supreme Court handed down a decision that caused outrage in the North. Dred Scott, a slave from Missouri, had been taken by his master, a United States army surgeon, to live in Rock Island, Illinois. Slavery was prohibited in Illinois according to the Northwest Ordinance and the state constitution. Scott's master later took him to live at Fort Snelling, Minnesota Territory, where slavery was excluded by the Missouri Compromise. After eventually returning to Missouri, Scott's master died, and Scott sued for his freedom based on the premise that he had been a resident of a free state and a free territory. The case finally ended up in the United States Supreme Court, where a majority decision was made against Scott. Chief Justice Roger B. Taney wrote the majority opinion. Taney ruled that Scott did not have the right to sue in court because, as a Negro, he was not a citizen of the United States. Taney went on to state that when the nation was formed, blacks were considered "so far inferior, that they had no rights which the white man was bound to respect." He argued that residence in free states and territories had no effect on the status of Scott's lack of freedom because all Congressional enactments that excluded slavery from the territories were "not warranted by the Constitution" and were "therefore void." Taney specifically cited the Missouri Compromise as one of the Congressional enactments that should be considered void.[1]

The decision of the court sent a shock wave across the nation. The majority justices had effectively ruled that slaves were not people, but property, and as such, could be taken by their owners anywhere in the county without fear of a change in status. Horace Greeley, the editor of the *New York Tribune*, expressed the outrage felt by many when he wrote that the Court's decision deserved no more respect than if it had been made by "a majority of those congregated in any Washington bar room." Southerners saw the decision as a judi-

Contemporary picture of Harpers Ferry, Virginia, at the time of John Brown's raid (Military History Institute, United States Army War College).

cial mandate against the intrusions of the abolitionists. Northerners viewed it as the Court interfering with the will of the people, as it was enacted by their representatives in Congress. Up to this point, most Americans felt that the Supreme Court was the guardian of the Constitution. The *Dred Scott* decision changed public opinion, mainly in the North, and caused many there to view the Court with suspicion. Abraham Lincoln, a member of the Illinois Bar, had always held a reverent respect for the judicial process. He felt that the judicial system provided checks and balances in a society where Democrats believed that the majority was always correct, and abolitionists sought to circumvent the Constitution to adhere to a higher law. The *Dred Scott* decision shook Lincoln's faith in the judiciary because it did "obvious violence to the plain unmistakable language of the Declaration," that all men are created equal. Lincoln felt that the Court had turned its back on the principles of the Founding Fathers, stating that the Declaration "is assailed, and sneered at, and construed, and hawked at, and torn, till, if its framers could rise from their graves, they would not at all recognize it." For the first time in his life, Lincoln lost his faith in the judicial process, and never again did he give deference to the rulings of the Supreme Court. The *Dred Scott* decision set in motion a practice of Court nullification that would be evident throughout Lincoln's administration.[2]

Dissatisfaction with the decision diminished the influence of the Court in the North, and would soon lead to the national government's being run by the executive and legislative branches, free from the intended checks and balances the Founding Fathers intended the judicial branch to hold. When the Republicans came to power, they were free to pursue their political agenda because of the reduced reputation of the Court with the people. As we will examine in later chapters, Court rulings would be ignored, and even defied, during the Lincoln administration, and the judicial branch became as Dred Scott: stripped of its rights under the Constitution.

The *Dred Scott* decision served to heighten tensions between the two sections of the country, and set the stage for an event that would show to all that the time for conciliation and compromise was over. In the North, the event would be heralded as the dawn of a new day, and its perpetrator would receive a martyr's crown and be held as a hero in a modern crusade. Citizens in the South viewed the event with shudders of horror, and questioned how their brethren to the north could possibly rejoice in its intended objective. The event was John Brown's raid on Harpers Ferry, Virginia, on the evening of October 16, 1859. The unpunished murderer of Potttawatomie Creek, Kansas, had again surfaced to strike a blow against slavery. Over the past few years, he had garnered the clandestine support of several members of the abolitionist movement who, while disinclined to resort to violence themselves, were not above financing others to do so. Among them were Dr. Thomas W. Higginson, a Unitarian minister in Boston; Professor Samuel G. Howe; and ex-slave Frederick Douglass. On the evening of October 16, Brown led a small private army of five black men and thirteen white men into the quiet town, where they quickly captured the Federal armory and arsenal, and the town engine house. His force brought two hundred muskets, two hundred pistols, and one thousand pikes with them, for the purpose of arming the slaves that were expected to flock to Brown's banner once the town was seized. It was the intention of the raiders to rally the slaves together, arm them, and lead them south along the Appalachian Mountains, breeding servile insurrection all along their path. Brown had said of his mission, "I expect to effect a mighty conquest, even though it be like the last victory of Samson." But Brown's plan was far more ambitious than simply freeing slaves or inciting servile uprisings. He blamed both North and South for slavery being allowed to exist in the country, and sought to divorce his cause from the influences of either side. It was Brown's intention to establish a new nation, Columbia, in the Appalachian Mountains, and naturally, he would serve as the first leader of this new country.[3]

Brown's plan began to come apart almost from the start. The first person killed by the raiders was the town's baggage master, a free black man. Brown then ordered the taking of hostages from the town. One of those taken was the great-grandnephew of George Washington, who was directed to bring with him a sword that had been given by Frederick the Great to the Father of the Country. John Brown appropriated the sword and strapped it on, symbolic of his perceived role as the creator of his new nation of Columbia. Instead of a mass rising of slaves, what the raiders found was the outrage of the residents of Harpers Ferry, who armed themselves and surrounded Brown's party in the

Drawing of John Brown with a hostage in the fire house during his raid on Harpers Ferry, Virginia (Military History Institute, United States Army War College).

engine house. A firefight ensued, and the first of Brown's followers fell dead. He was Dangerfield Newby, an ex-slave who had accompanied Brown in the hope of freeing his wife and family from a Virginia plantation. Harpers Ferry notified the state of Virginia and the government in Washington of what was transpiring in the town, and immediate steps were taken to deal with the situation. On the morning of October 17, ninety Marines arrived from Washington. They were under the command of Lieutenant Colonel Robert E. Lee, who happened to be on leave at his home in Arlington, Virginia, from his command of the 2nd United States Cavalry. Lee ordered the Marines to storm the engine house as soon as they were formed. What resulted was a quick victory for the Marines, the death of nine more of Brown's men, including two of his own sons, and the felling of Brown by a saber wound.[4]

Brown's guilt was a foregone conclusion, and his trial was merely a matter of formality. In a letter to his wife, Brown wrote, "I have been whipped, as the saying is, but I am sure I can recover all the lost capital occasioned by that disaster; by only hanging a few moments by the neck; and I feel quite determined to make the utmost possible out of a defeat." Brown's greatest fear was that he would be lynched, and not have the opportunity to get his day in court.

He earnestly petitioned his captors to guard against this possibility and was given an armed guard at all times. The trial itself became a huge media event, attracting reporters from all over the country. Brown used the trial as a means to express his views on slavery to the world, and the reporters present willingly complied by printing his words on a daily basis. In the end, he was found guilty of treason, inciting servile insurrection, and murder, and sentenced to hang by the neck until dead. On December 2, 1859, the sentence was executed at Charles Town, Virginia. Fifteen hundred troops were on hand to guard against any disturbance. Among them was a contingent from the Virginia Military Institute, under the command of Thomas J. Jackson. Another soldier in the ranks who would later gain fame was John Wilkes Booth. In addition to the military, there were more than one thousand civilian spectators. Brown ascended the steps to the gallows, and to the surprise of most of those in attendance, refrained from making a speech or remarks of any kind. Instead, he simply handed a note to one of the guards. "I, John Brown, am now quite certain that the crimes of this guilty land will never be purged away but with Blood."[5]

Brown's death did not bring the matter to a close. Instead, it served as a starting point for discussion and debate. In the North, many citizens not previously known for their opposition to slavery hailed his bravery and devotion. Herman Melville called him "the meteor of war." On the day Brown was hanged, Henry Wadsworth Longfellow noted in his diary, "This day will be a great day in our history, the date of a new Revolution — quite as much needed as the old one." Henry David Thoreau made comparison between Brown's execution and the crucifixion of Christ as "two ends of a chain which is not without its links. He is not old Brown any longer; he is an angel of light."[6] These and countless other expressions of support and admiration gushed forth from the pens and mouths of many Northerners, breeding consternation and contempt among the people of the South. The average Southerner was at a loss to explain the manner in which the North was embracing John Brown and his raid. They wondered how sensible people could honor this murderer and common criminal whose avowed purpose had been to incite servile insurrection. To the people of the South, the abolitionists favored anarchy and open revolt, and posed a threat to their entire region. The average Southern man felt as if abolitionists sought to not only effect his murder, but the murder of his wife and children as well. If these people could honor and support John Brown, what were they capable of? In this incendiary environment, there could be no common ground between the two sides. The nation was moving steadily forward toward making John Brown's written death statement a reality.

The day after the execution of John Brown, the Thirty-sixth Congress of the United States convened in session. The mood of the Congress was one of division and distrust. Ex-President John Tyler summed up the attitude of the South when he wrote, "Virginia is arming to the teeth. More than fifty thousand stand of arms already distributed, and the demand for more daily increasing. Party is silent and has no voice. But one sentiment pervades the country; security in the Union, or separation. An indiscreet move in any direction may produce results deeply to be deplored. I fear the debates in Congress, and above all, the speaker's election. If excitement prevails in Congress, it will add fuel to the flame which already burns so terrifically." Tyler's words were prophetic.

The first order of business for the members of the House of Representatives was to elect a new speaker, and in the current state of affairs, the process would take on a sectional aspect unprecedented in the annals of American government. The House was made up of 108 Republicans, 101 Democrats, and 27 Know-Nothings, with 23 of the latter being from Southern states. The leading candidates were John Sherman of Ohio and Galusha Grow of Pennsylvania, both Republicans. The first ballot resulted in a split of the Republican vote between the two men, causing Grow to remove his name from consideration. Democrats took the opportunity to assail the Republican leadership. Allegations were made that William Seward and John Sherman had a hand in the raid on Harpers Ferry, and that the Republican Party was actively pursuing a covert war against the South. Reuben Davis of Mississippi went so far as to call Seward a traitor to his country. One Southern representative voiced the opinion of his peers by stating, "The South here asks nothing but its rights.... I would have no more; but, as God is my judge, as one of its Representatives, I would shatter this republic from turret to foundation stone before I would take one tittle less." Thaddeus Stevens rose in response. "I do not blame the gentlemen of the South for the language of intimidation, for using this threat of rendering God's creation from the turret to the foundation. All this is right in them, for they have tried it fifty times, and fifty times they have found weak and recreant tremblers in the North who have been affected by it, and who have acted from those intimidations." The Republican Party, however, did not intend to be cowed by Southern threats to split apart the Union.

Tensions rose to a fever pitch over the next few days as the representatives voted on succeeding ballots. So great was the passion within the halls of Congress that every man felt obliged to carry a knife or pistol for personal protection. On January 30, 1860, with the House still in deadlock, Sherman withdrew his name from consideration. William Pennington, a Republican from New Jersey, was then nominated. On February 1, after forty-four ballots and almost two months, Pennington received the number of votes necessary to secure election as Speaker of the House.

The contest in the House had furthered the antagonism between the two sides, and had spilled over into the general populace. General Winfield Scott wrote, "The state of the country almost deprives me of sleep."[7] 1860 was already in its second month. In a few months more the parties would meet to select their candidates for the fall presidential election. The lines of sectionalism had already been drawn, and the election would accentuate the differences between the two regions. It would also come full face with the specter of disunion.

To this point, one might logically assume that the conflict between the two sections was entirely based on the question of slavery. From the various compromises over the status of the territories, to Bloody Kansas, to *Uncle Tom's Cabin*, to the raid on Harpers Ferry, to the struggle to elect the Speaker of the House, it would seem that the common strain of all differences between the North and South was the peculiar institution of slavery. In fact, the abiding difference between North and South came from differing political and economic ideologies. The North was founded on manufacturing and commerce, and favored high tariffs and investment in industrial concerns. The South was largely agricultural, and would be injured by such measures. As such, the South continually blocked the North's efforts to protect its factories and merchants, earning the ire of prominent Northern industrialists. Northern politicians were predominantly of the Federalist/Whig/Republican persuasion, supporters of the strong central government that most Jeffersonian Democrats abhorred. The ideological and economic differences had existed between the two sections since the time of the Constitutional Convention, and had been the source of national debate in most of the government business from that time to 1860. Indeed, Northern states had more than once threatened to separate themselves from the Union because of what they viewed to be an inability to establish the forms of government and economy they wished under the current political system. In the end, the Federalist/Whig/Republican line of politicians adopted the advice of the British agent and settled upon slavery to become the vehicle with which to drive a wedge between the two sections of the nation, and the advice proved to be sound. It became a rallying cry for division, crumbled the foundation of support from common New Englanders for the Constitutional Union, and bred a feeling of superiority to the residents of each section.

It should be remembered that there was no Federal income tax in the years before the Civil War. The primary source of revenue for the central government was by means of the tariff. It has been estimated that 80 percent of all tariff revenue was collected in the South, where the agrarian society existed on the exportation of raw materials and the importation of manufactured goods. For its part, the North could not conduct the business of government without the revenue collected in Southern ports. Southerners felt as if they were being punished for their economic system, forced to pay exorbitant taxes to a government in which they experienced ever-diminishing influence and control. Northern merchants and shipping interests amassed huge profits, while Southerners footed the bill. Most Southerners could see no difference between the current arrangement with the Federal government and the situation that had existed between England and the Colonies.

To the South, the actions of Northern politicians signified a continual effort to subjugate its people to the political and economic interests of the North. Southerners, and a majority of Democrats, believed the actions of the Northern Republicans to be in violation of the Constitution, and worse, in violation of the actions of a civilized people. The raid on Harpers Ferry, and its subsequent celebration in the North, had struck fear in the hearts of the average Southerner, who viewed himself in danger from an irresponsible and power-hungry political foe.

Further, the South felt that Northern interests could not be appeased. The South had previously acted upon the issue of gradual emancipation of the slaves, only to be informed that gradual emancipation was not good enough. Only immediate action would do. When the South asked what was to be done with all the freedmen once this was accomplished, its question fell on deaf ears. Still, the region looked to the eradication of slavery. Amazingly, it was the abolitionists who caused Southerners to abandon their own plans for emancipation and to entrench themselves in staunch resistance to any efforts to free the slaves. Abolitionists not only made violent attacks on the institution of slavery, they made even stronger assaults on the white people of the South for allowing the institution to exist. Southern society was slandered as being a barbarous race of villains, and its citizens were under constant recrimination. For their part, Southerners responded in the only manner available to them — they fought back, in defense of themselves and their institutions. Both sides proclaimed their superiority, and this sense of superiority deepened the chasm between them.

The question that had to be resolved was the relation of the states to the government they had created in 1787. Did true power rest with the states and their citizens, or did it reside with the central government? The controversy was rooted in politics, and in a struggle for one side to gain advantage over the other. The various compromises taking place over the last four decades had been an attempt by statesmen to maintain a balance of power that both sides could live with, but compromise was no longer an option. One side or the other must gain control. The struggle for power had come to a stalemate, and while a balance was acceptable to both sides, a stalemate was not. Slavery had indeed become the main point of contention, but it was the rallying cry, and not the cause of the conflict, as will be made clear in later discussion of the actions of the Republican Party.

In April of 1860, the Democrats met in Charleston to hold their national convention to select a presidential candidate. Up to this point, the Democrats were a national party, boasting strength from such Northern strongholds as New Hampshire and Pennsylvania. When they met in convention, however, delegations from the deep South, led by men like William Yancey and Robert Toombs, pressed to adopt extreme measures that would protect the institutions of the South from Northern intrusion. The extremists failed to push forward their platform, causing all of the delegates from the "cotton states" to withdraw from the convention. Without the possibility of the two-thirds majority of the party to make a nomination, the convention was adjourned, with plans made to meet again, in Baltimore in June. The delegates from the deep South also planned a second convention, originally slated to be held in Richmond, but eventually it was moved to Baltimore. What resulted was the nomination of two different Democratic candidates for president. The northern faction of the party backed Stephen A. Douglas of Illinois, while the southern faction put its weight behind John C. Breckinridge of Kentucky. A third party arose from old-line Whigs, Know-Nothings, and Democrats who could not bring themselves to back either of the two candidates already nominated. Calling themselves the Constitutional Union Party, they nominated John Bell of Tennessee.[8]

Differing political agendas were only part of the reason for the split in the Democratic Party. Personal animosities also played a key role. Stephen Douglas had been acknowledged by all factions of the party to be the front-runner going into the nominating convention. President Buchanan was noted for having such a strong personal dislike for Douglas that the mere mention of his name almost gave him apoplexy, and he set about on a campaign to diminish the support he would receive for his nomination. Buchanan made no bones about the fact that his sole intention was that of ensuring Douglas's overthrow as the Democratic candidate for president. To accomplish this, he used the power of the executive to seduce potential delegates through the use of government contracts, land patents, and appointments as postmasters, marshals and revenue collectors. As George Fort Milton explains it in his book *The Eve of Conflict: Stephen A. Douglas and the Needless War*, "Buchanan was a dull and flabby Samson, but he exhibited great energy and resource in pulling down the pillars of his temple and destroying his enemy along with his party, his country and himself." Buchanan's personal war against Douglas was extremely successful, and contributed greatly to the latter not receiving the universal nomination of the party.[9]

While all this was taking place, the Republican Party met in Chicago in May to hold its convention. William Seward was acknowledged to be the front-runner for the nomination. He was one of the most powerful and well-known members of the party, and had positioned himself, over the course of the past four years, to bear the Republican mantle to the White House. Seward's competition for the nomination came primarily from Abraham Lincoln of Illinois and Simon Cameron from Pennsylvania.

Many of the party leaders felt that they had to appeal to a larger portion of the voters if they were to have a hope of defeating Douglas in the fall election. To be sure, the slavery issue fired the passions of many voters in the North, but the party could not win on that issue alone. In fact, running an election based on the eradication of slavery alone threatened to alienate large numbers of potential voters who might see the campaign as an effort to break up the Union. The leaders decided to adopt the additional platforms of a higher tariff, federally sponsored internal improvements, a homestead bill, and federal assistance for a transcontinental railroad to be built over a central line. The tariff and the central improvements would appeal to voters in the Northeast and

Middle Atlantic states, while the homestead bill and the transcontinental railroad would attract votes from the Old Northwest and Midwest. The adoption of these platforms would also allow the Republicans a chance to escape the label of being the aggressor between the two parties.

These platform moves may have made the party more palatable to the masses, but they needed a candidate to match the platforms. Party leaders began to question whether Seward would be able to appeal to the masses, or if he was merely a one-issue candidate. President Buchanan left an impression of Seward that exemplifies the fears the party leaders held over his candidacy.

> Senator Seward, of New York, was at this period the acknowledged head and leader of the Republican party. Indeed, his utterances had become its oracies. He was much more of a politician than a statesman. Without strong convictions, he understood the art of preparing in his closet, and uttering before the public, antithetical sentences well calculated both to inflame the ardor of his slavery friends and to exasperate his pro-slavery opponents. If he was not the author of the 'irrepressible conflict,' he appropriated it to himself and converted it into a party oracle. He thus aroused passions, probably without so intending, which it was beyond his power to afterwards control. He raised a storm which, like others of whom we read in history, he wanted both the courage and the power to quell.[10]

Seward led on the first two ballots, but did not receive the votes necessary to secure the nomination. On the third ballot, a dark horse candidate came out of the shadows to acquire the votes necessary to receive the nomination: Abraham Lincoln. While a respected politician within the borders of Illinois, Lincoln was not a well-known player on the national stage. His appeal to the delegates stemmed from the fact that he was a talented speaker, a known moderate, and a Westerner who it was felt could challenge Douglas for Western votes. Lincoln's campaign managers also played a pivotal role in securing the nomination with widespread promises of patronage to delegates who aligned themselves with their candidate.

Four men were now actively seeking the presidency. Douglas and Breckinridge were already well known, and had been associated with particular political views for years. Lincoln and Bell were lesser figures who would have to be introduced to many of the electorate.

Stephen Douglas, considered by most to be the front-runner in the election, was the senior senator from Illinois, though he had been born in Brandon, Vermont, in 1813. After being admitted to the bar, Douglas began his political career by becoming the attorney general of the state. He was elected to the state legislature in 1835, then became secretary of the state in 1840 and judge of the Illinois Supreme Court in 1841. In 1847, Douglas was elected to the United States House of Representatives, where he quickly gained stature in national politics. Douglas proved to be skilled at debates and influential in the passage of legislation. After being appointed chairman of the Committee on Territories, he dominated the Senate through the 1850s, gaining ever-increasing influence in national affairs. Douglas was largely responsible for passage of the Compromise of 1850 that briefly put an end to the issue of slavery in the territo-

ries. In 1854, his Kansas-Nebraska Act reopened a festering wound by allowing the citizens of new territories to decide for themselves if they wanted to be slave or free. This had been prohibited in the previous compromises. In a very real sense, Douglas was responsible for the creation of the Republican Party, which was formed in protest of the Kansas-Nebraska Act. In 1857, he supported the *Dred Scott* decision, but denied that it was any part of a Southern plot to introduce slavery into the Northern states. Up to this point, Douglas had emerged as the spokesman of Southern Democrats, and was the leading candidate to be elected president in 1860. But when President Buchanan, supported by Southern allies, tried to pass a Federal slave code that would have overruled the wishes of the people of Kansas, Douglas declared the code to be undemocratic and was largely responsible for defeating the bill. By this action, he alienated himself from many Democratic leaders in the South, which set

Stephen Douglas. Known throughout the country as the "Little Giant," Douglas was the face of the Democratic Party in the years leading up to the election of Lincoln and the Civil War (Military History Institute, United States Army War College).

the stage for the split in the party in 1860, when the more radical Democrats withdrew their support from him. Though still a powerful force in national politics, Douglas would have to rely on a coalition of Southern moderates and Northern Democrats if he wished to win the election. Even with the split in the party, Douglas was considered the man to beat in the fall campaign.

John C. Breckinridge was born near Lexington, Kentucky, on January 15, 1821. After graduating from Centre College in 1839, he attended Transylvania University, where he majored in the study of law. By 1845, Breckinridge had been admitted to the bar and was practicing at Lexington. His rise in political prominence was meteoric. In 1849, he was elected to the Kentucky legislature, and in 1851 he won election to the United States House of Representatives. Five years later, Breckinridge would become vice president of the United States, under Buchanan, at the young age of thirty-five. Though his political career was closely associated with Southern concerns over Northern encroachment,

Breckinridge was himself somewhat of a moderate in his views. A defender of Southern rights, he was nevertheless opposed to secession, and supported

Southerners' addressing their grievances within the parameters of the Union. In 1859, with about a year and a half remaining in his term as vice president, Breckinridge was elected to the United States Senate from Kentucky. His high profile in national politics had made him a viable candidate for president, and his association with the Buchanan administration, by means of the Federal slave code it had tried to pass, made him popular with Southern extremists within the party. Breckinridge's candidacy would serve as the dissent movement to what Southerners viewed as an ever-enlarging influence of Northerners in the Federal government, and a growing threat to the autonomy of Southern states to conduct their own affairs.[11]

John C. Breckinridge. Vice president under Buchanan and Democratic candidate for the presidency in 1860, Breckinridge would go on to become a general in the Confederate Army and Confederate Secretary of War. (Military History Institute, United States Army War College).

John Bell, the third candidate to emerge because of the split in the Democratic Party, was born at Mill Creek, Tennessee, on February 15, 1797. Bell studied law after his graduation from Cumberland College in 1814, and was admitted to the bar in 1816. He established his practice in Franklin, and soon after launched his political career, being elected to the Tennessee State Senate in 1817. Bell served only one term in the Senate, declining to run for reelection. At the conclusion of his term, he moved to Nashville, where he reestablished his law practice. In 1826, he was elected to the United States House of Representatives, an office he would retain until 1841, holding important positions as Speaker of the House and chairman of the Committee of Indian Affairs. Following his time in Congress, Bell served briefly as Secretary of War under Presidents William Henry Harrison and John Tyler. He resigned, with the rest of Tyler's cabinet, in protest over the president's vetoes of Whig legislation. He had originally been elected to office as a Democrat, but had changed his affiliation to the Whig Party following a fight with Jacksonian Democrats over the controversial Bank of the

United States. Bell returned to Tennessee, where he spent the next several years devoting his time to business matters. In 1847, he became involved in politics again, being elected to the Tennessee House of Representatives. He was subsequently selected to represent Tennessee in the United States Senate, serving in that capacity until 1859. He was one of only two Southern senators to vote against the Kansas-Nebraska Act, the other being Sam Houston. On the eve of the 1860 presidential campaign, Bell was a well-known national figure, and served as the leader of a small group of border and middle-state Whigs who were attempting to keep the defunct party alive. His support base would come from Southern Whigs and Northern Nativists, or Know-Nothings. It was derisively dubbed the "Old Gentleman's Party" by the rest of the country.

John Bell, one of the three Democratic candidates in the presidential election of 1860. Bell did well in the border states with former Whigs (Military History Institute, United States Army War College).

On the national stage, Abraham Lincoln was the least known of any of the four candidates in the 1860 election, though he was a well-established and respected member of the Republican Party in Illinois. Lincoln was born on February 12, 1809, at Nolin Creek, Kentucky, three miles south of Hodgenville. When Lincoln was still a child, his father lost the family farm in court cases and the Lincolns were forced to live in a dugout on the side of a hill in Indiana. The family moved to Perry County, Indiana, in 1816. In 1818, Lincoln's mother died at the age of thirty-four, and his father quickly remarried. The Lincolns continued to experience economic difficulties, and in 1830 they settled on public land in Macon County, Illinois. In 1831, Lincoln struck out on his own, settling in New Salem, Illinois, where he secured employment transporting goods from New Salem to New Orleans, Louisiana. Denied the educational advantages of his opponents, Lincoln had only had about eighteen months of formal education in his life. He was an avid reader who educated himself. Nevertheless, he decided to throw his hat into the political arena in 1832 when he made an unsuccessful run for the Illinois General Assembly. Over the next several years, Lincoln supported himself through a variety of occupations, including being a representative in the Illinois Legislature, while he studied the law. In 1837, he was admitted to the Illinois bar and moved from New Salem to Springfield. Lincoln served four successive terms in the Illinois House of Representatives. During this time, he became acknowledged as one of the best lawyers in Illinois and a leader of the Whig Party in the legislature. In 1842, he was elected to the United States House of Representatives. A speech in Congress condemning President Polk and the Mexican War hurt his popularity at home to the extent that he decided not to run for reelection. Lincoln then devoted his energies to his law practice, while he cautiously avoided politics. His representation of Illinois railroad interests brought him into contact with many powerful and influential men, and while Lincoln was running for no elected office, he was cultivating the good will of powerful backers who would later lend their money and influence to his political aspirations. The Kansas-Nebraska Act, in 1854, prodded him back into the political arena. That same year, he joined the new Republican Party. In 1858, Lincoln was the Republican candidate who opposed Stephen Douglas's reelection to the United States Senate. Douglas handily defeated Lincoln in the election, but the Lincoln-Douglas debates brought Abe to national prominence as a defender against the expansion of slavery. His "House Divided" speech served to rally Republicans throughout the North, and set the stage for the 1860 presidential election to be largely a fight to limit the expansion of slavery. While his Senate campaign in 1858 had brought him national recognition, Lincoln was by far the least known and least experienced of any of the four candidates on the eve of the 1860 election. As compared with the many and varied national posts held by the other nominees, he had served a single term in the House of Representatives, and had left that office because of disaffection from the voters who had elected him. Since he was the inexperienced candidate of a new political party, few had faith in his ability to mount a successful challenge to the opponents arrayed against him. Lincoln had done a

President Abraham Lincoln. Lincoln became the face of sectional turmoil for many in the South, and his election was seen as final proof that the North intended to subject the South to its political rule. He would later become the face of the Republican Party and a rallying influence in national politics for decades after the war (Military History Institute, United States Army War College).

great deal to promote his public image in a tour of speaking engagements through the Northeast in the winter of 1859-1860. His speech about the responsibility of Congress to police the expansion of slavery, delivered at Cooper Union Hall in New York City in February of 1860, was met with thunderous applause by those in attendance, and was widely reported in the press. Lincoln had gained approval on Seward's home ground, a fact that had not been lost upon the delegates at the Chicago convention.[12]

For their part, the Republican Party adopted the same "man of the people" theme that had brought them such a good showing in Frémont's campaign in 1856. Lincoln was portrayed as the ultimate commoner. From his humble log-cabin beginnings, to the loss of his mother, to his days splitting rails, he epitomized the hardships and trials endured by a multitude of voters. His subsequent successes, as a lawyer and a politician, exemplified the quality of his character and the superiority of his mind. Just as they had done in 1856, the Republicans did everything they could to distance themselves from the aristocracy and privilege associated with the other candidates. Lincoln's campaign may have been financed by some of the largest railroad and business concerns in the North, but the party took care to keep its own moneyed interests out of the headlines as it portrayed the other candidates as being the mouthpieces of the wealthy, powerful class who advanced their own agendas at the expense of the common masses.

The Republicans did make a fundamental change in their campaigning from the 1856 election, however. During that campaign, neither candidate took to the stump to drum up support for his cause. This time around, Lincoln went on an extensive campaign tour, and even ventured into the South, where he preached the virtues of the Union and warned against secession. He pledged to act with the same conviction Andrew Jackson had shown in the nullification crisis thirty years before should secession come about. This did him little good in the South, but he gained increasing support in the North. Though Lincoln had been selected by the party because he was felt to be a candidate less abrasive to Southern extremists, the election was shaping up along the sectional lines that the party leaders had hoped to avert.

Indeed, the differences between the parties and the sections of the country had become so acute by this time that no Republican candidate could have hoped to conciliate voters on the other side. This can be seen in the actions of Lincoln's own family, friends, and neighbors. In Lincoln's own family, none of his father's relatives voted for him, and only one of his mother's relatives did so. In his home town of Springfield, Lincoln conducted a pre-election canvass of the town's ministers to test his support. Only three of the twenty-three ministers were found to support his candidacy. Lincoln spoke out bitterly against these church leaders, stating, "They pretend to believe in the Bible and be God-fearing Christians; yet by their ballots they are demonstrating that they don't care whether slavery is voted up or down." This is an interesting comment,

Newspaper cartoon showing Stephen Douglas and John Breckinridge as oysters on the half-shell, with Lincoln about to devour them (from *Lincoln's Yarns and Stories: A Complete Collection of the Funny and Witty Anecdotes That Made Abraham Lincoln Famous as America's Greatest Story Teller*, by Colonel Alexander K. McClure, The John C. Winston Company, Chicago, Ill., n.d.).

given the fact that Lincoln had no church affiliation of his own, and was neither religious nor spiritual in his daily life.[13]

The state elections were held in September and October of 1860, and the results were a sweeping victory for Republicans in the North. By the time the ballots were tallied, the Republicans had gained control of all but two of the Northern legislatures, and excepting the Pacific Coast states, every Northern governor was now a Republican.[14]

On November 6, 1860, the voters went to the polls to decide what direction the Federal government would assume. The election was witness to the largest voter turnout in history to that time, with 81.2 percent of the registered voters casting their ballots. Popular opinion was still running decidedly against Lincoln, as most voters planned to vote against the Republicans. Lincoln was not even on the ballot in nine of the states of the deep South: Alabama, Arkansas, Florida, Georgia, Louisiana, Mississippi, North Carolina, Tennessee, and Texas. Lincoln did not have a single vote cast for him in any of these nine states, and carried only nine of the 996 counties in the South. When the votes were tallied, Lincoln had accumulated 1,865,593, or thirty-nine percent of those cast. The three opposition candidates amassed 2,823,975 votes between them,

Newspaper cartoon from the 1860 presidential election showing the four candidates ripping up a map of the country and symbolically tearing the nation apart (Military History Institute, United States Army War College).

with Stephen Douglas gathering 1,382,713 of those to himself. Breckinridge received 848,356, and Bell garnered 592,906. Clearly, the popular mandate was against the Republican Party and its platforms, with more than three out of every five voters casting their ballots against the new party.

But the electoral college was quite another matter. Lincoln's strength came from the Northeast and Northwest, states rich in electoral votes. He carried seventeen states, amounting to 180 electoral votes, enough to secure victory in the election and win the White House. Breckinridge was next in line with 72 votes, followed by Bell with 39 and Douglas with only 12. Though Douglas had made a strong national showing, and had won almost thirty percent of the popular vote, he only carried Missouri, with its nine electoral votes. He received the other three from New Jersey, which split its electoral tally between Douglas and Lincoln. As expected, Bell did well in the border states, and Breckinridge carried all of the deep South.[15]

Lincoln and the Republicans had won the election, but in doing so they had served to deepen the division between the contending sections. Southern extremists had vowed that they would not live under the rule of the Republicans, and threatened disunion if such an event was to transpire. Popular sentiment in the South was reflected at the polls. Lincoln received only 26,395 votes from all of the states where slavery was permitted. The totals were as follows: Virginia, 1,887; Missouri, 17,028; Maryland, 2294; Delaware, 3,822; and Kentucky, 1,364. Though he was born in Kentucky and was touted as a native son, Lincoln won less than one percent of the 146,216 votes cast there. Even in Missouri, where the Republicans secured the highest total of votes in a slave state, Douglas enjoyed more than a three-to-one margin in the ballot box.

The people had spoken, and the result was unmistakable. The split between the two sections of the country were irreconcilable, and the nation was speeding toward open rebellion. To Southerners, who had cast less than one half of one percent of the popular vote for Lincoln, living under Republican rule was viewed as tyranny akin to being under the

William Seward, Lincoln's Secretary of State. Seward believed that even though he had failed to secure his party's nomination for president, he would still exert the controlling influence in Lincoln's administration. He soon found out that Lincoln was the man in charge and he would not be controlled by Seward or any other Republican leader (Military History Institute, United States Army War College).

rule of a foreign power. Ninety-eight percent of the voting South had cast their ballots against the Republicans, with only 26,395 of the 1,214,042 votes cast there going for Lincoln, and they would never consent to hand over their political rights to a Federal government in which they felt they were no longer represented. The balance of power that had long epitomized the national government had been toppled. Southerners, convinced that their political, social, and economic foundations would be ravaged by a Republican administration, began to take steps to ensure the survival of these institutions. Between the time of Lincoln's election and his inauguration, secession would become the most talked-about topic in American society. Many in the North felt that the South was making idle threats in order to secure concessions from the new administration. The mandate of Southern voters was lost upon those of this inclination. The South was no longer looking for concessions. It was seeking representation, and if that could not be found in the old Union, then the South would establish its own government and withdraw from the compact it had made in 1787.

CHAPTER THREE

Sectional Crisis and the Outbreak of War

Fiery talk of disunion emerged from the South almost as soon as the polls had closed in the presidential election. Unknowingly, these Southern firebrands were playing right into the hands of the Republican Party. Ever since the time of the Constitutional Convention, the two sections of the country had been developing along different social and economic lines, and a clash between the cultures had been almost inevitable.

The United States was plunging head-long into the Industrial Revolution, and was on the verge of becoming a great nation in the world community. Blessed with what seemed a limitless supply of raw materials, America possessed more industrial potential than any other country in the world in the 1850s, and had the most to gain by embracing industrialization. The citizens of the country were becoming less self-reliant than had been their forbearers. They were producing less and less of the things they needed for working and living. Spinning wheels and candle molds were being stored, as people found it more convenient to buy their daily necessities than to make them themselves. Through the decade of the 1850s, homemade production dropped from $27,000,000 to $24,000,000, despite the fact that the nation was experiencing a huge growth in population.[1]

This growth and development of industry had overwhelmingly taken place in the North. The South had remained largely agricultural. On the surface, it appeared to be a perfect arrangement. One half of the country would provide raw resources, while the other produced manufactured goods. The South served as a built-in market for the manufactured products of the industrialized North. Southerners themselves would probably not have had a problem with this arrangement if it had not been for the insistence of the North to impose high tariffs on imported goods from Europe. While American industrialization was growing at a terrific rate, it was still hard to compete with products made in Europe. For that reason, Northerners sought to protect their interests by placing a tax, or tariff, on imported goods to make them more expensive than those

The Old Capitol Prison in Washington, D.C. The walls of this prison held hundreds of political prisoners during the course of the war (Military History Institute, United States Army War College).

produced in America. In the South, this was viewed as creating an unfair monopoly. Southerners felt that they were being exploited like colonies by the North, not allowed to spend their money where it would go the furthest, and forced to purchase the higher-priced, often inferior, products made in Northern factories. John C. Calhoun, the outspoken political defender of Southern rights, had stated it thus:

> We are told, by those who pretend to understand our interest better than we do, that the excess of production and not the Tariff, is the evil which afflicts us.... We would feel more disposed to respect the spirit in which the advice is offered, if those from whom it comes accompanied it with the weight of their example. They also occasionally, complain of low prices; but instead of diminishing the supply, as a remedy for the evil, demanded an enlargement of the market, by the execution of all competition.[2]

The division over the character of the nation, industrial or agricultural, had been festering for as long as the slavery issue. In fact, when one considers that the abolition movement had almost died by 1840, it had been around longer.

Slavery, disagreement over strong central government, and differing economic systems had long divided the country. The events of the previous decade had only served to illuminate and define these differences in the minds of the people, creating distrust and animosity from one section for the other. The election of Abraham Lincoln to the presidency served as the fuse to a powder keg that had been in place for decades. Both sides prepared themselves for a contest to decide the future direction of the nation. Most citizens, both North and South, felt that the differences could be addressed through negotiations. The public had become used to compromise in national affairs as a political staple, and even though most American citizens favored this sort of resolution, those in power, particularly in the North, were opposed to it.

Cassius Clay, a United States senator from Kentucky and relative of "The Great Compromiser," Henry Clay, saw clearly the mood of the nation, even before the Republicans won the election. While attending the convention in Chicago, Clay addressed a number of the delegates, stating, "Gentlemen, we are on the brink of a great civil war." Even though he was a Republican himself, and his name had been forwarded as a possible running mate with Lincoln, Clay warned that the South would fight if the Republicans captured the White House with their adopted platforms.[3] Clay's warning went largely unheeded. Most still felt that diplomacy would win the day. They were mistaken. The South had come to distrust the political leaders of the North, and those same Northern leaders were in no mood to make concessions to keep the Union intact. Instead, they were bent on pursuing an agenda intended to recreate the nation according to their own ideas of government.

The firebrands in the South lost little time in addressing Lincoln's election to the presidency. Sectional leaders had long since learned that a united South was a myth when it came to standing against the Federal government. In the crisis of 1850, Southerners had split along regional and social lines, instead of standing as a solid bloc. Therefore, states did not wait for a consensus of Southern leaders to act, knowing that such a consensus would be almost impossible to achieve, even with the almost universal resentment caused by the Republican victory.

South Carolina was the first to take action. The state legislature was still in session when news of Lincoln's victory was announced, prompting Governor William H. Gist to submit a bill calling for the election of delegates to a state convention. The legislature immediately approved the bill, setting January 8 as the election day, and January 15 as the day the convention would commence. All understood that this was to be a secession convention. On November 10, Gist learned that large secession meetings were taking place in Alabama and Mississippi, and that Governor Joseph E. Brown of Georgia was calling for a state convention. Desiring to take the lead in any secession movement, Gist and his supporters convinced the South Carolina legislature to move up the election of delegates to December 6, and the convention to December 17. Gist's speedy action prompted Governor Andrew B. Moore of Alabama and Governor J.J. Pettus of Mississippi to call for delegate elections on December 24, with conventions to meet on January 7. On November 18, the Georgia legislature set January 2 as the date to elect delegates, and January 16 for its convention. The Florida legislature followed suit in late November, followed by Louisiana in early December. All of the deep South states, with the exception of Texas, were now on a path to secession. Sam Houston, the governor of Texas, was a Unionist, and refused to call the state's legislature into special session. Texas secessionists circumvented their governor, however, by making their own call for a convention to be held in January. One month after Lincoln's election, seven Southern states had already taken the necessary steps to remove themselves from the Union. While the secession movement was gaining momentum, the Federal government was doing little or nothing to prevent it. In fact, President Buchanan, while condemning the breaking up of the Union, openly declared that the Federal government lacked the legal authority to prevent secession.[4]

The United States Congress convened in Washington on December 3, 1860, and the House of Representatives appointed a Committee of Thirty-three, composed of one representative from each state, to evaluate compromise measures. A similar committee was proposed in the Senate, but was, for a time, blocked by heated debates between Northern Republicans and Southerners. The Senate eventually formed a Committee of Thirteen, made up of five Republicans, five Southern Democrats, and three Northern Democrats. Given the explosive nature of the events at hand, it would seem inexplicable why the Committee of Thirty-three waited until December 14 to hold its first meeting. The Committee of Thirteen did not meet until a week later, and when they did so the initial proceedings made it impossible for any compromise to be attained. The Committee "resolved that no proposition shall be reported as adopted, unless sustained by a majority of each of the classes of the Committee; Senators of the Republican Party to constitute one class, and Senators of the other parties to constitute the other class." In this way, the Republicans effectually gained veto power in any proceedings of the Committee.[5]

On December 22, 1860, during the second day of meetings of the Committee of Thirteen, Senator John J. Crittenden of Kentucky proposed an amendment to the Constitution that became popularly known as the Crittenden Compromise. In essence, his proposal advocated a constitutional reinstatement of the Compromise of 1850, which had been rendered null and void by the Kansas-Nebraska Act of 1854. Crittenden advocated that the old Missouri Compromise line be adopted, in regard to slavery in the territories. Southerners would relinquish their right to take slaves into all of the territories, and would, by passage of the amendment, be restricted from doing so in any territory north of the Missouri line, even though the Supreme Court had already ruled such practice to be legal. All of the existing territories in the Union would be ceded to the North, with the exception of New Mexico, where all sides believed the climate and terrain were prohibitive of creating a slave state.

The measure Crittenden proposed would have guaranteed Northern Republicans the eventual mastery of national politics as the various territories were organized and brought into the Union as states. It would maintain the balance of power between North and South only temporarily, until these various territories could be admitted as free states. Thus, what Crittenden proposed was an eventual passing of power to the Republicans, protected by constitutional amendment. When one considers the fact that the Republican Party was, in large measure, formed out of protest over the Kansas-Nebraska Act's repealing the Compromise of 1850, it would appear that the Crittenden Compromise was a complete victory for the party. Republicans had successfully gained the repeal of the Kansas-Nebraska Act, and in doing so had guaranteed their eventual dominance of the Federal government.

Senator John J. Crittenden. Author of the Crittenden Compromise, a plan to negotiate a resolution to the crisis of secession, which Republicans refused to even consider (Military History Institute, United States Army War College).

But Republican leaders were not willing to endure any period of status quo while waiting for this shift of power to take place. The Crittenden Compromise failed to receive the approval of a single Republican member of the Committee of Thirteen, and could not be reported to the Senate as adopted, even though eight of the thirteen members voted for it, because the Republicans invoked the veto power they had previously insisted upon as a criterion for the committee. Crittenden's compromise was an olive branch presented to the Republicans by the South. It showed a resolve on the part of the South to accept great concessions in order to preserve the Union. It conceded to the North all of the demands that had led to the formation of the Republican Party in the first place, while doing injury to the agenda of Southern extremists. Even so, the proposal was welcomed by many in the South who would later be numbered among the most ardent supporters of secession. Stephen Douglas, a member of the Committee of Thirteen, wrote, "I can confirm ... that Senator [Jefferson] Davis himself, when on the Committee of Thirteen, was ready at all times to compromise on the Crittenden proposition. I will go further, and say that [Robert] Toombs was also ready to do so."[6]

But the Republicans refused to even contemplate compromise, prompting President Buchanan to ponder:

Indeed, who could fail to believe that when the alternative was presented to the Senators and Representatives of the Northern States, either to yield to their brethren in the South, the barren abstraction of carrying their slaves into New Mexico, or to expose the country to the imminent peril of civil war, they would choose the side of peace and union? The period for action was still propitious. It will be recollected that Mr. Crittenden's amendment was submitted before any of our forts had been seized, before any of the cotton States except South Carolina, had seceded, and before any of the conventions which had been called in the remaining of these States had been assembled. Under such circumstances it could have been true wisdom to seize the propitious moment before it fled forever, and even yield, if need be, a trifling concession to patriotic policy, if not to abstract justice, rather than expose the country to a great impending calamity. And how small the concession required, even from a sincere Anti-Slavery Republican.[7]

Senator Crittenden was confounded at the stance taken by his Republican peers on the committee. In an effort to try to sway their opinions, he stated, "The sacrifice to be made for its [that of the Union] preservation is comparatively worthless. Peace, harmony and union in a great nation were never purchased at so cheap a rate, as we now have it in our power to do. It is a scruple only, a scruple of as little value as a barley corn that stands between us and peace, reconciliation and union; and we stand here pausing and hesitating about that little atom which is to be sacrificed."[8] But the Republican senators could not be moved. They remained steadfast in their opposition to the measure even though it was receiving unprecedented support from the people of the nation. Tens of thousands of voters affixed their names to petitions addressed to Congress, imploring their elected officials to adopt the proposal. From Boston came one such petition, signed by the mayor, members of the Board of Aldermen and Common Council of the City, which contained the signatures of more than 32,000 citizens of Massachusetts. A similar petition from New York City had been signed by more than 38,000 voters. A greater number of people petitioned the Congress to adopt the Crittenden Compromise than for any other measure that had ever been before Congress, and still the Republicans refused to allow the proposal to even be discussed outside of committee.[9]

While all this was going on, a little-known army officer was facing a stalemate of his own in Charleston, South Carolina. Major Robert Anderson, a Kentuckian, was in command of the Federal-held forts in Charleston Harbor. With an undersized force of sixty-eight enlisted men and eight officers, he was charged with the mission of defending this Federal property from being seized by the state authorities of South Carolina, who demanded the immediate withdrawal of all Federal troops from military sites within their borders. Anderson had taken refuge with his men in Fort Moultrie, an antiquated masonry fortification originally used during the Revolutionary War to defend Charleston from the British. The fort was in a bad state of repair, and its brick walls contained so many gaps that an attacking force could easily shoot through them and into the works. Worse still, the fort was surrounded by sand hills and build-ings, giving any attacking force the advantage of being able to shoot down into the interior of the structure at will. There were already thousands of state mili-tia assembled in the city, and Anderson felt that it was impossible for him to hold the crumbling old fort with the force at his disposal, so he decided to effect a change of base to a more tenable position.

On December 26, under cover of darkness, Anderson secretly moved his command from Fort Moultrie to Fort Sumter, constructed on a man-made island in the middle of Charleston Harbor. Its fifty-foot-high walls, and its position in the harbor, made Fort Sumter a more defensible position than Moul-trie had been, but Anderson's command was still woefully inadequate for the mission assigned to them. Sumter had been built to hold 650 men. Anderson had barely more than one-tenth that number. With his command in slightly more secure surroundings, Anderson waited for additional word from Wash-ington. Abandoned and cut off from the rest of the nation, he waited to find out if he was to be reinforced or ordered to withdraw, or for news that some compromise had been reached that would put an end to the tensions that were rising daily in Charleston.[10]

For their part, the Republicans were not interested in compromise, how-ever. They felt concessions to the South would be viewed as weakness to a party that had not come to office with a popular mandate for its platforms or ideol-ogy. Leaders were well aware of the fact that 60.1 percent of the voters had cast their ballots against them in the election. With both the Supreme Court and Congress controlled by the Democrats, it would be almost impossible to form a coalition in which the Republicans could survive, and Republican dominance of the government would be out of the question. But Republican control of the government was exactly what the party sought to achieve, even though they were not willing to wait for it under the provisions of the Crittenden Compromise. Republicans denounced the threats of secession publicly, but they also realized privately that the South was playing right into their hands by advocating such a move. The Republican Party was dominant in the Northeast and Northwest, and held an advantage over the Democratic Party in those sections of the coun-try. However, it could not overcome the weight of the Democratic Party's influ-ence on a national scale. As evidenced in the 1860 election, the South voted in a solid Democratic bloc, with virtually no support for the Republicans. If the Southern voice were removed from the equation, it would shift the balance of power in national politics firmly in favor of the Republicans.

Nothing could give more emphasis to this assertion than a review of how the already seceded Southern states conducted themselves in regard to the national government in Washington. In little over a month following the first meeting of the Committee of Thirty-three, all seven of the deep South states had convened their conventions and voted for secession. It was agreed that a convention be held no later than February 15, in Montgomery, Alabama, for the purpose of organizing a Southern Confederacy. The convention was actually held a week prior to the deadline of February 15. In the meantime, it was determined that the senators and representatives of these states would retain their seats in Congress until March, to impede the Buchanan administration and hinder Republican efforts to strengthen their hold on the government prior to the inauguration of Lincoln.[11] Southern leadership fully recognized the stranglehold the Democrats had on Republican designs to take control of the central government, and used the advantage to blunt any steps by the Republicans to increase their influence in national affairs. This ploy was not lost upon Lincoln or other key members of his party. Republican leadership realized that Lincoln's administration would be akin to a lame-duck presidency if it was forced to constantly confront Democratic opposition in Congress.

Republican leadership faced a dilemma. In order for the party to seize control of the national government, the Democratic bloc that was the South had to be neutralized. Southern firebrands seemed to be accommodating this by virtue of their moves toward secession. The elimination of Southern Democrats in Congress would give the Republicans a secure numerical advantage, and enable them to push through all of their government reforms and pet legislation. Seemingly, events could not have been working out better for them. But Republican leaders were intelligent enough to understand that their short-term victory could be the catalyst to cause their long-term ruin.

Only six years old, with no heritage of great accomplishments, no great statesmen or heroes at its helm, the party knew its legacy would lie in becoming the political entity that broke up the Union and destroyed the nation created by the Founding Fathers. Republican leaders acknowledged that most voters supported the Union, regardless of any other political ideology they might adhere to. The Declaration of Independence, the Constitution, and the legends that were Washington, Jefferson, and Adams formed a fraternal bond between all sections of the country. The common masses, North and South, Democrat and Republican, cherished the old Union, and took justifiable pride in the government their forefathers had created. Passions and sectional interests had brought the country to the brink of disunion, largely perpetuated by the agenda of the Republican Party. The Republicans could make no compromises with the Democrats, else the party appear to be seeking permission from their opponents to govern. The removal of Southern senators and representatives would give the party the majority it sought, but would cast it in the light of being the instigator and aggressor, and, in all probability, sound its death knell in national politics. A way had to be found to achieve majority without alienating the electorate or casting the party as the Simon Legree in this test of wills between the opposing sections of the country. What resulted was a passive-aggressive policy that ensured the Republican Party would be able to save face with the nation. It also eliminated the possibility of compromise and assured that civil war would be the only viable remedy for the issues then facing the country.

Senator Crittenden had been feverishly at work trying to win support for his proposal and fend off the impending crisis. Crittenden sought to bring the bill to the floor of the Senate directly, since he could not get it out of committee. The move was blocked several times by the Republicans, but on January 16, 1861, by a single-vote margin, it was allowed to go before the main body. Every Republican in the Senate had voted against allowing the proposal to be introduced. When Crittenden introduced his compromise to the senators the Republicans evinced a new tactic. They eliminated Crittenden's preamble and resolution and "in lieu thereof insert[ed] those of a directly opposite character, and such as were in accord with the Chicago platform." This motion passed the Senate by a vote of 25 to 23, with every Republican voting for it and six senators from the seceded states abstaining.[12]

Knowing the support his proposition had with the people, Crittenden then sought to take his compromise directly to the voters in the hope of starting a national referendum. This campaign never really got off the ground, however. Rallies and meetings all over the country were planned, but in every case they were not allowed to take place. Republican thugs and bully-boys interrupted and interfered with these proceedings, working in much the same manner as strike busters would later do in the early twentieth century. In the end, the Crittenden Compromise was killed for no other reason than that the Republicans did not want to compromise. The party had gained all of the concessions that had served as the reasons for its formation.

How can these actions be viewed in light of the historical record? If the Republicans were not intentionally pushing the nation to the brink of war, then they were being incompetent and irresponsible. They were intentionally defying the will of the vast majority of voters who had elected them. They were turning their backs on a compromise that guaranteed concessions on all of the issues that had caused their formation as a protest party in 1854. Crittenden's proposal had even promised an eventual majority to the North that would be irreversible. But the Republicans did not want to wait. They did not want to achieve their goals because the South made concessions. They did not want to rule because the South had given them permission to do so. The Republicans wanted to seize control of the government now, and they wanted to do so from a position of power.

Following the death of Crittenden Compromise, a series of conciliation plans were forwarded by politicians wishing to avert war, but all met with the same fate as the Crittenden proposal. On January 19, the General Assembly of Virginia adopted a resolution inviting all the states to appoint commissioners who would meet in Washington on February 4, where an effort would be made "to adjust the present unhappy controversies in the spirit in which the Constitution was originally framed." These resolutions expressed the belief that the Crittenden Compromise, with some revisions, would be the best possible way to avert the coming disaster, and the method favored by a majority of the citizens. All classes were willing to support Virginia's call for a Peace Conference, except the Republicans. A few of the Northern states refused to even appoint commissioners to the conference, and those that did selected delegates known to oppose compromise in any form, men like Salmon P. Chase and David Wilmont. Zacariah Chandler telegraphed the governor of Michigan urging him to appoint only radical abolitionists to the conference, in order that no compromise could be reached.[13]

The historic record speaks for itself. Democratic politicians from the South made repeated efforts to save the Union. They offered concessions and appeasements to the Republicans in a spirit of patriotism, only to have their efforts shunned and thwarted at every turn. Publicly, the Republicans were making violent denunciations that the Southerners were out to break up the old Union, and condemned the leaders who advised for secession as traitors and madmen. Privately, they refused to even talk about any proposal that would bring about a peaceful resolution to the problems at hand. It seemed as if the members of the party had all taken to heart the words and sentiment expressed by John Brown as he faced the gallows little more than a year before, that the "crimes of this guilty land will never be purged away but with blood."

Even so, Republicans were aware of the widespread support for compromise among the people, and it would not do to portray themselves in such a negative manner. It must appear to the folks back home that a sincere effort was being made. For that reason alone, Republicans agreed to send commissioners to the conference. On February 27, John Tyler, president of the conference, sent a diluted version of the Crittenden Compromise to the Senate, where it died, never being brought to a direct vote by that body. On March 2, after so many disappointing efforts, Senator Crittenden was finally successful in pushing his compromise to a vote of the Senate. It was defeated by a vote of 20 to 19, with all the dissenting votes coming from Republicans. On the eve of the Lincoln administration's being inaugurated into power, the options for a peaceful solution of the nation's difficulties were running out. Lincoln would assume his position as commander in chief of a country that seemed destined for division and war.

Let us pause here to make a cursory examination of the charge leveled by Republicans that the leaders of the secession movement were traitors to the nation, or to the compact their forefathers had entered into when they ratified the Constitution. It would be proper here to submit the farewell speech made in the Senate by a man held to be among the top instigators in the movement, one who was actually arrested, held in confinement, and threatened with execution for treason at the conclusion of the war: Jefferson Davis. Read for yourself the magnanimous words, and draw your own conclusion as to whether they were the expressions of a traitor, or those of a patriot.

> For we have proclaimed our independence. This is done with no hostility or desire to injure any section of the country, nor even for our pecuniary benefit, but solely

from the high and solid motives of defending and protecting the rights we inherited, and transmitting them unshorn to our posterity. I know that I feel no hostility to you, Senators here, and am sure that there is not one of you, whatever may
have been the sharp discussion between us, to whom I cannot say now, in the presence of my God, I wish you well. And such is the feeling, I am sure, the people I
represent have towards those you represent. I therefore feel I but express their
desire, when I say, I hope, and they hope, for those peaceful relations with you
(though we must part) that may be mutually beneficial to us in the future.

There will be peace if you will it; and you may bring disaster upon the whole
country if you thus will have it. And if you will have it thus we invoke the God of
our fathers, who delivered them from the paw of the lion, to protect us from the
ravages of the bear; and thus putting our trust in God, and our own firm hearts
and strong arms, we will vindicate and defend the rights we claim.

In the course of my long career I have met with a great variety of men here, and
there have been points of collision between us. Whatever of offense I have given
which has not been redressed, I offer my apology for anything I may have done,
and I go thus released from obligation, remembering no injury I have received,
and having discharged what I deem the duty of a man, offer the only reparation in
my power for doing any injury I ever inflicted.[14]

Seeing no hope of a satisfactory resolution from the government in Washington, the leaders of the seven seceded Southern states pushed forward with
plans to create a new nation and, accordingly met in Montgomery, Alabama,
on February 4, 1861, for the purpose of adopting a constitution. The document
they adopted bore a striking resemblance to the United States Constitution. The
nation was to be called the Confederate States of America, though Thomas R.
Cobb of Georgia had preferred to name it the Republic of Washington. On February 9, Jefferson Davis was named provisional president of the Confederacy.
Davis had secretly desired a military commission, wanting to lead an army in
battle rather than direct the affairs of state, but he accepted the honor and was
inaugurated in Montgomery. Alexander H. Stephens was selected to be vice
president. Stephens had fought against secession until his state adopted that
measure, at which time he loyally followed it out of the Union.[15]

Davis took the control of a nation that had to create everything from an
army to a postal system. All of the inner mechanisms of a national government
had to be built from scratch. His administration also assumed the liabilities of
the seven states which made up the Confederacy, including compensation they
now owed to the Federal government in Washington. The United States government had owned sixteen military posts located in the newly seceded Southern states. Twelve of these had been occupied by state authorities by the time
of Davis's inauguration, with only four remaining in Federal hands: Fort
Sumter, in Charleston; Fort Pickens, in Pensacola; and two other forts in
Florida, at Key West and the Dry Tortugas. The liability to the states was now
transferred to the Confederate government, and commissioners were sent to
Washington to make settlement with the United States for the value of the

seized property. The commissioners arrived too late to open negotiations with the Buchanan administration, and determined to wait until Lincoln had been inaugurated.

In the meantime, those Southern forts still in Federal hands occupied the attention of most members of the new government. Since the states in which they were located had formally severed their ties with the United States, Federal occupation of these facilities was viewed as an encroachment on sovereign and independent soil. Southerners felt the presence of Federal troops in their midst to be the same as an intrusion by any other foreign power, and demanded their removal. The forts at Key West and the Dry Tortugas posed no immediate threat to the Confederacy, could be taken only by a massive naval effort, and were largely left out of the equation. Sumter and Pickens were quite another matter, and of the two, Sumter was fast becoming the focus of attention, both North and South.

Situated in the middle of Charleston Harbor, Fort Sumter posed a threat to Charleston's shipping trade, while the Stars and Stripes that flew over it served as an insult to the people of the city. South Carolina officials were pressing for a conclusion to the stalemate at Sumter, prompting President Davis to appoint Pierre Gustave Toutant Beauregard a brigadier general in the provisional Confederate army and to send him to Charleston to assume direction of the military preparations taking place there. Beauregard arrived in the city on March 3, 1861, the day before Lincoln was to be inaugurated as president of the United States.

Beauregard was well known to Major Anderson, the defender of Fort Sumter. Anderson had been Beauregard's artillery instructor at West Point, and had been so impressed by the young New Orleans Creole's expertise that he made him his assistant instructor as soon as he graduated. Upon assuming command, the student fully utilized the lessons of the teacher, as Beauregard supervised the placement of cannon around the harbor in such a fashion as to effectively produce a ring of fire which the fort's defenders could not hope to survive.[16]

General P.G.T. Beauregard. Popularly nicknamed the "Napoleon in Gray," Beauregard was given the responsibility for seizing Fort Sumter from its Union defenders (Military History Institute, United States Army War College).

While Jefferson Davis had been greeted by throngs of cheering citizens at his inauguration at Montgomery, Alabama, Abraham Lincoln made an inauspicious entrance into Washington, D.C., to assume the mantle of Federal leadership. Private detectives had uncovered what they were sure was a plot to assassinate the president-elect as he passed through Baltimore on the way to Washington. On February 22, Lincoln had stopped in Harrisburg, Pennsylvania, to make a speaking engagement, and to presumably spend the night. Lincoln made his speech as planned, but he did not remain in the city. Instead, he left the hotel at approximately 6:00 P.M., disguised in an old threadbare coat and a soft wool hat, the likes of which he had never worn before. He was secretly driven to an unlighted railway coach, and a few minutes later was on his way to Philadelphia. Lincoln and his party had to change trains at Philadelphia, and were to be delayed in doing so for an hour. To prevent him from being recognized, Allan Pinkerton, the nationally famous detective, drove Lincoln around the streets of the city in a darkened coach until it was time to board the train. Lincoln used a side door to enter the railroad station. He leaned on Pinkerton's arm, and stooped so as not to draw attention to his height. An old traveling shawl was pulled up over his shoulders and clutched in front to almost obscure his face from view. In

THE LATE ALLAN PINKERTON.

Allen Pinkerton. An associate of both Abraham Lincoln and George B. McClellan, Pinkerton was regarded to be America's foremost detective at the outbreak of the war. His wildly inflated estimates of Confederate troop strength, however, prompted McClellan to exercise caution in many instances, believing that the enemy forces were superior to his own (Military History Institute, United States Army War College).

this manner, he boarded the train to Baltimore. Lincoln and his party snuck into Washington to assume control of the government.

This picture is hard for us to imagine today. Abraham Lincoln has come to symbolize all things American, and has become, along with Washington, the most famous of American presidents. He has been linked to every manner of patriotic, nationalistic, human rights, and even religious issue until he has become an immortal character in the fabric of American society. As a people, we have come to accept the legend of Lincoln so completely that all one needs to do to elevate the status of one's product or argument is make a connection between it and "Old Honest Abe." It is beyond our ability to fathom that he was so disliked, so unpopular with a majority of those whom he was about to govern that it was necessary for him to sneak into Washington in a disguise, surrounded by personal security and bodyguards, but that was certainly the case. The sixteenth president of the United States was going to the White House as possibly the single most hated and despised man in the nation.[17]

Among the many problems Lincoln would have to face after his inauguration was a growing sentiment in the North to allow the seceded Southern states to go in peace. The majority of public opinion in both sections of the country was that states had the right to withdraw from the Union and sever their ties with the Federal government. To be sure, South Carolina had tested the waters in the time of Andrew Jackson's presidency, but there had been numerous other instances where portions of the country had contemplated or pursued an agenda of secession. During the War of 1812, it had been the New England states that had sought to unite and form their own confederacy, in protest over dissatisfaction with the Madison administration. All in all, secession had been contemplated or threatened more than a half dozen times in the history of the nation, and only one of those times had been in the South. All others had occurred in the North. Ask people which was the first state to secede from the Union and you will invariably receive the answer: South Carolina. The first state to declare its independence from the Union was actually Vermont, during the War of 1812. As late as 1854, the state of Wisconsin considered secession out of protest over the Dred Scott decision. Massachusetts had considered or threatened the expedient on four different occasions. In the debates over the adjustment of state debts incurred during the Revolutionary War, in protest of the Louisiana Purchase, during the War of 1812, and upon the annexation of Texas, the state resorted to threats of secession as a political remedy for situations it felt to be intolerable. When Louisiana petitioned for statehood, Massachusetts Representative Josiah Quincy rose in Congress to state "it as my deliberate opinion that, if this bill passes, the bonds of this Union are virtually dissolved; that the States which compose it are free from their moral obligations; and that as it will be the right of all, it will be the duty of some, definitely to prepare for a separation, amicably, if they can — violently, if they must. It is to preserve, to guard the Constitution of my country that I denounce this attempt." How does this stance differ from the position taken by the Southern states in 1860? Sufficient precedent had been established for the right of secession so that most citizens of the North willingly accepted that the seven cotton states of the deep South were acting within the bounds of constitutional authority in leaving the Union and declaring themselves a new nation. Abraham Lincoln himself had addressed this topic in a speech made before Congress during the Mexican War. Lincoln declared, "Any people anywhere being inclined and having the power have the right to rise up and shake off the existing government, and form a new one that suits them better." New York abolitionist leader and famed newspaper editor of the *New York Tribune*, Horace Greeley, expressed the opinion of the majority when he wrote, "If the Cotton States shall become satisfied that they can do better out of the Union than in it, we insist on letting them go in peace.... Whenever a considerable section of our Union shall deliberately resolve to go out, we shall resist all coercive measures designed to keep it in. We hope never to live in a republic whereof one section is pinned to the residue by bayonets."[18] In New York City, with its large Democratic population, residents clamored for conciliation between the two sides, and blamed the Republicans for the lack of compromise. The situation became so acute in the city that Mayor Fernando Wood actually proposed that New York City secede with the South, to become a free port of entry, like Bremen or Hamburg in Germany.[19] War protests would once more bring the city to the attention of the world in the summer of 1863, when a United States army would invade and occupy the city of New York as if it had indeed seceded and formed an alliance with the Confederacy.

Lincoln's administration would inherit a nation whose general attitude was one of nonintervention. Though the vast majority of citizens favored the continuation of the Union, when compromise failed, they were more than willing to allow the seceded states to go their separate ways. Even such prominent abolitionist men as Henry Ward Beecher of Boston advocated allowing the Southern states to depart in peace, and Senator Charles Sumner stated that "nothing would be so horrible, so wicked or so senseless as a war."[20] During this period, Lincoln and the Republicans could not have hoped to secure the needed support to mount a military intervention against the Southern states. Such a move was considered illegal and in violation of the Constitution by the majority of the electorate, who would not have volunteered to serve in an army raised for the sole purpose of subjugating another section of the country. Lincoln knew that without an incident that would inflame and outrage the people of the North, there could be no action taken against the seceded states. Up to this point, the South had conducted no overt actions against the Federal government. It had done nothing to hamper or interfere with the business of the United States, desiring only to be excluded from any further affiliation with that government. It was this posture that had won it the consent of a majority in the North, and Lincoln and the Republicans recognized that unless this situation was altered, the nation was destined to become two countries. After that took place, any attempts at reunification would necessarily involve large concessions on the part of the Republicans, and that would be out of the question, given the intolerance of the party to enter into compromise to avert the crisis in the first place.

Therefore, the question of Federal property then existing within the boundaries of the seceded states was brought to the forefront, and made to be the prime issue between the two sides. Chief of these was to be Fort Sumter. This was the situation on March 4, 1861, when Abraham Lincoln was sworn in as the sixteenth president of the United States. Fear for Lincoln's safety had led General Winfield Scott to place sixty soldiers around the platform upon which

General Winfield Scott. Though a Virginian by birth, this elder statesman of the United States Army remained with the Union and directed the early military operations against the Confederacy (Military History Institute, United States Army War College).

Lincoln would take the oath of office. Following his being sworn in, Lincoln delivered his inaugural address in which he made it clear that the government would not consent to its own destruction through secession. He avowed that the nation would maintain its authority: "The power confided to me, will be used to hold, occupy, and possess the property, and places belonging to the government." But Lincoln was quick to add that there would be "no bloodshed or violence" involved in the maintaining of government property. There "will be no invasion," he stated, "no using of force against, or among the people anywhere." Lincoln stressed the bonds that connected the two sides, and asked if "aliens" could "make treaties easier than friends can make laws?" In regard to the question of slavery, he pledged that his administration had "no purpose, directly or indirectly, to interfere with the institution of slavery in the States where it exists," promising that "the property, peace and security of no section are in anywise endangered by the now incoming administration." Lincoln ended his speech with the following words:

> In your hands, my dissatisfied countrymen is the momentous issue of civil war. The government will not assail you. You can have no conflict without being yourselves the aggressors. You have no oath registered in Heaven to destroy the government, while I shall have the most solemn one to "preserve, protect, and defend" it.
>
> We are not enemies, but friends. We must not be enemies. The mystic chords of memory, stretching from every patriot grave to every living heart and hearthstone, all over this broad land, will yet swell the chorus of the Union, when again touched, as surely they will be, by the better angels of our nature.[21]

If Lincoln's words were to be believed, his inaugural address repudiated the very platforms upon which his party had run for election, and under which he had secured the presidency. On the surface, Lincoln's words appeared to be conciliatory toward the South. His official policy would have protected slavery, contrary to the intentions of the abolitionist core that had control over party policy. The tone of the speech portrayed his administration as being willing to compromise, and thus garnered the favor of the Northern electorate. But this hand of peace was offered with full knowledge that Northern Republicans had already quashed every offer of compromise that had thus far been proposed. The real genius of Lincoln's inaugural speech was that it set the tempo to begin depicting the seceded states as being the aggressors in the crisis. Lincoln had promised that there would be "no invasion," no "use of force" against those Southern states that had left the Union, but had added the admonition that these guarantees were valid only so long as the South refrained from any aggressive actions toward the Union. Therein lay the key to Lincoln's policy in regard to the South. A passive Northern electorate had compelled him to employ subterfuge in creating an incident that he was sure would galvanize public opinion for the war he and other Republican leaders knew must come. Fort Sumter was to become the catalyst that would change public opinion, while shielding the party from allegations of being the perpetrators of the conflict. Charleston, South Carolina, was to become the site of an elaborate game of chess, and Lincoln was to prove himself the grand master of the game.

The question of Federal property within the Southern states had been broached before the secession of the seven "cotton" states. In fact, it had been brought up before Lincoln had secured his victory at the polls, setting the stage for such discussions to be relevant. General Winfield Scott, the aging general in chief of the United States Army, foresaw the impending crisis occasioned by the upcoming election, and attempted to mitigate potential events by sending President Buchanan a written statement of his advice. In it, Scott said, "From a knowledge of our Southern population it is my solemn conviction that there is some danger of an early act of rashness preliminary to secession, viz, the seizure of some or all of the following posts: Forts Jackson and St. Philip, on the Mississippi, below New Orleans, both without garrisons; Fort Morgan, below Mobile, without a garrison; Forts Pickens and McKee [McRee], Pensacola Harbor, with an insufficient garrison for one; Fort Pulaski, below Savannah, without a garrison; Forts Moultrie and Sumter, Charleston harbor, the former with an insufficient garrison, the latter without any; and Fort Monroe, Hampton Roads, without a sufficient garrison. In my opinion all these works should be immediately so garrisoned as to make any attempt to take any one of them, by surprise or coup de main, ridiculous." Scott, a Southerner himself, further suggested that exports be left perfectly free, without being taxed by tariffs, with all duties on imports being collected outside of the cities, in forts or ships of war.[22]

Scott's advice was to avert Southern takeover of Federal property by a passive-aggressive show of force. If the Southern states could not seize these installations, then there could be no insult to the Federal government, and no incident upon which to instigate open hostilities. Buchanan, for his part, ignored Scott's advice. In fairness, however, there was little he could do to adopt the measures Scott promoted. The United States Army contained a mere 16,000 officers and men on the eve of the Civil War. Of the 198 companies of regulars that made up the army, 183 were assigned to duty on the western frontier. The government simply did not have the available manpower to put Scott's measures into action, and it was feared by Buchanan that attempting to reinforce the forts, with the limited resources at hand, would merely embolden the Southerners by showing how weak the government truly was. The truth was that the government needed the various state militias in order to be able to prosecute any military interventions against the South. With popular sentiment running strongly against such intervention, an incident, such as was warned against by General Scott, was needed to gain the support of state and local leaders to release those militias for Federal service.[23]

With Forts Sumter and Pickens now being the only significant Federal property in the seceded states still in the hands of the Union, the stage was set for precisely the sort of catalyst Scott had envisioned and warned against. Of the two, the situation at Sumter was the more precarious. Charleston was one of the South's most important ports, and the city was dependent upon maritime trade for its existence. The prospect of having a Union garrisoned fort in the middle of its harbor was repugnant to Charlestonians, South Carolinians, and Southerners as a whole.

In truth, the Civil War had already begun, but the timing of open hostilities was not convenient for the Republican agenda. On January 9, 1861, Cadet George E. Haynsworth of the Citadel Military Academy had fired the first of several hostile shots against the United States, though the incident caused little more than a ripple on the national scene. The *Star of the West*, an unarmed side-wheel steamer, had been loaded with provisions and two hundred New York recruits and sent on a secret mission to reinforce Fort Sumter. The ship arrived off the coast of Charleston on the night of January 8, and attempted to reach the garrison early the following morning. A little before 7:00 A.M., Haynsworth pulled the lanyard that sent the first shell fired against the flag of the United States arcing toward the *Star of the West* as the ship passed by defenses on Morris Island. The shell flew harmlessly over the vessel, but was followed by a barrage, first from the Morris Island batteries, then from the guns at Fort Moultrie. The ship was struck twice, though little damage resulted from the shot and shell.

Major Anderson, at Fort Sumter, held his command in check during the shelling, refusing to provide covering fire for the *Star of the West*. His orders from the War Department had been to act strictly on the defensive and to take no action that might be judged to be offensive. Anderson had been given no notice of the mission of the *Star of the West*, having learned about it and its covert operation only through the pages of the *Charleston Mercury*. Anderson fully realized that if he fired on any South Carolina positions he would be entering into open conflict from which there could be no turning back. As he had received no orders to countermand those already in his possession, he restrained his men from answering the shells that were being fired from the South Carolina state militia, as the garrison became spectators in the dramatic chapter that was unfolding. Without supporting fire from Sumter, and faced with the prospect of an increasing fire at decreasing range, the captain of the *Star of the West* decided to abort the mission. The ship turned, headed down the channel, and out to sea.[24]

At the time of the incident, South Carolina was the only state that had seceded from the Union, even though secession conventions were scheduled for the other six cotton states. The nation was still convinced that the crisis could be averted through compromise, causing the public to overlook the incident. Embarrassment, not outrage, was the prevailing sentiment in the North. Instead of relieving the fort from a position of power, with a fighting ship of the line sailing boldly up to Sumter, a hired merchant steamship had tried to sneak the men and supplies ashore. To the people, it looked as if the government was afraid of the secessionists. The Buchanan administration suffered severe criticism for the failure. Southern nationalists were given yet another example of the bad faith with which the Federal government was negotiating.

But that was January. In the two months that followed, a great deal had changed on the national landscape. By March, the Confederate States of America was a reality, complete with a provisional government and army. Compromise negotiations had proved to be a farce. Lincoln had been sworn in as president. The situation at Fort Sumter was increasingly occupying the attention of both the government and the people, held in the spotlight by the clever manipulation of the Lincoln administration. The importance of the position, in a military sense, was almost useless. Its walls were unfinished. There were cannon yet to be mounted. The defending garrison numbered only about ten percent of that required to hold the fort. Lastly, Sumter was ringed by Confederate batteries with the capacity to reduce the structure by bombardment any time the Rebel leaders decided to do so. Though it held almost no real military value, Sumter was being elevated to high symbolic value by the Lincoln administration. Everything hinged on Sumter. If the fort fell without incident, the division of the nation would probably be effected without interference from the Federal government.

Major Anderson held an untenable position. He and his garrison were short on everything, including food and ammunition. By the first week in April, the Confederates were on the verge of gaining a bloodless victory, by reason of this shortage of food supplies. All that was required was a little more time, and Anderson's garrison would be compelled to surrender from hunger. This fact had been communicated to Washington, prompting Lincoln to authorize another resupply mission, in opposition to advice he had been given by General Winfield Scott. When Lincoln had solicited the general's opinion about what should be done regarding Fort Sumter, Scott reported, "Evacuation seems almost inevitable, and in this view our distinguished Chief Engineer concurs."[25] Lincoln rejected Scott's advice, opting instead on the naval expedition to reinforce and resupply the base. Secrecy was impossible, and the Confederates knew of the plan almost as soon as it was authorized. To the Confederate government, provisioning a fort lying within the boundaries of the Confederacy, in spite of demands for the surrender of the illegally held property, constituted an act of aggression, and justified the use of force to prevent it. The Northern public did not see it this way. To most Northerners, the firing of the first gun would signify the start of the war. Lincoln had maneuvered the South into a corner, and had manipulated the situation to provide the incident he sought in order to declare war.

After three days of failed negotiations, the Confederate government telegraphed orders to Beauregard to capture the fort on April 11. Early that afternoon, Beauregard presented his formal demand for surrender to Anderson, which was promptly declined. At 4:30 A.M. on the morning of April 12, a signal shot was fired from Johnson Island, and the bombardment of Sumter began. By 6:00 A.M., the ships of the relief fleet arrived outside the harbor and prepared to cross the bar. Only one of the vessels had entered the harbor before the entire fleet was turned back by a heavy volume of Confederate fire. Anderson responded as best he could, with the men and guns at his disposal, but the result was predestined from the firing of the very first shell. After two days of bombardment, he was forced to surrender his post at 7:00 P.M. on April 13. The United States flag was lowered from its staff, and the Confederate military took possession of Sumter. The victory had cost no more than would have been the case if the garrison had been forced to surrender from hunger, as not one of Anderson's men had been killed during the bombardment. The intrinsic differ-

Drawing of the firing on Fort Sumter by the Confederate forces under the command of General P.G.T. Beauregard. Lincoln skillfully maneuvered the South into firing the first shots of the war, and by so doing was able to portray the Confederacy as being the aggressor in the conflict (Military History Institute, United States Army War College).

ence, however, was that the fort and the flag of the Union had been fired upon. In the winning of this victory, Confederate authorities had played right into the hands of the Lincoln administration, and had accomplished for the Republicans what they could not do for themselves—they had galvanized what had previously been a wavering spirit among the people of the North.[26]

There is little doubt but that Lincoln and the Republicans desired war. They had done all in their power to avoid compromise, the compromise favored by the vast majority of the very people who had elected them to the presidency. Lincoln had maneuvered the Confederate leaders into firing the first shot, knowing that this act would inflame the passions of the North, and allow him to open hostilities against states that sought only a peaceful departure from their old compact. Historians J.G. Randall and David Herbert Donald, in their book *The Civil War and Reconstruction*, ponder: "Did Lincoln anticipate that sending this expedition to provision Fort Sumter would precipitate a civil war? Even at the time there were those who claimed that Lincoln well knew the consequences of his action and deliberately tricked the Confederacy into firing the first shot. There is indeed some evidence to support this view."[27] This "evidence" comes from several sources, mostly from the mouth or pen of Lincoln himself. In May of 1861, Lincoln wrote to Captain Gustavus Fox, the commander of the relief expedition to Sumter, "You and I both anticipated that the cause of the country would be advanced by making the attempt to provision Fort Sumpter [*sic*], even if it should fail; and it is no small consolation now to feel that our anticipation is justified by the result."[28] On July 3 of that same year, Lincoln confided to Orville H. Browning, a personal friend, "The plan [sending supplies to Major Anderson] succeeded. They attacked Sumter—it fell, and thus, did more service than it otherwise could."[29] Southern historian Charles W. Ramsdell believed that "Lincoln, having decided that there was no other way than war for the salvation of his administration, his party, and

Major General Robert Anderson. This Kentucky-born Union officer commanded the garrison at Fort Sumter, South Carolina, where the first shots of the Civil War were fired (Military History Institute, United States Army War College).

the Union, maneuvered the Confederates into firing the first shot in order that they, rather than he, should take the blame of beginning bloodshed."[30]

The Republicans had been successful in achieving all of their designs in regard to the South. They had blocked the possibility of compromise, eliminated the solid Democratic bloc of the Southern states, and had set in motion events that led to the Confederate forces' firing on Fort Sumter. All of this had been done while portraying themselves as the non-aggressors in the crisis, swaying public opinion in their favor, as an enraged North demanded satisfaction for the disrespect shown to their flag in Charleston Harbor. Northerners, who a week before had resigned themselves to the division of the nation, were now clamoring for military action, and proclaiming their willingness to enlist in the army to put down the rebellion. It was a coup de main for the Republican Party. With Northern opinion now solidly in their favor, the party could proceed with their war in certain knowledge that the state militias of the North would be theirs for the asking.

In the months between the secession of the cotton states and the firing on Fort Sumter, Republicans received a large measure of the blame for instigating the crisis that was at hand. The party suffered a loss of popularity even within its own rank and file, leading J.W. Kane of Pittsburgh to write to Stephen Douglas: "The Republican party would not have a majority in any state of the Union if the election were to come off tomorrow."[31] Lincoln's stealth in forcing the South into firing the first shot changed all that. Lincoln was a master of public relations. He knew that constitutional abstractions carried little weight in the minds of the common people. All the masses cared about was who fired the first shot. In talking about the actions of the Republicans during the time between Lincoln's election and the firing on Fort Sumter, one noted historian stated it thus: "But if they must choose between saving the party, at the cost of civil war, and saving the Union through sacrificing the party, they placed party first."[32]

CHAPTER FOUR

Securing the Borders

News of the firing on Fort Sumter sent a shock wave through both sections of the country. North and South, the towns and cities were alive with excitement. It was almost as if a great weight had been lifted. Tension had been escalating between the two sections for decades, and the firing on Fort Sumter gave an outlet for the tension to finally be over. True, it would probably require the use of military power to establish a united nation once and for all, but no one on either side speculated that it would be much of a war. One prominent politician stated that he would be able to wipe up all the blood that would be spilled with his handkerchief. Most saw the coming conflict as the great adventure of their lifetime, not as a violent social upheaval that would tear apart the existing fabric of America and redefine what the country was, and would become.

On April 15, 1861, Lincoln issued a call for 75,000 volunteers, to serve for a period of nine months, to put down the rebellion in South Carolina, and for Congress to reconvene on July 4, 1861. On the previous day, the nation had sustained the first casualties of the young war. Major Anderson had been granted permission from General Beauregard to fire a departing salute of 100 guns before evacuating the fort. While in the process of firing the salute, Private Daniel Hough inserted a charge into the muzzle of a cannon that had not been thoroughly sponged. A spark of flame still burned inside the tube, causing the charge to explode prematurely, severing Hough's right arm and killing him almost instantly. Fire from the mouth of the cannon was carried by the breeze, igniting a pile of charges nearby. When these exploded, five more Union soldiers were wounded.[1]

In terms of intent, let us first examine Lincoln's call for the Congress to reconvene. Congress was scheduled to adjourn in mid–April. As noted Civil War historian William C. Davis states the case, "This situation would permit him [Lincoln] to put emergency measures into effect without an embarrassing clash with Congress over the proper executive and legislative authority in the matter." Facing the prospect of open hostilities, Lincoln allowed the current session of the legislature to expire, without any request to keep them in Washington to help deal with the impending crisis. The result was that the administration would have a period of two and one-half months to pursue its war agenda without interference from Congress. William C. Davis suggests that Congress was not to be reassembled "until public opinion had time to solidify behind him [Lincoln], as he felt sure it would."[2]

Without Congress in session to challenge his actions, Lincoln was free to pursue military interventions on the basis that the current emergency was an insurrection. As such, he could proceed with authority reserved to him under the Militia Act of 1792, as amended in 1795. In simplest terms, this meant that Lincoln was taking "police" action against the South, not declaring war. If the question of "sovereign" states, as they were referenced in the Constitution, was brought up, then Lincoln's call for volunteers and preparations to invade the South could be viewed in no other way than being a war. Since the sole authority for declaring war rested with Congress, there was a strong possibility that Lincoln's call to arms, and his subsequent military initiatives, might have been blocked by a Congress that felt he was usurping its authority to decide such matters. The resulting cooling-off period may have averted the war altogether. As it was, Lincoln would be free to embroil the nation in civil war before Congress could have an opportunity to stop him. When the legislative body reconvened, the situation would already be beyond its power to effect a reversal of policy. Lincoln would have already voted the proxy of Congress, and its members would be compelled to lend their support to a policy they had no say in creating.

Given the fact that Lincoln, in his own words, acknowledged that the expedition to resupply Fort Sumter had been undertaken with a view to create an incident, the timing of that action now comes into question. Lincoln waited to take any action regarding Fort Sumter for more than a month following his inauguration. He did so only when Congress was about to conclude its current session, knowing full well that this would give him a chance to direct events without being impeded by legislative constraints. Were these events a matter of coincidence or convenience? Viewing each in and of itself, it is possible to arrive at the conclusion that coincidence played a major role. When examined in the context of the actions of Republican leaders leading up to the firing on Fort Sumter, however, it is hard to conceive that they were not intentional acts, designed to bring about the conflict, and to allow Lincoln a grace period to commit the nation to a war that would be beyond the power of Congress to reverse when it met again in July. On April 20, 1861, Lincoln imposed a naval blockade on all Southern ports.[3] This action was not consistent with a police action against insurrectionists. In the world community, it was viewed as an act of war from one nation against another. As such, it should not have been within Lincoln's authority as president to do so. But with Congress in recess, Lincoln merely continued to refuse to recognize the fact that the Southern states had formed a new nation, declaring that as long as they were part of the United

States, he was only acting within the limits of the law in taking military action against them.

The president's call for 75,000 volunteers, instead of being an act of coercion and containment, further exacerbated the crisis. The upper slave states, as well as the border states, were faced with a difficult decision. Union sentiment had been very strong in these states, but if they remained in the Union, they would be called upon to furnish troops to the Federal army for the purpose of invading their sister states to the South. While most residents of these states favored Union and rejected secession, they also were staunch advocates of state's rights, and viewed Lincoln's action to be in violation of the Constitution. Loyalty to the old Union was put in conflict with their fundamental belief in Jeffersonian principles of government. The result was inevitable. Leaders in the border and upper South states felt that they were standing against what they saw to be violations of the Constitution by the Lincoln administration when they not only refused to provide troops to coerce the Confederacy, but also took steps to join that Confederacy. The situation in Virginia was similar to that in all of the slave states still in the Union at the time of the firing on Fort Sumter.

Moderate Democrats, and those remaining old-line Whigs, who had voted for Bell for President, banded together to overrule the secessionist factions within their borders. In a secret session, the Virginia legislature had voted against secession by a margin of 88 to 45.[4] The Reverend Edward Ames, a bishop of the Methodist Episcopal Church, stated: "There has been held a grand Union convention amid the fortresses of the everlasting hills. The Rocky Mountains presided, the mighty Mississippi made the motion, and the Allegheny Mountains seconded it and every mountain and hill, valley and plain, in this vast country, sent up a unanimous voice; Resolved, that we are one, and inseparable and what God has joined together, let no man put asunder." Parson Brownlow, a newspaper editor in Knoxville, Tennessee, vowed that he would "fight Secession leaders till Hell froze over and then fight them on the ice."[5] But all this was before Lincoln made his call for 75,000 volunteers to invade the South.

The administration seemed to be going against its own policy in making this call. On March 8, shortly after the inauguration, Seward had stated, "I have built up the Republican Party, I have brought it to triumph, but its advent to power is accompanied by great difficulties and perils. I must save the party, and save the government in its hands. To do this, war must be averted, the Negro question must be dropped, the irrepressible conflict ignored, and a Union party to embrace the Border Slave States inaugurated."[6] Lincoln's actions were contrary to everything Seward had proposed, and the result was an overnight shifting of public opinion in the slave states still remaining in the Union.

Reaction to Lincoln's call was swift and decisive. In Virginia, the Richmond convention brought the secession issue to a vote on April 17, two days after the president's announcement. The result was almost the exact opposite

Newspaper cartoon showing Lincoln being supported by bayonets in his efforts to save the Union (*Lincoln's Yarns and Stories*).

of that which had taken place in the secret session, with 88 votes in favor of severing ties with the Federal government and 55 votes against, with the majority of the dissenting votes coming from the western, mountainous counties of the Commonwealth. May 23 was set as the date to hold a public referendum on secession, but the result was a foregone conclusion. By that date, Virginia had already transferred all of its state military forces to the service of the Confederacy. Arkansas, Tennessee, and North Carolina all were forced to reevaluate their previous decision to remain in the Union, and in each state Lincoln's anticipated use of military force against the Southern states swung the balance of power in favor of the secessionists. Arkansas went out of the Union on May 6, followed by Tennessee on May 7, and North Carolina on May 20.[7] In February, Tennessee had voted against secession by a margin of two to one. Following Lincoln's call for troops, secession was approved by a margin of three to one.[8] The Confederacy had grown to eleven states, and Maryland, Kentucky, and Missouri were all leaning toward leaving the Union. Lincoln's call held the portent of doubling the size of the Confederacy, as the defections from the Union became a common event. Historian Elbert J. Benton noted that while the states of the Upper South and Border States favored Union, they were convinced "that the beginning of all tyranny was in centralization, the security of human liberty in America, and for that matter in the World, bound up in maintaining unimpaired States' Rights."[9]

Lincoln and the Republican leadership realized that the loss of all of the Upper South and the Border States would result in a situation where the North would have an almost impossible task in subordinating the South to its will. With all the slave states of the Upper South already on the road to secession, the administration focused its efforts on keeping the Border States in the Union, with or without the consent of the citizens residing within those states. Maryland, Kentucky, and Missouri were seen as the keys to victory for both sides. In the case of Maryland, the very existence of the national capital at Washington depended on the state's remaining in the Union. If Maryland joined its sister states in the Confederacy, Washington, D.C., would be surrounded by enemy territory, and would have to be abandoned. The Federal government had good reason for concern. As in Virginia, the majority of public opinion in Maryland had shifted toward secession after Lincoln's call for troops. Also like Virginia, the main source of opposition was to be found in the mountainous, western portion of the state. The counties immediately surrounding Washington were firmly secessionist in their sentiments, and had already displayed their hostility toward Lincoln and the Federal government.

On April 19, 1861, the 6th Massachusetts Infantry was passing through Baltimore on its way to Washington in response to Lincoln's call. Angry citizens had lined the streets to watch the regiment pass through. Tempers within the mob increased, and eventually the insults they were hurling at the troops were replaced by rocks and other items. The Massachusetts troops, without orders, fired into the crowd at will, but the mob did not disperse. Instead, it returned fire. Casualties sustained by both sides have been variously reported, but it seems that the total of four soldiers and nine civilians killed is reasonable. Many more soldiers and citizens were wounded. The 6th Massachusetts at length arrived in Washington, where it was quartered in the Capitol building.[10]

The Baltimore riot, combined with acts of sabotage like the burning of bridges to prevent Union troops from reaching Washington, convinced the Federal government that Maryland was on the verge of secession. A Confederate Maryland would be in position to choke off the flow of men and supplies to Washington, and effectually besiege the capital into submission.

In response to the threat posed by the situation in Maryland, President Lincoln made one of the most blatant attacks on the Constitution committed by the administration during the entire course of the war. Lincoln authorized General Scott to suspend the writ of habeas corpus. Initiated as a means of combating hostile elements in Maryland, the suspension would have far-reaching effects throughout the North, and would be used as a weapon to punish and deter anyone who dared to speak out against Lincoln, his administration, or his policies. Scott invested General Robert Patterson, commander of the

Major General Ben Butler. Sent to Maryland following the Baltimore Massacre, Butler was among the first to be ordered to implement Lincoln's suspension of the writ of habeas corpus and to oversee the arrest of political prisoners in the state (Military History Institute, United States Army War College).

Department of Pennsylvania, Delaware and Maryland, General Benjamin Butler, commander of the Department of Annapolis, and General Joseph Mansfield, commander of the Department of Washington, with authority to suspend the writ, opening the door for summary political arrests.

In early May, John Merryman, a resident of Maryland living near Cockeysville, was arrested in the night by a detachment of soldiers and imprisoned at Fort McHenry. No warrant had been issued for his arrest, and he was held at the fort without charges. According to the military, Merryman had been detained because he was a lieutenant in a company of militia suspected to be secessionist in their sentiments. The company had in its possession weapons belonging to the United States government, and it was feared these would be used against the administration. Further, Merryman had been heard to utter sentiments that were considered to be disloyal. A review of the case reveals that Merryman was indeed an officer in a state militia unit. The weapons used by the company, however, were of state issue, and did not belong to the Federal government. Furthermore, it was only natural if the company was feared to have secessionist sentiments, as all of the men were from the area around Baltimore, where secession sentiments were high. Merryman's commission in the militia was for state service. If, as expected, Maryland voted to leave the Union, it was his duty to defend his state from all aggressors. Simply put, the issue was merely part of an overall attempt, on the part of the administration, to forcibly keep Maryland in the Union, with or without legal methods.

When he learned the details of the case, the U.S. Supreme Court's Chief Justice Roger Taney issued a writ of habeas corpus, which was presented to General George Cadwalader, in command at Fort McHenry. Cadwalader ignored Taney's writ, citing his authority to do so as coming directly from the president. Chief Justice Taney, in *Ex parte Merryman*, ruled that the suspension of the writ of habeas corpus was unconstitutional, since it could only be suspended by an act of Congress. President Lincoln and the military likewise ignored this ruling of the Supreme Court, and the writ was not reinstated until 1866, when it was officially restored by the Supreme Court in *Ex parte Milligan*. Thus, for the duration of the war, Lincoln and the Republicans were in open defiance of the Supreme Court, clinging to an act ruled unconstitutional by the highest law in the land.[11]

On May 11, the Union commander on the Florida coast was authorized to suspend the writ of habeas corpus on the islands of Key West, Tortugas, and Santa Rosa. On July 2, General Scott was empowered to make military arrests, without interference from the writ, on a line from New York City to Washington, D.C., and on October 14, that line was extended from Washington to Bangor, Maine.[12]

In the meantime, the policy had been put to the test in Maryland. The arrest of John Merryman was soon followed by the mass arrest of the Baltimore police commissioners, members of the police board, and the marshal of police. The police commissioners, in protest over this violation of constitutional rights, effectively disbanded the Baltimore police force, paving the way for General Nathaniel Banks to proclaim marshal law and appoint a military provost marshal to

Roger Taney. As Chief Justice of the United States, Taney ruled that Lincoln's suspension of the writ of habeas corpus was unconstitutional. Lincoln ignored Taney's ruling and continued to incarcerate political prisoners throughout the war without formally charging them with a crime (Military History Institute, United States Army War College).

rule over the city. The members of the Maryland state assembly were the next to feel the sting of military rule. General Banks was instructed by the Secretary of War to arrest any member of that body suspected of disloyalty to the administration. Accordingly, the majority of the members of the Maryland legislature were rounded up and incarcerated without charges. It is unknown whether or not Lincoln's call for troops to invade the South would have been reason enough for the Maryland representatives to vote for secession, but the heavy-handed tactics of the military since that time had definitely swung the balance in favor of the secessionists. The order to arrest the members of the legislature was carried out in an effort to prevent them from voting Maryland out of the Union. The *London Saturday Review* denounced the action and said their arrest "before they had time to meet, without any form of law or prospect of trial, merely because President Lincoln conceived they might, in their legislative capacity, do acts at variance with his interpretation of the American Constitution, was as perfect an act of despotism as can be conceived. It was a coup d'etat in every essential feature."[13] The administration attempted to quash all resistance when they arrested the legislators by also rounding up editors of Baltimore newspapers that had run disparaging or critical articles about the administration. Lincoln and the Republicans were not only trampling on the constitutional rights of the writ of habeas corpus, they were also putting freedom of speech to the sword.

The editor of the London newspaper had been exactly correct in his opinion of the military arrests. Lincoln had indeed intervened to prevent the rep-

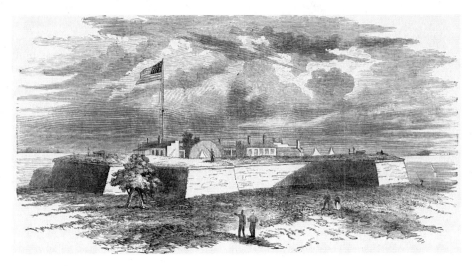

Drawing of Fort McHenry in Baltimore, Maryland. Though the fort had become a symbol of American freedom because of its association with "The Star Spangled Banner," its primary Civil War usage was as a prison for political prisoners (Military History Institute, United States Army War College).

resentatives from voting the will of the people of their state because he was convinced that the result would go against him. In so doing, Lincoln and the Federal government directly interfered with the proceedings of a state government, and, by force of arms, rendered null and void the will of its citizens. Furthermore, the editor was correct in his suspicion that the legislators were to be held without trial. In some cases, members of the Maryland assembly were detained for more than two years without ever being officially charged with a crime, and without the opportunity to take their case to trial. It was despotism of gigantic proportions. The border states were crucial to Lincoln's ability to win a war against the Confederacy. Maryland was now secure, held in the Union at the point of a bayonet, and policed by an army of occupation. All told, 171 military arrests were made in the state in the early phases of the war, with a large number of them being the representatives of the Maryland state legislature.[14] But the administration's policy of coercion and military force was not to be confined to Maryland.

General William Harney. His efforts to keep peace in St. Louis, Missouri, were undermined by Nathaniel Lyon and members of the Lincoln administration (Military History Institute, United States Army War College).

During the first year of the war, the responsibility for making arbitrary arrests fell under the jurisdiction of the State Department. On February 15, 1862, authority for such arrests was transferred to the War Department. In all, 866 people were the victims of arbitrary arrest during the first year of the war, according to the State Department records. No definitive numbers exist for the total for the remainder of the war, once the War Department was in charge. The most conservative estimates place it at 13,535, and it could have topped out at more than 30,000. If the lower totals are to be used, then one out of every 1,563 persons living in the North was arrested during the war. If one accepts the higher total, the ratio of arrests becomes 1 in 750.[15]

In Missouri, the secessionists were led by Governor Claiborne Jackson, while the Unionists followed Francis P. Blair, Jr. Former governor Sterling Price and Brigadier General William S. Harney were the leaders of the state moderates, holding sympathies for the South and North, respectively. Tensions in the state were heightened following the firing on Sumter, and were further exacerbated after Lincoln's call for troops, but it appeared that Price and Harney would be successful in keeping the peace. Lincoln recognized the importance of holding both Missouri and Kentucky in the Union. Each state had a population of around 1.2 million people, second in population only to Virginia. If these states seceded, they would potentially increase the Confederate military by 25 percent. Of the two, Missouri was of the more pressing importance. If Missouri left the Union, Kentucky was almost sure to follow. Aside from the manpower that such a move would give to the Confederacy, the strategic placement of the two states would create a nightmare for the Union. The Confederacy would be in control of key stretches of the Mississippi and Ohio Rivers, and would be able to block traffic to the west. If Missouri and Kentucky sided with the Confederacy, the North would be hard-pressed to win a military conflict. Furthermore, the Confederacy would be able to strike an economic blow at the North by restricting the flow of goods to and from Northern manufacturing bases, and would be able to isolate Kansas, southern Illinois, and the western territories. Lincoln and the Republicans did not wait to see what course the citizens of Missouri adopted in regard to Union. Instead, he authorized the military to make a preemptive strike that would assure Federal control and hopefully eliminate the possibility that Missouri would follow its sister states into the Confederacy.[16]

In early May, the state militia turned out for its two weeks of summer training at Camp Jackson in St. Louis. General Harney, commander of the Department of the West, was temporarily absent from his headquarters, leaving Captain Nathaniel Lyon to oversee the department. In fact, the absence of Harney had been contrived by Francis Blair, Jr., who had used his influence with the administration to have the general called away to Washington just as matters were heating up at St. Louis. Blair had already taken the measure of Nathaniel Lyon, and found in him an ally willing to assist in tipping the scales in Missouri in favor of the Republicans and the administration. Lyon was a passionate Unionist, in the mold of John Brown. An army doctor had once described him as "honest to the core, truthful and intelligent," but had also stated that he was "Narrow-minded, mentally unbalanced," and filled with an "anger that was almost insane." He was just the sort that Blair could use to instigate an incident in Missouri designed to effect Federal control over the region.

Though the state militia had committed no subversive acts, maintained its allegiance to the Union, and flew the banner of the United States over its camp, Lyon determined that it posed a threat and decided upon a course of action that forced all residents to choose sides once and for all. The militia was composed of some 700 men under the command of General D.M. Frost. Lyon, with some 5,000 Union troops, surrounded the camp and summoned Frost's immediate surrender. Caught in the open, and with no reasonable alternative options, General Frost complied. When Lyon's troops marched their prisoners through St. Louis, angry citizens lined the streets in protest over Lyon's arbitrary action. Passion erupted into violence when the crowd fired into the closed ranks of the soldiers, prompting the troops to return their fire. By the time it was over, there were twenty-eight dead and many more wounded.

Anarchy ruled the city until Harney's return, when he and Sterling Price worked out a truce and pacified the people. Harney issued a public apology for the violence that had taken place. In a public broadside, he stated: "I have just returned to this Post, and have assumed the Military Command of this Department. No one can more deeply regret the deplorable state of things existing here than myself. The past cannot be recalled, I can only deal with the present and the future. I most anxiously desire to discharge the delicate and onerous duties devolved upon me, so as to preserve the public peace. I shall carefully abstain from the exercise of any unnecessary powers, and from all interference with the proper functions of the public officers of the State and City."

This solution was not to the administration's liking, however, and in less than three weeks Harney was removed from command. Lyon was promoted to the rank of brigadier general and temporarily assigned to replace him in command of the Department of the West. Francis Blair, Jr., wanted Lyon to receive the job permanently, but the rash young officer's tactics had caused authorities in Washington to deny this request, since they feared that Lyon's heavy-handed tactics would have the reverse effect of pushing the state's moderates firmly into the secessionist camp. General John C. Frémont, the first to carry the banner of Presidential aspirations for the Republican Party, was sent to assume command of the department in Lyon's stead.[17]

Lyon wanted nothing to do with the truce Harney and Price had established. Once Harney was gone, and before Frémont had arrived, he demanded that the state authorities and the militia immediately submit to his orders, in essence establishing martial law. Convinced that there was no further hope of peace, Price withdrew from the city with his followers, and joined Governor Jackson and the legislature at Jefferson City. Lyon marshaled his forces and marched on the capital. On June 17, at Boonville, he met and defeated a force of 1,300 militia that Governor Jackson was organizing to defend Jefferson City. The civil and military leadership of Missouri fled to the southwest corner of the state, as General Lyon consolidated his control over the state he had won through force of arms. A Union convention was held in Jefferson City that declared all of the state's elected offices vacant. A loyal governor was then appointed to replace Jackson, and Unionist politicians were placed in all of the other vacancies. Lyon's actions were committed with the full knowledge and approval of the Lincoln administration. Missouri, to be sure, contained a strong secessionist faction within its borders, but the state had remained loyal to the Union. Fearing that this loyalty would not endure, Lyon was allowed to make war on the legitimate civil and military authority of Missouri. He was granted permission to effect a military takeover of the state, and to use his forces as an army of occupation once the legal and elected authorities were overthrown.[18]

From June till August of 1861, both sides prepared for the decisive military showdown that would decide who controlled Missouri. Sterling Price's Missouri militia had received the support of General Ben McCulloch and his Confederate forces from Arkansas and Texas. Lyon marched on this combined force with 5,000 troops, and made contact at Wilson's Creek, in the southwestern portion of the state, on August 10, 1861. The Confederates, numbering some 15,000 men, attacked Lyon's little army, threatening to overwhelm it. The Federals fought valiantly, however, repulsing the first two Southern assaults. General Lyon was shot dead during the third Confederate charge, and in the precipitating confusion resulting from his death the Union forces were driven from the field.

For his part, Frémont's time in command of the Department of the West was one of graft, corruption, and incompetence. Frémont spent great sums of money to arm and outfit the volunteers coming into his ranks, but most of the arms and supplies he received from those with whom he had contracted were of shoddy, inferior quality. He distributed generals' commissions liberally, and without the consent or approval of Congress. But most importantly, Frémont took it upon himself to initiate government policy. Immediately following the defeat at Wilson's Creek, he issued a proclamation decreeing that the state was under martial law. Any man captured in the act of rebellion against the military was to be summarily executed.

If Frémont had stopped there, he might have received the approval of Washington, but the general decided to take one step further. Of his own volition, and without prior consultation with his superiors, Frémont took it upon himself to order the immediate freeing of the slaves. The effect of his declaration was horrific, both North and South. Moderate Missourians were pushed into the secessionist camp. Those already aligned against the administration were quick to retaliate. Jeff Thompson, leader of a force of Confederate guerrillas operating within the state, vowed to "hang, draw and quarter a minion of said Abraham Lincoln" for every secessionist Frémont ordered executed. Frémont had opened a veritable Pandora's Box, and now the administration had to scramble to put the lid back on. Lincoln sent his personal secretary, John Hay, to meet with Frémont, and to deliver a letter asking the general to modify his proclamation dealing with the slaves. Frémont refused to do so. As the general assembled an army of some 50,000 men and marched out of St. Louis in search of the Confederates, Lincoln decided his fate. The President stated that Frémont had become the "prey of wicked and designing men" and voiced his opinion that he had "absolutely no military capacity," and directed Winfield Scott to relieve him from command.[19]

The war in Missouri would become one of the saddest chapters in American history, with neighbor fighting neighbor in a blood feud that degenerated from warfare into bushwhacking between armed mobs. Civil war visited the state in all its horror, and had been brought about by the manipulation of the administration and its appointed military officials. The actions of Lyon and Frémont had been the cause of this bloodshed. While the latter had merely intensified the situation, the former had brought them to a head. In doing so, however, he had put in motion events that would lead to Union control over the civil and political operation of the state, and had effected the military occupation of key points in the state, depriving a base of organization or a political voice to anyone who might oppose the will of the administration. As was the case in Maryland, Missouri was to be held in the Union by force of arms.

General Frémont's actions are essential in examining the war goals of the North, however. If, as has been avowed in almost a century and a half that has passed since its occurrence, the North was fighting to free the slaves, why did Frémont's proclamation cause such a stir with the politicians in Washington? Why did it cause Lincoln to have him removed, and why was the proclamation repealed? The reason is that the war was not being fought to free the slaves. It was being fought for political power and control. The freeing of the slaves was not an expedient measure, it served no purpose at this time and therefore, was denounced by the Republican-controlled government as being a radical act. It was only when such a move benefited the administration that it would be considered, as it did little more than a year after Frémont's declaration. An examination of the reasons for the Emancipation Proclamation will be reserved for later chapters. Mention of it is only made here so that the reader may ponder the incongruity of what he or she has previously been taught. If the war was fought to free the slaves, then why did the Lincoln administration recoil with horror when General Frémont did just that?

The situation in Kentucky provided what was possibly the most complex and sensitive situation of any of the Border States. Though they were Southerners by virtue of their culture, economy, and affiliations, Kentuckians were known for their fierce devotion to the Union. One New York editor proclaimed that "there are no people on the globe who have evinced more national feeling, more disinterested patriotism, or displayed a more noble enthusiasm to defend the honor and rights of their common country." A Bostonian declared Kentuckians "are the most patriotic people I have ever seen or heard of."[20] Truly, the people of the Bluegrass State wrestled with a mighty problem at the outset of the Civil War. They were faced with what appeared to be conflicting loyalties: to the Union and to their state and region.

There was no doubt in anyone's mind that Kentucky was a Southern state, especially not in the mind of any Kentuckian. But the attachment to the Union was particularly strong here, possibly because the geographic location of Kentucky gave it shared borders with several different states, and because it was a main thoroughfare for the commerce and trade of the entire nation. If Kentuckians were conflicted in their sentiments, they were just as conflicted in their beliefs. On the subject of secession, the state legislature had drafted the Kentucky Resolutions in 1798 and 1799, declaring that Congress, created as it was by a compact between the individual states, was subject to the judgment and approval of those states. If the Federal government passed legislation that was considered unjust, or ignored the will of the states, it was the right of any state to nullify that legislation and prevent its enforcement, even if it had to be done by use of force. The Kentucky Resolutions were largely written by Thomas Jefferson, even though they were presented by John Breckinridge. Henry Clay, Kentucky's favorite son, known as "The Great Compromiser," voiced what would seem to be a contradictory belief during the crisis which eventually led to the Compromise of 1850 when he said, "If Kentucky Tomorrow unfurls the banner of resistance, I will never fight under that banner. I owe a paramount allegiance to the whole Union; a subordinate one to my own state." The citizens of the state made known their feelings on the subject when later that same year they sent a block of native stone to be used in the construction of the Washington Monument. Chiseled into the stone was the inscription: "Under the auspices of Heaven and the precepts of Washington, Kentucky will be the last to give up the Union." On the surface, it might appear that these two beliefs could not possibly coexist. Kentuckians, however, were very jealous of their rights. They felt they had the right to oppose tyranny from the central government, but they also felt they had a duty to defend the common good of that union. For decades the two beliefs had been able to live together. Even with the crisis of the nation almost upon them, Kentuckians tried to balance those beliefs. In the 1860 election, the state boasted two native sons as presidential candidates: Abraham Lincoln and John C. Breckinridge. Lincoln bore the banner of the Northern extremists, while Breckinridge carried the torch for the Southern extremists. Kentuckians responded by casting their votes for John Bell, the Constitutional Union candidate.[21]

With the outbreak of war, Kentuckians found themselves caught in the middle. Northerners fully expected Henry Clay's home state to stand firmly with the Union. Southerners were convinced that the state would follow the cultural and economic ties it had with the other slave states and join the new Confederacy. Most Kentuckians were opposed to secession, but they were equally adamant in their condemnation of the Federal government's proposed use of force against the seceded states. What resulted was a sort of standoff in which Kentucky refused to be part or party to either side. The state officially adopted a policy of neutrality, and took steps to protect its neutral status from any and all assailants. In March of 1860, the legislature had passed a bill that called for every able-bodied male between the ages of eighteen and forty-five to be a member of the enrolled militia. Thus, at the outbreak of hostilities, Kentucky boasted one of the largest and best-trained military bodies of any state in the Union. In the current crisis, the Kentucky State Guard was mobilized to defend the borders against any aggressor that sought to violate its neutrality. The policy was doomed to failure from the start, but to most Kentuckians, it was a natural solution to the dilemma they faced. The Bluegrass State would simply sit this one out.

When President Lincoln made his call for 75,000 troops, the state of Kentucky was informed that its quota would be four regiments, or 4,000 men. Governor Beriah Magoffin quickly informed the administration: "Kentucky will furnish no troops for the wicked purpose of subduing her sister Southern States." On May 16, the Kentucky legislature officially approved the position of neutrality and gave its endorsement to Magoffin's refusal to provide troops to the Federal government. Simon B. Buckner had been selected as inspector general of the Kentucky State Guard, and though his personal sentiments favored secession, he worked diligently to enforce the neutrality adopted by his state. Along with Governor Magoffin, he tried to establish a confederation of neutral states, including Tennessee and Ohio. Magoffin and Buckner felt that such an alliance would be strong enough to confront any hostile forces, while also being strong enough to protect its neutrality. Governor Isham G. Harris of Tennessee agreed, at least in principle, with the proposal, as did George B. McClellan, commander of the volunteer military forces of Ohio. But Magoffin's attempt at neutrality would prove to be a pipe dream almost from the start. While most of the citizens of the state favored neutrality, the firing on Fort Sumter had forced them to search their individual souls, and to choose sides. Within the Kentucky State Guard, sentiments ran strongly for secession, so much so that a worried legislature made a second call for militia to create a Home Guard to counter the influence of the State Guard. Union men came forward in droves to answer the call, establishing a tense standoff within the state. The United States and the Confederacy were also locked in a standoff. Both sides knew that whoever violated Kentucky's neutrality would be responsible for driving the state into the other side's camp.[22]

For its part, the Confederacy strictly observed the neutrality. As soon as it had been proclaimed, Jefferson Davis ordered all Confederate recruiters out of the state. For his part, Lincoln took an entirely different approach. On the surface, the administration recognized the neutrality, while it secretly made covert efforts to shift the balance of power in favor of the North. As early as May 14, Lincoln advised General Robert Anderson that he was providing covert aid to the Unionist forces within the state. Thousands of muskets from the North found their way into the hands of the Home Guard units that were forming. When Buckner ordered muskets with which to arm units of the State Guard, Republicans and Unionists in the North generally saw to it that what he received were antiquated or unserviceable weapons. In mid–June, a special congressional election was held within the state, resulting in a majority of Unionist candidates' being elected. Magoffin's fragile neutrality was already starting to come unraveled.

The administration, sensing this, took steps to complete its demise. By

July, recruiting camps were established for loyal men just across the border in Ohio and Indiana, followed closely by the establishment of a recruiting camp within the state by General William Nelson. When Union troops from George B. McClellan's command crossed into Kentucky to invade Columbus, for the purpose of removing a Confederate flag flying there, it was the beginning of the end. More and more "Lincoln rifles," as they were called, poured into the state, while the newly elected Unionist legislators consolidated their control. By September, the pro–North element in Kentucky had grown strong enough to officially declare neutrality at an end.[23]

To John C. Breckinridge, neutrality was never a solution to the problem facing his home state. Breckinridge had worked diligently following Lincoln's inauguration to try to find a compromise that both sides could agree to. Lincoln's call for troops to put down the rebellion caused him to shift his allegiance to the Confederacy, and he attempted to organize a convention for the purpose of taking Kentucky out of the Union. Failing in this, he decided to abide by the legislature's neutrality stance, even though he disagreed with it. Breckinridge took his seat in the U.S. Senate in July of 1861, and he was quite vocal in attacking the Lincoln administration for its role in bringing on the war. Senator Edward P. Baker of Oregon openly accused Breckinridge of treason for his scathing attacks, and the Kentucky state legislature at length requested his resignation from the Senate. By the time of his recall, Breckinridge had already accepted a commission as a brigadier general in the Confederate army, and had gone south. If he could not fight against the administration in the halls of Congress, he would do so on the field of battle.[24]

Control of the Border States was crucial to both sides in the Civil War. Both sides felt that these states held the balance of power, and that the outcome of the war rested in who controlled them. In the end, Lincoln was successful in keeping all three in the Union. Maryland and Missouri had been coerced through the use of direct military force, augmented by political arrests that undermined any opposition movement before it could be organized. In Kentucky, the administration proclaimed a policy of nonintervention, officially respecting the state's neutrality, while it covertly armed the pro–Unionist Home Guard and tipped the balance of power from within. Once they were organized and armed, the Home Guard assumed a threatening posture within the state, openly denouncing neutrality in favor of alignment with the Union. The strength and swagger of the Home Guard influenced the special congressional elections in June, giving the Unionists political control as well as military superiority. Neutrality was abandoned, and Kentucky was embraced by Lincoln and the administration. The border was secured, and the Northern war effort had been materially strengthened. Though the Union army had suffered a humiliating defeat in the first major battle of the war at Manassas, Lincoln and the Republicans had scored a victory greater than any that could be won on a battlefield. With Maryland, Missouri, and Kentucky firmly in its grasp, the Union was now ready to win the war. Four bloody years of conflict would end in a result that was already decided when the Border States were retained in the Union.

But it was not only in the Border States where opposition to the administration was to be found. Horace Greeley would write: "There is, or has been quite a general impression, backed by constant and confident assertions, that the people of the free States were united in support of the war, until an Anti-Slavery aspect was given to it by the administration. Yet that is very far from the truth. There was no moment wherein a large portion of the Northern Democracy were not at least passively hostile to any form or shade of 'coercion' while many openly condemned and stigmatized it as atrocious, unjustifiable aggression. And this opposition, when least vociferous, sensibly subtracted from the power and diminished the efficiency of the North." This undercurrent of discontent existed in all of the states of the Union, and would, at various times, erupt into open confrontations with the administration.[25]

CHAPTER FIVE

Elections and Endorsements

The first year of the war was a disaster for the Union. Two different "On to Richmond" drives had resulted in defeats and bloody repulses. Everywhere in the East, the Confederates seemed to hold the upper hand. From 1st Manassas to "Stonewall" Jackson's Valley Campaign, from the Seven Day's Battles to the rematch at Manassas, the Northern military was outgeneraled and outfought. At least that was the opinion of the people on the home front. The expectation of the people, on both sides, had been for a short war, nothing longer than ninety days. By the time the first year had passed, even the most optimistic observer had to admit that the conflict was no closer to a conclusion than it had been when the initial call to arms had been made, during those first patriotic and giddy days.

The situation was slightly more promising in the Western Theater, where the Union boasted its only string of victories in this young war. General Albert Sidney Johnston's defensive line had been breached, causing Nashville and Memphis to fall into Union hands. The Union army had prevailed at Mill Springs, Kentucky, and had captured Forts Henry and Donelson in Tennessee.

Then, in the spring of 1862, when human minds are usually filled with the promise of renewal, came the Battle of Shiloh. The two-day struggle resulted in the retreat of the Confederate army, and was counted a victory for Northern arms, though both sides were bloodied and bruised to an extent never dreamed of by the American public. To a nation accustomed to the relatively small losses of the American Revolution, the carnage of Shiloh came as a horrifying shock. Total losses in the battle amounted to 23,741, with the North suffering 10,694 and the South sustaining 13,047.[1] It was commonly stated in the Confederacy that the South never smiled again after Shiloh. In the North, a stunned and dazed population scanned the casualty rolls in search of loved ones. This was not panning out to be the thrilling adventure that had motivated men to swarm to the banner of their respective sides. The size of the armies and the length of the casualty lists more closely resembled the great bloodletting wars of Europe. In Northern papers, editors compared Shiloh to Waterloo.

No one could imagine that the conflict could become bloodier than Shiloh, but in the fall of 1862 came Antietam, the bloodiest single day of the entire war. Between sunrise and sunset on September 17, 1862, some 26,134 Americans became casualties.[2] Most historians consider the battle to be a draw, but Robert E. Lee's Army of Northern Virginia quit the field, leaving it to George B. McClellan's Army of the Potomac. It was the first battle that even looked like a victory in the East, and as such, it was embraced by the Lincoln administration as a sign of the turning tide of fortune. Lincoln and the Republicans were in dire need of a victory. Public opinion was running sharply against the war, and the administration that had led them into it. War-weariness had already surfaced in the North, where most citizens felt that it was becoming impossible to subdue the Confederacy on the battlefield. The Southern army seemed almost invincible. The notion of a negotiated peace was gaining support, and the Republicans were in real danger of losing their grip on the national government.

Northern Democrats took advantage of the discontent of the civilian population by proclaiming the war to be a failure and advocating its termination, with or without the reinstatement of the Southern states. Democrats not only attacked the administration's handling of the war effort, but also the right of Lincoln and the Republicans to intervene in the social and economic interests of the South. Standing on a platform of nonintervention, the Democrats styled themselves as the "Peace Party," and gained a large following from among the working class with their reasoning that tampering with the institution of slavery was tantamount to sacrificing the jobs and economic welfare of the people of the North. Their portrayal of ex-slaves as a cheap, transient work force struck fear in the hearts of factory workers across the region. With a slogan of "The Union as it was and the preservation of the Constitution as it is," they garnered a grassroots support that threatened to sweep the fall Congressional elections.

The Lincoln administration thus faced war on two fronts, military and political. The Confederacy was maintaining its independence on the battlefield, and seemed wholly capable of being able to foil any Northern efforts to coerce it back into the Union. But the greater threat to the Republican Party came from the "Peace Party" and the Northern Democrats. If something was not done to stem the tide of their growing popularity, the Republicans would surely lose their majority in the House of Representatives, and be forced to admit failure and seek a negotiated peace with the Confederacy. Andrew Curtin, the Republican governor of Pennsylvania and a close personal friend of Abraham Lincoln, chose this moment to step into a position of leadership in national affairs. Colonel A.K. McClure, a contemporary of both Curtin and Lincoln, in talking about the personal and political bond between the two men, states that there "was not a phase of the war, at any time that did not summon Curtin to the councils of Lincoln."[3]

Curtin, considered to be a moderate, first sought out the advice of like-minded Republicans. He contacted Governors F.H. Pierpont of West Virginia and David Tod of Ohio, and all agreed that something must be done to make a show of support for the administration. It was felt that the best way to achieve this would be through a conference of the loyal Northern governors. Curtin's next move was to sound out the feelings of a prominent member of the radical faction of the Republican Party, and Governor John Andrew of Massachusetts was his selection. On September 6, 1862, Curtin wired Andrew: "In the present emergency would it not be well if the loyal governors should meet at some point in the border states to take measures for a more active support of the Federal government?" Andrew replied that he was in agreement with Curtin's suggestion, bringing himself under a great deal of criticism for doing so. Many of Andrew's political adversaries used his acceptance of Curtin's invitation to claim that he was compromising the interests of his home state. The fact that he was unwilling to discuss any details of the meeting publicly led to charges that he was conspiring against the government. Nevertheless, on September 14, 1862, invitations were sent out to all the Northern governors: "We

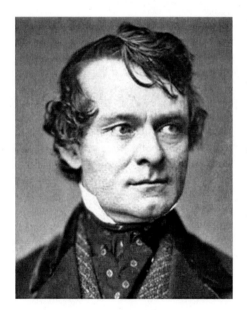

invite a meeting of the governors of the loyal states to be held at Altoona, Pennsylvania on the Twenty-fourth instant. A.G. Curtin, Pennsylvania, David Tod, Ohio, F.H. Pierpont, West Virginia."[4]

Governor Curtin organized the conference in the face of two impending emergencies. The first was, of course, the danger posed to the Republican Party by the Democratic movement. The second was of a far more immediate nature, and was a threat to the selection of the conference site. Lee's Army of Northern Virginia was invading Maryland, and Curtin feared that Harrisburg or Philadelphia would be its final objective. The day before he sent out the invitations to the Northern governors he had wired Lincoln requesting "not less than eighty thousand disciplined forces," plus state militia forces from every state in the mid–Atlantic "to concentrate here at once." Curtin wildly estimated the size of Lee's army at "not

Andrew Curtin. A staunch supporter of Lincoln and his policies, Curtin was the motivating force in organizing the Altoona War Governors' Conference in Altoona, Pennsylvania, for the purpose of solidifying support of the loyal Northern governors behind the administration (Military History Institute, United States Army War College).

12079— *Logan House & P. R. R. Train Shed & Station, Altoona, Pa.*

Picture of the Logan House in Altoona, Pennsylvania, where the War Governors' Conference was held in 1862 (from a 1905 postcard in author's possession).

less than one hundred twenty thousand men with a large force of artillery," giving the Confederate commander credit for having almost three times the number of men he actually had. Lincoln responded that he did not have an additional 80,000 men to send to Pennsylvania. He further stated his opinion that if Lee did indeed invade the state, it would be the best possible situation for Union arms, as the army would then be able to seal him off from his lines of supply and communication and effect his destruction. The whole matter was made moot when General McClellan attacked Lee's army at South Mountain, Maryland, on September 14.[5]

Altoona had been selected for a variety of reasons. First, it was removed from the bustling political and industrial centers of the North, allowing the conference to be held with a minimum of interference from swarming crowds of reporters or groups of curious citizens. Secondly, it lay along the line of the Pennsylvania Railroad, the main east-west artery in the state, making it an easy destination for most of the governors who would be attending. Lastly, there was the Logan House, the hotel in which the conference would be held. It had been built by the Pennsylvania Railroad in 1853 to accommodate overnight passengers, and was regarded as one of the most luxurious hotels of its age. Named for an Indian chief of the region, the Logan House boasted the highest standards in comfort and atmosphere. Its 106 rooms were lavishly furnished, most with balconies. There was a dining room, three large parlors, a laundry, a commissary, and a bakery for the convenience of the guests. The parlors where the governors would meet were adjoining and could be made into one large room by rolling back the folding doors that partitioned them. Curtin hoped that in such a cozy atmosphere the various factions of the Republican Party could find some common ground and begin to act in unison to counter the advances of the Northern Democrats.

Before the conference convened, Curtin and Andrew traveled to Washington for a private meeting with Lincoln. The secrecy surrounding the gathering had led to allegations that the governors were preparing to pressure Lincoln into assuming a more radical stance on the war by refusing to provide men or money if he didn't make freeing the slaves the issue of the war and remove all non-abolitionist officers from high command. Curtin and Andrew wished to apprise the President of the true meaning of the conference, and dispel any apprehensions he might have arising from the rumors that were circulating. Lincoln heartily approved of the meeting, and offered Curtin and Andrew insight into his plans to issue a proclamation of emancipation. Lincoln told them that he had made up his mind to issue such a proclamation in the event that Lee's invasion of Maryland was turned back. The Battle of Antietam had already been fought, and though it was considered to be a draw in most military and political circles, the public viewed it as a victory, giving Lincoln the opportunity to make his proclamation from a point of strength. He was, however, concerned over the timing of the issuance. Lincoln offered to delay the proclamation until after the governors had held their conference, at which time they could publicly call on him to do so. After some discussion, it was determined not to pursue this course of action. All felt that the sooner the proclamation could be issued, the better.

By the time Curtin and Andrew made their way from Washington to Altoona, several of the other governors were already starting to arrive. Those who had accepted the invitation included Israel Washburn of Maine; John Andrew of Massachusetts; William Sprague, a manufacturing giant and the youngest member of the group, from Rhode Island; Richard Yates, radical Republican leader and the man who had recommended U.S. Grant for field command, from Illinois; Austin Blair of Michigan; Edward Salomon of Wisconsin; N.S. Berry, a Democrat until slavery began to become an issue, at which time he switched to the Republican side and was elected governor of New Hampshire; Samuel Kirkwood of Iowa, who had been offered several positions by the Lincoln administration but declined them to become governor; and Augustus Bradford of Maryland.[6]

Of the governors not in attendance, Oliver Morton of Indiana was unable to attend because his state was in danger of Confederate attack from General Braxton Bragg's army in Kentucky, so he sent a representative in the person of Colonel D.G. Rose. Governor Frederick Holbrook of Vermont expressed sympathy for the conference but declined to attend because he was readying troops for the army and the legislature was about to convene. Governor Charles Olden of New Jersey also expressed sympathy for the conference but was influenced not to attend by Governor Edwin D. Morgan of New York, who was openly hostile to Lincoln and his policies. No reason was given as to why the governors of the other Northern states were not in attendance.

Andrew Curtin opened the conference with a welcoming speech, reminding those in attendance that their purpose was "to enable the President to secure a more vigorous and successful prosecution" of the war. In the first order of business, Augustus Bradford was elected chairman of the group. Lincoln had issued the Emancipation Proclamation two days earlier, on September 22, and the initial discussion centered upon that topic. All present agreed, at least in theory, to the Emancipation Proclamation, and it was decided that some sort of formal address should be drafted to thank Lincoln for taking that step.

It is ironic that the Northern governors were discussing Lincoln's freeing of the slaves on the same day that the President was enacting measures to enslave the free. On the day the governors met in Altoona, Lincoln issued another proclamation equally as important as the Emancipation Proclamation, though not nearly so well known, then or now. By executive decree, the writ of habeas corpus was suspended for anyone deemed guilty of "discouraging volunteer enlistments, resisting militia drafts, or guilty of any disloyal practice, affording comfort to the enemy." The wording of this proclamation made it a crime to resist the authority of the Federal government in any manner, including public criticism of the administration or its policies. It made anyone who did not agree with Lincoln or the Republicans a potential criminal, subject to arrest and confinement without charges.[7]

Back in Altoona, the governors had hit a snag in achieving the desired cohesion in supporting the administration. Following a break for dinner, the meeting reconvened, at which time Governor Andrew gained the floor for the purpose of making an hour-long attack on General McClellan's fitness to command, and demanding his immediate recall. Curtin, Tod, and Bradford all rose to McClellan's defense, with Curtin emphatically stating that the general had saved Pennsylvania from invasion, winning the first major Union victory in the East in the process. Tod expressed the utmost confidence of the people of Ohio in the general's abilities, and Bradford added that he did not feel this was the time or place to remove him. When asked who could possibly take over the Army of the Potomac and administer its operation better than McClellan, Andrew responded that John C. Frémont's staff was "perfect and ready."

Debate over the matter swayed back and forth for hours, during which time the real reason for this demand by the radical Republicans became evident. McClellan was a prominent Democrat, and it would not do to have a leader of the opposing party become a military hero. The radicals advocated the removal of all Union officers having affiliations with the Democratic Party, as well as those who were known to be sympathetic in any way to the South.

At about 8:00 P.M., with no resolution to the debate in sight, it was decided to take a one-hour recess.

Andrew Curtin used the recess to do considerable buttonholing among the governors, as he sought to reestablish the feeling of cooperation that had been shattered by the military question. During the hour-long break, he was to be seen everywhere, exerting his persuasive nature with individual governors and among small groups. Shortly after 9:00 P.M., when the meeting resumed, it became evident that Curtin's efforts had been successful. All talk of replacing McClellan was dropped, with Andrew proposing instead that an address be sent to President Lincoln approving of the Emancipation Proclamation and promising the resolute support of the governors for his war policies. Governors Tod and Salomon voiced their opinions that the endorsement be made in less radical terms, and for the next three hours variations of the address were debated. At about 12:30 A.M., the debate ceased, and Andrew spent the next 20 minutes making corrections to the address he had originally proposed. Once completed, all of the governors present affixed their names to the document, with the exception of Bradford. In explanation for his refusal to sign, Bradford stated, "Gentlemen, I am with you heart and soul, but I am a poor man, and if I sign that address I may be a ruined one."[8]

The address the governors adopted praised Lincoln for the Emancipation Proclamation and urged him to make a call for 100,000 additional volunteers to form a reserve army. Its most important feature, however, was the fact that it pledged the president the unconditional support of each of the state executives who had signed it. From this point forward, it would be political suicide for any of them to threaten the withholding of men or means, as had been done in the past. A telegraph operator from the Pennsylvania Railroad was summoned to wire the address to Lincoln, and upon its receipt, the President invited the assembly to come to Washington to meet with him personally. Later that same morning, the governors boarded different trains for the trip to the capital. They were split up for reasons of security, and the action proved to be well-founded. Pennsylvania may have been a Union state, but it contained a large number of antiwar and anti-administration citizens, as well as a smaller number having Southern sympathies. Several shots were fired at the railroad cars transporting the governors as they traveled through the Commonwealth.

Upon reaching Washington and meeting with Lincoln, Governor Andrew suggested that the address be sent to all of the governors who had not been at the conference, so that they might have the opportunity to add their names to it. Holbrook of Vermont, William Buckingham of Connecticut, Alexander Ramsey of Minnesota, Charles Robinson of Kansas, A.C. Gibbs of Oregon, and Leland Stanford of California all acquiesced and affixed their names. Robinson of Kentucky, Hamilton Gamble of Missouri, William Burton of Delaware, Olden of New Jersey, and Morgan of New York joined Bradford in refusing. Several of the governors cited the Emancipation Proclamation as their reason for declining.

The Altoona War Governors' Conference had not set down any bold new programs in policy, but that was not Curtin's intention when he invited the governors to hold a meeting. His intention was to defuse a potentially dangerous political situation by getting the governors together to present a combined front in supporting Lincoln and the administration, and in this the conference was a huge success. The combination of the conference, Lincoln's emancipation, and McClellan's victory at Antietam served to breathe new life into the Republican Party, thwarting the designs of the Peace Party and the Northern Democrats. Though many of the results of the War Governors' Conference were subtle, it is certain that the outcome of the war could have been drastically altered had it not occurred. Many historians have rated the event second only to the Emancipation Proclamation in importance for civil or political actions taken during the war. Governor Sprague is quoted as saying, "There are unnumbered reasons, as facts, to show that the meeting or its effects made it possible for the Union armies to win."

With Lee's first invasion of the North turned back, the state executives presenting a somewhat united front of support for the administration, and Lincoln's proclamation concerning disloyalty and the writ of habeas corpus all now in place, the Federal government was ready to face the prospect of the fall Congressional elections, and try to retain its grip on the Federal government. The threat of the Democratic peace movement had received a serious check. The issuing of the Emancipation Proclamation had served to drastically diminish the prospect of foreign intervention on behalf of the Confederacy, as was its intent. But that will be saved for later discussion. The domestic situation that existed during the Congressional elections of 1862, and how it was dealt with by the Republican administration, will be the present focus of attention.

The military reverses suffered by Union arms during the summer of 1862 fueled Democratic attacks on the administration. The faltering condition of military affairs gave them an opportunity not only to assail the Republican handling of the war, but also to rehash the administration's culpability for initiating the conflict in the first place. The Peace Democrat faction of the party believed that the only way to secure reunion was to end the war, with or without the attainment of its objective. During the summer of 1862, the war effort would definitely be far short of its goal. Clement Vallandigham, the acknowledged leader of the peace movement, advised the Union: "Withdraw your armies, call back your soldiers, and you will have peace." The resolution adopted by the Peace Democrats' convention, held in Shelby County, Indiana, became a rallying cry for the movement as a whole. "That we earnestly recommend a cessation of hostilities for such a period as may be necessary to allow the people of the North and the South to express through a National Convention, their desire for peace, and a maintenance of the Union as it was and the Constitution as it is."[9]

The platform of the Peace Democrats enticed large numbers of war-weary voters to join forces with the core of Northern Democrats who had opposed Lincoln and the Republicans from the start. Their strongest support came from Northern factory workers who feared the effect that the abolition of slavery would have on their jobs and economic welfare. Democrats portrayed the freed slaves as a transient work force that would infiltrate the North, willing to work for a fraction of the money then being paid to Northern workers.

On September 17, the day that was to witness the Battle of Antietam, the *Democratic Standard,* printed in Hollidaysburg, Pennsylvania, featured two stories on the front page that preached the doctrine of opposition. The first article was a critical evaluation of African society throughout the ages, and declared that the black race had never made a contribution to civilization in the world. It declared that blacks in Africa still lived as they had in the Stone Age, devoid of written language, recorded history, or the arts. The tone of the article is clear to today's reader, and its veiled suggestion that blacks were of an inferior race is readily evident. In the fall of 1862, however, such articles played on the fears of Northern workers, and provided an argument against emancipation. The second article, titled "Patriotism and Politics," was a direct attack on the Lincoln administration and its policies:

> The Republican leaders tell us that our duty consists in supporting and sustaining the administration, in abandoning the Democratic organization, and giving in our adhesion to the principles of the party in power — not to support the Government merely — for that we have all done, and are doing with men and money, voice and pen — but to re-elect the members of the dominant party, or to fill their places with others of like views, and to perpetuate — so long as the war shall last — the reign of the present irresponsible and incompetent ruling power. This, according to the radical Republicans, is the length and breadth, and height and depth, in short, of patriotism. With all respect for those who give us such advice, we repudiate the teaching, and reject, emphatically and totally, the invitation to abandon our principles — the principles upon which the country rose to greatness, prosperity and power, and to adopt those under the practical workings of which it has been brought to peril, and is now threatened with total destruction. If the country is to be preserved from impending ruin — if the Constitution is to be maintained and the Union restored, there is a high and imperative duty for all patriots to perform — a duty, indeed above partisan and political advantage — involving the dearest rights and noblest institutions ever possessed by man. The duty appeals not to Democrats alone, but to every true friend of his country, and it consists in the most powerful and determined effort to procure a return, in all branches of the Government, Executive, Legislative, and Judicial, to the sound principles which governed the nation for almost three quarters of a century, during its unparalleled growth and success, but whose partial abandonment has speedily brought disaster and evil of the most appalling character."[10]

As more and more people in the North sided with the Democrats in the summer of 1862, it began to appear as if the Republicans would be turned out of power in the fall elections, a possibility that had provided the impetus for Andrew Curtin to call the War Governors' Conference. Republican response to the growing wave of opposition was to pronounce its instigators disloyal. Republicans argued that these Democrats were pro–Southern, to the point of being Confederate activists. To be sure, the Confederate government welcomed any assistance to its cause occasioned by the Northern Democratic opposition, but it did not agree with any of the platforms or policies of the Peace Democrats, and was not part or party to the movement. The die had been cast, and the South was not interested in reunion, with or without compromise. Nevertheless, Peace Democrats were denounced in Republican orations as being disloyal and subversive, and acting as the puppets of the government in Richmond. Indeed, the Republican Party put anyone who dared criticize it into this category, and to speak out against the party or the administration was tantamount, in their eyes, to a confession of Southern loyalty.

Lincoln's September 24 proclamation concerning the suspension of the writ of habeas corpus found direct application in combating the expansion of Democratic influence in the North. Its vague wording that citizens "guilty of any disloyal practice" should be viewed as "affording comfort to Rebels" cast all opponents of the administration as being traitors, guilty of subverting the Union. This application found usage during the upcoming Congressional elections, and proved a means by which the Republicans could ensure their grasp on national affairs. Democratic leaders were targeted for persecution by the administration, and their character and motives were brought into question in the pages of Republican newspapers across the North.

At the same time, the Republicans took steps to censure the voice of Democratic editors by proclaiming their articles to be seditious. Democratic newspaper offices were destroyed, and their editors threatened with imprisonment, violence, or worse. In Uniontown, Pennsylvania, Edward G. Roddy, the editor of the pro–Democrat *Genius of Liberty*, was told that if he did not comply with popular Union sentiments, "forcible means will be used to compel you to surrender your possessions." In Haverhill, Massachusetts, the editor of the local Democratic paper was tarred and feathered, and ridden through town by soldiers who forced him to swear he would never again publish articles "against the North." The story was the same throughout the Northern states, as the administration sought not only to silence the opposition, but also to defame it.[11] In Connecticut a crippled young boy was arrested on board a train on the Naugatuck Railroad. His crime was being the paperboy on the train, selling the *New York Daily News*, a newspaper critical of the administration.[12]

The persecution of Francis W. Hughes is but an example of smear tactics employed by Republicans leading up to the fall elections. By 1862, Hughes had risen to become chairman of the Pennsylvania Democratic convention. During the Congressional campaigns of that summer, he was highly critical of the administration's handling of the war, especially noting the Republican attacks on civil liberties by means of censorship and the suspension of the writ of habeas corpus. Republicans responded by claiming Hughes was disloyal and held disunionist sentiments. As proof, they offered evidence that Hughes had supported Breckinridge in the 1860 election, and that he and his family had ties to Southern interests. Hughes acknowledged his prior voting record, as well as family ties to the South, pointing out that Lincoln himself had brothers-in-law currently serving in the Confederate army. Though Hughes was successfully able to defend his loyalty to the Union and fend off allegations of treason, his reputation was so stained as to warrant his removal from Democratic Party leadership. Over the course of the summer and fall of 1862, the political careers of many Democratic candidates suffered similar smear campaigns from the incumbent party.[13]

The Union victory at Antietam, the War Governors Conference, and the attempt to link any and all opposition to treason all played a part in lessening the influence of the Democratic Party through the fall of 1862. During the actual elections, the government attempted to further emphasize its stance that Democratic candidates were in league with the enemy by posting armed soldiers at a number of polling places throughout the North. It was claimed that this was a necessary evil, brought about by threats from enemies of the Union to interfere with the voting. The reality was that it was an overt attempt on the part of the administration to intimidate the electorate and lessen the turnout for the opposition.

For the reasons previously listed, the 1862 election did not witness the destruction of the Republican Party, but it showed a definite erosion of its base of support, as Northern Democrats made substantial inroads in Congress, where the Republicans lost twenty-two seats and the Democrats gained twenty-eight. Republicans, while losing the majority, still dominated the all–Union Congress, having eighty-six representatives, as opposed to the seventy-two Democrats seated there. The balance of power hung with the members of the Unionist Party, Northern Democrats who had aligned themselves to the Republicans during the first days of the war. Their twenty-five representatives could have swayed the Congress against the administration if they had cast their lot with fellow Northern Democrats. New York and New Jersey were the only states holding gubernatorial elections in 1862, and both states voted Democrats into office.

All in all, the Republicans were still in very good shape. They still held the executive mansion in seventeen of the nineteen states in the Union. They had lost the majority in the legislatures of New Jersey, Illinois, and Indiana, but still held the upper hand in sixteen of the nineteen states. Though the Democrats were hailing their gains as "a great, sweeping revolution of public sentiment" and "a most serious and severe reproof" of Republican policies, the truth was that the Republican incumbents still held the upper hand in national affairs. What was clear was the growing dissatisfaction of Northern citizens with the war and the people responsible for it. Lincoln lamented the 1862 election results by saying, "It is like the boy who stubbed his toe on the way to see his girl; he was too big to cry, and it hurt too much to laugh."

With the fall elections concluded, the administration took steps to eliminate Democratic influence in the army. The three main armies of the Union contained many generals who were either Democrats, or who were closely allied to Democrats. It had been charged by the Republicans that these Democratic officers were too soft in their prosecution of the war, owing to their pro–Southern sentiments. Now, with the elections over and the Republicans still in control, the time had come to purge these officers from the armies. On October 30, General Don Carlos Buell, commander of the western army, was relieved of command. He was followed on November 5 by the removal of George B. McClellan, commander of the Army of the Potomac, and on November 8, Benjamin Butler was replaced as commander of the Department of the Gulf. Numerous other Democratic officers suffered the same fate as their commanders. A thorough examination of the purging of Democrats from the army will be reserved for the next chapter.[14]

The army was not the only place where the Republicans attempted to purge Democrats from power. In the United States Congress, several Democratic members came under attack for allegedly having Southern sympathies. Senator Lazarus W. Powell of Kentucky became one of the main targets for these attacks when accusations were made that he had, through his actions, supported the Confederacy. Expulsion proceedings were begun in the Senate, but Powell was able to successfully defend himself from the charges, and retained his seat in the upper chamber until 1865.

The Republican campaign to maintain its grasp in the workings of government had been highly successful in the 1862 elections. In 1863, the ever-rising cost of the war, and the institution of a national draft, served to increase the war-weariness that had threatened to unseat them the previous year. Bold measures would again be necessary in the 1863 elections if the Republicans hoped to once more stem the tide of protest. Emboldened by their previous efforts. the administration resorted to drastic measures and outright tampering in an effort to influence the outcome of the 1863 elections.

At Frankfort, Kentucky, a Democratic convention, held to nominate candidates for state office, was dispersed by Colonel Gilbert and a regiment of United States troops. When Kentucky leaders made formal protest of the act and demanded an investigation, the demand was refused. Lazarus Powell, the same Senator who had faced charges of disloyalty in 1862, condemned the actions of the military in his home state when he rose in the Senate chamber to charge the administration with tampering in the 1863 elections:

> In many counties the name of the whole Democratic ticket was stricken from the poll book by the military authorities. In many voting places, and in entire counties of Kentucky, no man was allowed to vote for the ticket. In the county in which I

live, the names on the Democratic ticket were stricken from or not allowed to go into the poll books of three or four of the voting precincts. It is asserted that in one precinct of that county sixteen votes were cast, all for the Wickliffe ticket. The military then came there, took the poll books from the judges and clerk, returned them to head-quarters and stopped the election.

Sir, there is abundant evidence of the facts that I have indicated. Since the beginning of time there never was a more atrocious assault on free elections, than took place in many counties of Kentucky. In many places the candidates were arrested. In the First Congressional District Judge Trimble, the candidate for Congress as a loyal man and as true to the Constitution and Union of his fathers as lives in the Union, was arrested by the military authority. He was brought to the City of Henderson, a town just without his district, and there he was kept in military confinement near a month until after the elections were over. They told him if he would decline being a candidate for Congress they would release him. He would not so degrade his manhood as to decline the canvass at the bidding of military tyrants and usurpers, and he was kept in prison. They found that he would be elected by a large majority, notwithstanding his imprisonment, and then they sent the military over his district, and had his name stricken from the polls in almost every voting precinct in the district. The gentleman who beat him got some four thousand votes in a district that polls twenty thousand.[15]

Some fourscore years later, Joseph Stalin would capture in words the spirit of the Republican actions in Kentucky when he said, "What matters is not who votes, what matters is who counts the votes."

Similar instances took place in other states of the Union, including Delaware and Maryland. Governor Augustus Bradford complained of voting interference in Maryland, but his complaint was forwarded to the Military Committee, where it received approval, not condemnation.

On the day preceding the election, the officer in command of the regiment, which had been distributed among the counties of the Eastern shore, and who by himself landed in Kent County, commenced his operations by arresting and sending across the bay some ten or more of the most estimable and distinguished of its citizens, including several of the most steadfast and uncompromising loyalists of the shore. The jail of the county was entered, the jailor seized, imprisoned, and afterwards sent to Baltimore, and the prisoners confined therein, under indictment, were set at liberty. The commanding officer referred to, gave the first clue to the character of the disloyalty against which he considered himself as particularly commissioned; by printing and publishing a proclamation, in which, referring to the election to take place the next day, he invited all the truly loyal to avail themselves of that opportunity to establish their loyalty "by giving a full and ardent support to the whole Government ticket, upon the platform adopted by the Union League Convention," declaring that "none other is recognized by the Federal authorities, as loyal or worthy of the support of any one, who desires the peace and restoration of the Union."

The message was obvious. Anyone who did not support the Republican ticket was to be enrolled on the "disloyal list" and faced the possibility of imprisonment.

In West Virginia, Maryland, and Missouri, state conventions to address and approve Lincoln's Emancipation Proclamation were elected under military dictation. In possibly the most reprehensible act of all, large numbers of Union voters were disenfranchised and denied the opportunity to cast a ballot by means of unconstitutional test oaths. Anyone having ties to the South, or accused of Southern sympathies, could be excluded from voting by the implementation of these test oaths. The reality was that anyone found guilty of extreme criticism of the administration was lumped into this category and disenfranchised. If one protested against the Republicans or their policies, then he would lose his most precious right as an American: the ability to vote his conscience. If forced to endure the same scrutiny as this mass of disenfranchised voters, Lincoln himself would have been denied the right to vote, by reason of his association through marriage to several officers serving in the Confederate army.[16]

N. Bushman, a Northern minister, captured the essence of the attacks on members of the Democratic Party when he wrote: "Old Abe has all the power in his hands. He split fence rails and now has split the Union. It is a burning shame to call everyone a traitor who does not agree with all that Mr. A. does and says. My pulpit in no way, shape or form shall be desecrated with this contemptible disease of this nation. I will at least help them to become good Christians, then I have fulfilled my mission."[17]

By 1863, the Republicans had created something akin to a police state in the North in order to crush the voice of the opposition party. The suspension of the writ of habeas corpus had only been the first step. Freedom of speech, freedom to gather, and the right to vote followed in quick succession as the party pledged to uphold the Constitution superceded that document whenever it was convenient to do so in order to retain power.

One notable difference of policy came from the Commonwealth of Pennsylvania, where Governor Andrew Curtin proposed a bold and innovative suggestion. Suffering from ill health, Curtin proposed that he would not run for reelection, and would retire from public life, if the Democratic Party would nominate General William B. Franklin as its candidate for the fall gubernatorial election. Curtin knew Franklin to be a "War Democrat" who could be counted on to support the suppression of the rebellion, unlike other possible Democratic candidates from the state. If Franklin received the Democratic nomination, Curtin advised that he also be nominated by the Republicans, so that his election would be unopposed. By attempting to choose the Democratic Party's candidate for them, Curtin was trying to assure that Pennsylvania would remain supportive of the Lincoln administration. If Curtin should be defeated in the fall election, the governor's mansion would undoubtedly be occupied by a Democrat openly opposed to the Republicans. But Curtin's plan to retain control of the state met with opposition from both parties. The Republicans were unwilling to lend their support to any Democrat, regardless of his loyal affiliation to the war effort, and the Democrats refused to accept a candidate whom they felt to be little more than a puppet of the administration. In the end, Curtin ran for reelection, and won in a narrowly decided victory.[18]

CHAPTER SIX

The Democrats Must
Leave the Army

In the early days of the war, the Republicans and the Lincoln administration were compelled to seek an alliance with the Northern Democrats in order to prosecute the war. This alliance was not confined merely to the political arena. The Republicans needed Democratic votes, to be sure, but they also needed Democratic money and Democratic men. The Lincoln administration employed a liberal system of patronage in creating the coalition needed to raise an army and induce men to volunteer. All factions of the Northern population were to be represented, as it was felt that men would more readily enlist if they were to serve under leaders they knew and trusted.

The 1860 Census showed that some 4,000,000 foreigners resided in the North, as opposed to 233,000 in the South, and special attention must be shown to each group. The large German segment of the population was induced to enlist by leaders such as Peter Osterhous, Carl Schurz, Franz Sigel, Alexander Schimmelfenig, and Adolph Von Steinwher.[1] In all, twelve German-born officers were commissioned to the rank of general during the war. The tactic worked to perfection. Some 31,000 Germans enlisted from the state of Missouri alone during the course of the war. At the beginning of the conflict, Germans volunteered in droves, forming ten full regiments in New York, six in Ohio, six in Missouri, five in Pennsylvania, and three in Illinois, with thousands of other Germans scattered throughout the rest of the army. The Irish immigrants were also to have their heroes, with another twelve commissions of general being granted to Irish-born leaders such as Michael Corcoran, James Shields, and Francis Meagher. Five Irish regiments were raised in New England, four in New York, and two each in Pennsylvania and Indiana.[2]

The Democratic Party received like consideration in the dispensing of politically motivated commissions in the army. To be sure, there were a number of officers already in the army who happened to be Democrats, like George B. McClellan and Don Carlos Buell, but the administration passed out many more commissions to prominent members of the party solely on the basis of patronage, to individuals who had no prior military experience or training. Men like Ben Butler, Dan Sickles, John Logan, and John McClernand received generals' stars simply because they wielded clout and influence within their home districts and could convince their constituents to enlist.

Most members of this group could not have passed the test oath to vote that the administration was now administering. Ben Butler had been a delegate at the Democratic presidential convention held at Charleston in 1860, where he cast a ballot to nominate Jefferson Davis to be the Democratic candidate. Dan Sickles had served as legal counsel for the corrupt Tammany Hall organization before achieving national notoriety for shooting down the son of Francis Scott Key in sight of the White House. Logan and McClernand both came from southern Illinois, where Southern sympathies ran so high that numbers of men from the area were crossing the border to join the Confederate army.[3] In fact, their districts had taken steps in April of 1861 to separate from the rest of the state and join the Confederacy. The administration hoped that giving Logan and McClernand commissions as generals would not only bring Democratic men into the ranks, but would also help in keeping the southern portion of the state from seceding. Logan was given a general's stars in the Union army even as John and Hibert Cunningham, his father-in-law and brother-in-law respectively, were actively seeking to raise a regiment of troops for Confederate service.[4]

Lincoln's system of patronage in handing out generals' commissions worked to perfection, as members of every group in the Union flocked to join units under the command of their own officers, including Northern War Democrats. By 1862, many of the top positions in the North's armies were held by Democrats, including the top command of the Army of the Potomac, the Army of the Ohio, and the Department of the Gulf. This was a situation that seemed deplorable to the administration. The war was not going well for the Union, and most Republicans assessed blame for that to the Democratic generals who were leading the armies, claiming that they all held pro–Southern sympathies that prevented them from an active prosecution of the fighting. While blame for the lack of Union success was heaped upon the Democrats, it was also certain that Republicans feared the results of Democratic victories in the field. Successful generals have always been able to convert their victories on the battlefield into votes at the polls, and win or lose, the Democrats simply had too much control over the Union armies for Republican peace of mind. George B. McClellan posed the most immediate threat. His popularity with the men in the Army of the Potomac, and the nation as a whole, combined with the fact that he was openly critical of the administration, made him a thorn in the side of the Republicans. There were too many potential Democratic heroes in the army. They had already served their purpose in funneling Democratic men into the ranks, and the time had now come to cleanse the army of Democratic influence and power.

George B. McClellan had been hailed as the new Napoleon by the Northern press when he took command of the Army of the Potomac following the disastrous defeat at First Manassas. Born in Philadelphia on December 3, 1826, he had attended West Point, graduating second in the class of 1846. Assigned to the elite Corps of Engineers, McClellan attracted a great deal of attention during the Mexican War by virtue of his expertise and ability, and was awarded brevets to first lieutenant and captain. He served as an instructor at West Point before being sent abroad as an observer to the Crimean War. He also developed the McClellan saddle, which became standard military issue for the next eighty years.

In 1857, McClellan resigned from the army to become chief engineer of the Illinois Central Railroad, a position he held until the outbreak of hostilities. On April 23, 1861, he was made major general of Ohio Volunteers by Governor William Dennison. Three weeks later, Lincoln appointed him a major general in the Regular Army, making him second in command only to Winfield Scott.

Major General George B. McClellan. "Little Mac," or "The Young Napoleon," as he was commonly called, was so popular with his men that Union officers spread false rumors that he was in command of the army again during the first day's fighting at Gettysburg in the hope of inspiring the men. He proved to be a thorn in the side of the Lincoln administration, however, and was relieved of command of the Army of the Potomac (Military History Institute, United States Army War College).

McClellan was personally responsible for holding the western counties of Virginia, which would later become West Virginia, in the Union through his Rich Mountain Campaign. This success, coupled with General Irvin McDowell's defeat at Manassas, prompted President Lincoln to appoint McClellan commander of the Army of the Potomac, and General-in-Chief of the United States Armies on November 1, 1861.[5]

McClellan proved to be a wonderful choice to organize an army out of the armed mob that had been the Army of the Potomac. To the disdain of the politicians in Washington, he allowed the summer and fall of 1861 to pass by without mounting an offensive campaign, as he drilled, equipped, and organized the ever-enlarging army into a finely tuned military machine. No one could question his abilities as an administrator and organizer. The proof was evident for all to see, in the form of an army of more than 100,000 men, that seemed to rival any to be found in Europe. But the public and the politicians were impatient for action. "On to Richmond" cries rang out from all quarters from those who felt that a precious opportunity for an early end of the war was being lost. But McClellan refused to be pushed into action before he was ready.

His refusal to march his army to battle before it was fully ready to do so was a source of irritation to politicians in the North, but was insignificant when compared with the ever-increasing dialogue of political dogma he espoused. Being a prominent Democrat, McClellan forwarded the platforms of his party, which were in direct conflict with those of the Republicans. His status with the military, and his political affiliation, brought him to the attention of Democratic Party leaders, who began to frequent the camp, sounding him out on his desire to run for high office. As early as the fall of 1861, he was already being touted as a leading candidate to represent the Democratic Party in the 1864 presidential election.

McClellan, for his part, remained silent concerning any political ambitions he might have had, but the attention he received from party leaders caused him to use his position as a political platform. As General-in-Chief, he directed General Henry Halleck, in Mississippi, to impress upon the people of that state that this war was being fought solely to restore the Union. To General Don Carlos Buell, in Kentucky, he wrote instructions to convince the people of Kentucky that he was fighting for the Union and the Constitution. Buell was to prepare his army for a march into East Tennessee, where it would liberate the Union-loving people there from rebel oppression. Fundamentally opposed to wartime emancipation, McClellan took Lincoln at his word when the president had stated that the government had no intention of interfering with the institutions of the South. He sought to completely dodge the issue of abolition, and to reassure his Confederate adversaries that, as Lincoln himself had stated, the war was being fought only to restore the Union. McClellan wrote to a Democratic member of Congress about the matter, asking him, "Help me to dodge the nigger — we want nothing to do with him." At an early date, McClellan's political views, and his willingness to give voice to them, placed him at odds with the administration and the Republican Party.[6]

For all the seeds of discontent that he was sowing with the administration, McClellan's popularity with the army was never in question. He was dubbed the "Young Napoleon" by the soldiers and the press, and his appearance and personality lent themselves easily to the comparison. Indeed, the "Young Napoleon" was adored by the soldiers he commanded. Under his supervision, the citizen volunteers had become soldiers, and they took justifiable pride in their accomplishment, and in the man who was responsible for the transformation.

But once he had succeeded in creating an army, McClellan chose not to march it out to fight the enemy. His biggest reason for this inactivity was his own conception that the enemy army contained many more men than it actually did. McClellan was constantly calling for reinforcements to enable him to be on par with a Confederate army that was actually much smaller than his own. The question is, where did McClellan come by these wild ideas of the enemy's strength and numbers? How was it that he could have been so grossly uninformed as to the size and composition of the Confederate army? Historian T. Harry Williams states bluntly, "His estimate of the size of the Confederate forces was based on the reports of the poorest intelligence service any general ever had."[7]

If this be the case, then where did this stream of misinformation come from? McClellan's reports originated with Allan Pinkerton and the operatives in his detective agency. Pinkerton enjoyed the reputation of being the most famous detective in the country at the outbreak of hostilities, and his services had been engaged early on by the Lincoln administration. It was Pinkerton, you will remember, who assisted Lincoln in sneaking into Washington prior to the inauguration. Following the inauguration, Pinkerton and his men were in the constant employment of the administration, spying on the actions of Southerners, carrying secret dispatches to Union commanders, and seeking to uncover plots and schemes directed against the president and his administration. In his own published memoir, Pinkerton relates how he or his detectives were constant visitors at the White House.[8] Indeed, Pinkerton had known both McClellan and Lincoln since the days when they had come in contact in dealings with the Illinois Central Railroad.

Pinkerton seems to have been quite accurate in his assessment of situations before and after Lincoln's inauguration, and the information provided to the administration by his agency rang true in the days before and after Fort Sumter. Why did his information become so inaccurate during the tenure of McClellan's command? T. Harry Williams ponders the answer when he addresses Pinkerton's reports on Southern forces that attributed almost twice the number of men to the Confederate army than they actually had. Williams states, "Either Pinkerton was incompetent, or he sensed that McClellan wanted the enemy army magnified as an excuse for inaction." I would submit that if Pinkerton was incompetent, it was a temporary affliction. His reports, and those of his operatives, were reasonably accurate both before and after the time of McClellan's command. It was only during the time of McClellan's tenure that enemy strength was doubled in scouting reports.

As to the suggestion that Pinkerton "sensed" a desire on the part of McClellan to have the size of the enemy magnified, then he would have been part of a conspiracy to keep the main Union army in the East inactive, and if such was indeed the case, he should have been charged with treason. The historical record shows that Pinkerton was not the target of accusations of treason, and did not even receive official censure for the shoddy intelligence work performed by his operatives in regard to reports on the Confederate army. That criticism was reserved for McClellan alone. Most present-day historians ridicule McClellan for crediting Pinkerton's fictitious reports, but Pinkerton escapes, as he did during the war, without assuming any blame for the misinformation. The purpose of intelligence is to provide the commander with information needed to plan appropriate strategy. In McClellan's case, the intelligence he received was faulty, but since it came from a credible source, he had no other option but to accept it as being accurate. That being the case, the general acted in the only way he could have. Committing his army to an offensive against a superior force in enemy territory would have been rash and irresponsible.

His hesitation to take the field was a constant complaint from the Republicans, but McClellan felt his efforts to organize and train the army were hampered by the very system of recruitment adopted by the administration, and cited that as a prime reason for the amount of time necessary to prepare the army to take the field. He stated, "The numbers of troops ... in the various parts of the country, were ample for the suppression of the rebellion, if they had been properly handled and their numbers made good by a constant stream of recruits poured into the old regiments, so as to keep them always at their full strength. Instead of this, spasmodic calls for large numbers of men were made, and the general rule was to organize them into new regiments, often allowing the old regiments to die out. This system was infinitely more expensive, but gave the opportunity to promote personal or political favorites. [In reality, it was just another manner in which the Republicans could dispense patronage.] The new regiments required a long time to make them serviceable, while the same men placed in the old regiments, under experienced officers and surrounded by veterans, would in a few days become efficient soldiers. Another grave defect of this system was the destructive effects of the espirit de corps of the old officers and men — an invaluable adjunct in war." Anyone familiar with the military knows that McClellan was right. Replacements, filtered into existing units, is the most effective and time-efficient method of building an army. But the Republicans were more interested in patronage than in building an effective army, and McClellan was then held responsible for the situation they created.[9] The Republicans chafed at the delays, just as they had earlier in the year when Lyman Trumball, a Republican senator from Illinois, along with fourteen other senators had passed a resolution demanding McDowell not only undertake the offensive, but capture Richmond by July 20, 1861.[10] McClellan was determined not to allow himself to be bullied by these same politicians into sending an army into battle before it was ready.

But the system of organization was only one factor, not of McClellan's doing, that influenced delays in active campaigning. Once his plans for the Peninsula Campaign had been approved by the administration, Lincoln threw a monkey wrench into the whole operation by refusing to release General Irvin McDowell's 40,000 men to McClellan. McDowell's Corps had been an integral part of the campaign devised by McClellan, and its exclusion from the operation upset all hopes of a successful advance. McClellan's assault force had been reduced by approximately one-third. Any commander would be hard-pressed to compensate for such a reduction, and to an officer as meticulous and organized as McClellan, the withholding of McDowell's men was akin to sabotaging his entire campaign.

McClellan had left some 67,000 men behind to guard the capital (19,000 at Washington, 7,800 at Harpers Ferry, 30,000 in the Shenandoah Valley, and 10,000 at Manassas) and felt that this total was sufficient to protect Washington from any incursions the Confederates might make. But Lincoln and the Republicans wanted more. They were obviously tainted by the same poor intelligence McClellan was receiving, for the force they demanded to protect the capital was larger than the Confederates actually had in their entire army. The results of the Peninsula Campaign are a matter of historical record, and it is not the purpose of this work to dwell upon any of the individual battles. McClellan's advance to the gates of Richmond, his subsequent withdrawal and change of base, and the shifting of the fighting from the Confederate capital to Northern Virginia have all been written about in exhaustive detail. In all cases, McClellan receives harsh criticism for his actions, and is blamed for the failure to capture Richmond and end the war in 1862.[11]

There is one important fact that is missing in every account of McClellan's career that I have ever read, however, and that involves the very topic we are discussing now: numbers. Every Union commander who ever defeated the Army of Northern Virginia in battle did so while enjoying a vast numerical superiority. This superiority in numbers did not always carry with it the promise of victory, however, as can be attested to by the defeats suffered by Joseph Hooker at Chancellorsville, by Ambrose Burnside at Fredericksburg, and by Ulysses S. Grant at the Wilderness, Spotsylvania, and Cold Harbor, even though they held an advantage over the enemy of more than two-to-one. But the fact remains that almost every Union victory was obtained through superior numbers on the battlefield. George McClellan is the only exception to that rule. During the Peninsula Campaign, for the only time during the war, the Union and Confederate armies in the East fought in relative parity to one another. McClellan was able to score several victories over the Army of Northern Virginia during this time, and not only at its final repulse of the Confederates at Malvern Hill. McClellan was the only Union commander in the East to ever face Robert E. Lee, or the Army of Northern Virginia, on equal terms, and defeat them.[12] This goes a long way toward explaining Lee's assessment of him as an army commander. Following the fighting, in one of only two interviews given by Lee concerning the war, the general was asked which Union general he had feared most. The reporter stated that Lee's response was "emphatic and instantaneous": "McClellan, at all odds!"

It is a matter of historical record that Lincoln and the administration interfered with and impeded McClellan's Peninsula Campaign almost from start to finish. The following is a chronological listing of the incidents that doomed the operation to failure:

• March 8, 1862 — Lincoln confronts McClellan about his Urbanna Plan, charging him with "Traitorous intent" in exposing Washington to attack, because of the number of troops the general's plan left in the capital. An angry McClellan convinces Lincoln to back down from the charges.

• March 8, 1862 — Lincoln and Stanton canvass twelve of McClellan's top generals about their opinion of the Urbanna Plan. Eight are in favor of it and four are opposed.

• March 8, 1862 — Lincoln issues General War Order No. 2. Without consulting McClellan, the president forms the Army of the Potomac into four corps. Three of the four generals that were against McClellan's plan are appointed to corps command. All four are Republicans.

• March 11, 1862 — Politician Edward Bates urges Lincoln to remove McClellan from the general-in-chief position and assume it himself. On that same day, Lincoln issues Special War Order No. 3, demoting McClellan to army commander. He also creates the Mountain Department, appointing Republican John Frémont as commander. McClellan is issued no orders regarding his demotion, and reads about it in the newspaper the following day.

• March 13, 1862 — Lincoln appoints James Wadsworth to command the defenses of Washington. McClellan protests the appointment on the grounds that Wadsworth is a New York Republican politician with no previous military experience.

• March 14, 1862 — Navy Secretary Gideon Welles refuses Naval cooperation for McClellan's invasion, declining to send supporting ships above Yorktown.

• March 15, 1862 — Stanton asks Ethan Allen Hitchcock, retired since 1855, to take command of the Army of the Potomac. Hitchcock declines.

• March 19, 1862 — General John Barnard, Admiral Louis Goldsborough, and General John Wool secretly divert resources away from McClellan's campaign to make an effort to capture Norfolk, Virginia.

• March 27, 1862 — General Hitchcock, now senior military advisor to the administration, advises that men be taken from Frémont's force to augment McClellan's army. Stanton ignores his advice and instead takes two divisions from McClellan to reinforce Frémont.

• April 1, 1862 — McClellan embarks his army for the Peninsula.

• March 4, 1862 — Lincoln removes McDowell's Corps from McClellan's invasion force, reducing the size of his army by some 40,000 men. Most of McClellan's cavalry, which has not yet embarked, is also withheld by the president. McDowell is made a department commander and placed under the direct orders of Lincoln and Stanton. McClellan has been stripped of control of Banks's and Frémont's forces, as well as McDowell's, the garrison at Fortress Monroe, and the men in the Washington defenses. He can neither coordinate their actions nor call on them for assistance.

• April 5, 1862 — The Navy commits a tiny four-ship flotilla to cooperate with the campaign. The Naval commander refuses to approach Yorktown, to conduct reconnaissance, or to even meet with McClellan.

• April 13, 1862 — McClellan requests the Navy to shell positions below Gloucester to support an advance, but the request is refused.

The incidents listed above are but a partial listing of the obstructions placed in McClellan's path by the administration, but they are sufficient to provide the reader with an understanding that the campaign was undermined from the very beginning, and destined to failure. It can readily be seen that McClellan's hesitation was caused by circumstances beyond his control, though all blame for tardiness was heaped upon his head, as was the overall failure of the campaign.

Following the end of the Peninsula Campaign, McClellan was effectively relieved of command, as his army was removed from the Peninsula and funneled into Major General John Pope's Army of Virginia. Pope, a Republican, enjoyed the confidence of the administration, and stood in line to become the leading Union general in the Eastern Theater. Then came the battle of Second Manassas. Pope suffered one of the worst Union defeats of the war, and the "skedaddle" back to Washington surpassed that of the first meeting on that very same field a year before. The army was beaten and demoralized, and badly in need of reorganization. Lee's army, flushed with victory, was advancing into Maryland, threatening Baltimore and Washington. With its own military in a shambles, the administration turned to George McClellan to once again command the army and bring order out of the chaos. More specifically, Lincoln turned to McClellan. Most of the members of his Cabinet, as well as most of the prominent Republicans in Congress, violently opposed McClellan's reinstatement to command.

John Pope's army of some 90,000 men had been thoroughly whipped by Lee's Confederate force of only about 55,000, and Lincoln believed that no other officer in the service could restore and rebuild the demoralized army. Secretary of the Navy Gideon Welles noted in his diary that "General surprise was expressed" when news of McClellan's reinstatement was announced to the Cabinet. Welles went on to state that all present agreed that McClellan was a "good engineer," that "there was no better organizer" in the army, and that McClellan "can be trusted to act on the defensive." The most important factor in Lincoln's decision was that McClellan "had beyond any officer the confidence of the army." But Salmon Chase voiced the mood of the majority when he "emphatically stated his conviction that it [McClellan's reinstatement] would prove a national calamity."[13]

The Cabinet members could take heart in the fact that McClellan's reinstatement to command was of a limited nature. Officially, he had been assigned only to command of the defenses of Washington, and not restored to command of the Army of the Potomac. This is a point of contention with many historians, who assert that McClellan was given that command on September

5, 1862. The facts of the situation are that Lincoln and General-in-Chief Henry Halleck visited McClellan on September 2, at which time he was assigned only command of the Washington defenses. McClellan's own written statements about this event are corroborated by entries in Salmon Chase's diary about his conversation with Lincoln about the meeting. On September 3, Lincoln ordered Halleck to organize a field army, independent of the defense forces. On September 5, Pope's Army of Virginia was ordered merged with the Army of the Potomac. Command of the combined forces was offered to General Ambrose Burnside. It was intended that Burnside would command the army in the field, while McClellan maintained the defenses at the capital, but Burnside declined to accept the position. On September 6, General Pope was reassigned to the Northwest. On that same day, McClellan named General Nathaniel Banks to command the defenses of Washington and personally took the field to oppose General Lee's invasion of Maryland, without orders or authority. Following this turn of events, Lincoln began telling people that Halleck had argued for McClellan's restoration to command of the Army of the Potomac, and had facilitated that objective on September 2. Halleck, for his part, testified to Congress that Lincoln was in error, and that it was his belief that Lincoln himself had reinstated McClellan. The fact of the matter is that McClellan was never officially given command of the Army of the Potomac. The general who was so often slighted for having the "slows" had taken the initiative to blunt Lee's invasion of Maryland, and was now operating on his own hook. As such, McClellan was probably correct, in sentiment at least, when he stated that if he lost the upcoming battle, the administration would "hang" him.

The majority of the criticism received by McClellan regarding the Antietam Campaign stems from the fact that he came into possession of General Lee's orders to his subordinates, outlining his plan of campaign and the position of his forces. Most critics feel that given this information, McClellan should have been able to crush the Confederate army, and cite McClellan's failure to do so as a shining example of his incompetence in command. There are, however, several points that need to be taken into account before rendering final judgment on McClellan's actions. McClellan had never been officially restored to command of the Army of the Potomac. He was acting on his own initiative in taking the army out to fight Lee, and such being the case, was naturally cautious in committing his forces to battle, knowing the recriminations that would be hurled his way in the case of a defeat.

While he possessed information regarding the plans and location of Lee's army, he had no reliable intelligence concerning its size. McClellan had no way of knowing that the Army of Northern Virginia had been reduced by up to 20,000 men for the campaign, as a large number of Southerners refused to cross the Potomac River and invade Maryland. These men felt that they had enlisted to defend the Confederacy and not to mount a war of aggression against the North. Many simply drifted away from the ranks, while many more threw away their shoes, taking advantage of an order that allowed men with bare feet to remain in Virginia.[14] One Confederate soldier noted, "From first one cause and then another, the regiments, brigades and divisions had dwindled into half of the strength which they carried to Manassas."[15] McClellan had no way of knowing that Lee's invading army had an effective strength of only about 40,000 men, and his actions were based on the sound assumption that the Confederates were advancing through Maryland at full strength. It is for this reason that he held General Fitz John Porter's Corps in reserve during the battle of Antietam.

McClellan's objective was twofold: to turn Lee's army back, and to guard against a defeat on the battlefield, under any circumstances. He considered Porter's Corps to be the best in his army, and Porter himself to be his finest subordinate officer. As such, this corps was held in reserve to guard against any contingencies that might arise to imperil the Army of the Potomac. Bear in mind McClellan's personal belief that the administration would "hang" him if he lost this battle. Given the fact that A.P. Hill's Division suddenly appeared from out of nowhere to crush General Burnside' advance in the latter part of the battle, McClellan's strategy would seem to be acceptable. He had no idea that the Confederates were short some 20,000 men, and was guarding against the eventuality that another force, like Hill's, would suddenly make its appearance on the field to turn the tide of battle against the Federals. In fact, McClellan had no reliable information at all concerning the numbers of the Confederate army.

In the final analysis, McClellan accomplished the goals he had set for the army when the campaign began. He successfully repulsed Lee's invasion of Maryland, saving Washington and compelling the Confederates to return to Virginia. He also avoided a defeat in the field that would have had severe implications, both at home and abroad. The English and French governments were poised to formally recognize the legitimacy of the Confederacy. The North had appeared unable to win the war, and the Southern invasions of Maryland and Kentucky lent credence to the belief abroad that the Confederacy was on the verge of winning its independence on the battlefield. A Confederate victory on Northern soil could possibly have provided the impetus for English and French intervention on the side of the South, and would have resulted in an escalation of the conflict that would have placed the Union in a position from which it could not have hoped to win.

Antietam was hailed by the public as a victory, though most military historians consider it to be a drawn battle. Lee had been turned back, and a grateful public gave McClellan the credit for it. Lincoln himself counted the battle in the win column, as it served as the basis for his issuance of the Emancipation Proclamation, which he had been waiting to make public until such time as a Union victory on the battlefield made it expedient to do so. No one could contest that the battle had been a hard-fought affair. With more than 23,000 casualties on both sides, it would forever be known as the bloodiest single day of the war, quite a testimonial to a general who the administration proclaimed was afraid to fight his army. Regardless of the positive outcome of the campaign, McClellan immediately came under fire from both Lincoln and the administration. He was publicly condemned for his failure to crush Lee's army on the battlefield, and for his reluctance to follow the Confederates and finish them off before they recrossed the Potomac River. The old charges of McClellan's slowness and his unwillingness to fight were revived, as prominent Republicans clamored for his removal.

A review of McClellan's actions reveal that on September 2, he was given command of the defenses of Washington, and charged with the task of reorganizing Pope's shattered army, which had been streaming into the capital ever since the battle of Second Manassas on August 29. On September 5, Pope's army of Virginia was folded into the Army of the Potomac. On September 7, less than a week after being posted to the command, McClellan had restored order to Pope's demoralized command, had reorganized and refitted the entire army, and had marched out of the capital in search of Lee. On September 14, less than two weeks after his reassignment, he engaged a portion of Lee's army at South Mountain, and three days later fought the decisive battle of the campaign, at Antietam. The outcome of this fight was to throw back the Confederate invasion of Maryland and remove the threat to Washington. Were McClellan's military actions really the source of his conflict with the administration, or was there another reason for the ever-widening chasm between himself and the Republicans? To be sure, McClellan was a prominent Democrat in a high-profile position, and that fact alone made him a target for many Republicans. When one considers that McClellan was politically opposed to immediate emancipation, and had voiced personal concerns over Lincoln's proclamation, the situation may be seen on a broader scope. From the time of the issuance of Lincoln's Emancipation Proclamation, McClellan had been advised and pressured by several ranking Republicans to lend his support to the policy. This he declined to do. In one instance, the general wrote to his wife about a politician who visited the army camp to tell McClellan that it was "my duty to submit to the President's proclamation and quietly continue doing my duty as a soldier."[16] McClellan's army was in motion, and had made contact with the enemy at the time of his removal from command, so how could delays and hesitation have been the reason given for his dismissal? The fact is that McClellan had become a political liability, not a military one, and the delays became a convenient reason to effect his ejection from high command, and the platform it gave him to concentrate Democratic opposition to the administration.

On the night of November 7, 1862, McClellan was visited by an emissary from the War Department bearing two written orders from the administration. The first relieved him of command of the army and directed him to proceed to Trenton, New Jersey, to await further orders. These orders never came. The man cited by Lee as being the commander he most feared in the war, and by

Lincoln as being the best officer in the Union army, was allowed to sit out the rest of the war without a command. The second order presented by the emissary placed Ambrose Burnside in command of the Army of the Potomac. Burnside requested that McClellan postpone his departure from the army for a few days, in order that he might familiarize the new commander with the location and dispositions of the army. To this McClellan readily assented.

He stated that he had a second, ulterior motive in postponing his departure, that being to calm the troops. The order for his removal had "created a deep feeling in the army — so much so that many were in favor of my refusing to obey the order, and of marching upon Washington to take possession of the government. My chief purpose in remaining with the army as long as I did after being relieved was to calm this feeling, in which I succeeded."[17] McClellan was so beloved by the army that it was within his power to have subverted the government and taken control of the army, but he instead chose to act in the best interests of the nation by calming the situation and convincing the men to pledge their support to Burnside. For anyone who doubts the esteem with which the army held its commander, I would submit that during the first day of the Battle of Gettysburg, when the men in the ranks were not yet informed of Meade's appointment to replace Hooker as commander of the army, officers intentionally spread the rumor that McClellan had been reinstated, knowing the positive effect it would have on the men. The Union army fought like men possessed that day, preventing the Confederates from gaining the heights at Cemetery Ridge, which would have turned the tide of the battle, and possibly the war, against them.

With the removal of McClellan came a purge of the Union army. Prominent Democrats, or officers aligned with McClellan, quickly fell under the axe of the administration, as the Army of the Potomac was cleansed of what was felt to be anti-administration officers. Chief among these was General Fitz John Porter, McClellan's most trusted corps commander, and commonly regarded to be one of the most promising officers in the army. When the Army of the Potomac was being removed from the Peninsula, its units were ordered to attach themselves to Pope's Army of Virginia as they came into supporting range. Porter had a low opinion of Pope as an officer, and spoke and wrote intemperately about him.

After the debacle that was Second Manassas, a scapegoat was needed to assume blame for the defeat, and Porter, McClellan's most trusted lieutenant, seemed the obvious choice. Pope charged Porter with disloyalty, disobedience, and misconduct in the face of the enemy. He was placed under arrest and tried by a military commission — all of whose members were hand-selected by Secretary Stanton. During the trial, defective maps, perjured and hearsay testimony, and Porter's own disparaging comments about Pope were used to secure a guilty verdict. Porter was dismissed from the army on January 21, 1863, and never again served in the military of the United States.

From the time of his dismissal, Porter sought to clear his name. Sixteen years after the guilty verdict had been pronounced, a second military commission, headed by General John Schofield, not only reversed the verdict of the previous court, but determined that Porter's actions at Second Manassas had saved the army from total annihilation. The court found Pope to have been completely unaware of the situation during the battle, and stated that his orders to Porter would have been impossible to execute. Even if Porter had been able to comply, he would have endangered the entire army. Porter's refusal to obey Pope's directive was stated to be the action that had saved the army from total ruin. This panel tendered Porter the appreciation of the nation for his actions, and recommended that he be restored to his former rank. Schofield was neither a Democrat nor a supporter of Porter. In fact, Porter had voted to expel Schofield from West

Major General Fitz John Porter. Porter's close personal and professional ties with George B. McClellan led to his being charged with dereliction of duty at the Battle of Second Manassas. It took Porter twenty-four years to clear his name and be completely exonerated of his charges (Military History Institute, United States Army War College).

Point many years before for disciplinary reasons. The recommendation of the board went unheeded by the government because the case had become a political issue. It was not until 1886 that President Grover Cleveland signed a bill that exonerated Porter of all charges and restored him to the rolls as a colonel of infantry. Politics had cost Porter his career and reputation, and politics kept him from clearing it for twenty-four years.[18]

In the West, General Don Carlos Buell had preceded McClellan by a few days in being relieved of army command. Buell, a Democrat, close personal friend of McClellan's, and husband of a Southern-born wife, had been the target of the same Republican detractors who sought to unseat McClellan from command.[19] Like McClellan, he had been called upon to gather a force to repel a Confederate invasion of Kentucky, which culminated in the decisive battle at Perryville, fought on October 8, 1862. While the results on the field were less than spectacular, partly owing to an acoustic shadow that prevented Buell from knowing that his army was being engaged until the fighting was almost concluded, the end result was the expulsion of the Southern army from Kentucky and the blunting of the Confederate campaign. On October 30, 1862, Buell was officially replaced in command by General William Rosecrans and accused of dilatory tactics.

A year later, Buell was called before the Committee on the Conduct of the War to testify as to his actions in the Kentucky Campaign. After hearing the

testimony of all the officers called, the Committee determined that Buell was guilty of poor judgment in conducting the campaign.[20] The decision of the Committee ruined Buell's reputation, and the general languished without a command until May of 1864, when he was mustered out of the volunteer service. In June of that year Buell resigned his commission in the regular army. No less an officer than Ulysses S. Grant would later request his reinstatement to command, but the War Department declined to act upon the request.

A secret military commission, chaired by General Lew Wallace, examined the charges that had been made against Buell, but neither the proceedings nor the verdict was ever published. What is known is that Buell was tendered an offer to serve in a subordinate capacity to either Phil Sheridan or William T. Sherman. Buell declined either choice, on grounds that he held higher rank than both men. General William Farrar Smith stated the stain that had been done to Buell's reputation in plain language when he described that officer as "a capital sol-

Major General Don Carlos Buell. A prominent Democrat and friend of George B. McClellan, Buell found himself without a command following the administration's purge of high-ranking Democratic officers. Despite the support of Ulysses S. Grant, Buell would never be reassigned by the War Department (Military History Institute, United States Army War College).

dier and a student of his profession. He fought a battle with courage, coolness, and intelligence, saving us from utter rout at Shiloh, into which false position Halleck's ambition and Grant's density had begotten us."[21] Unlike Porter, Buell never pushed for a court-martial to clear his name, and therefore never had the slight to his reputation expunged. In 1864, he actively campaigned for McClellan for president, but he had no further dealing with either the government or the military, earning his living in the private sector for the remainder of his life.

General John McClernand was serving as a Democratic Congressman from southern Illinois when the war broke out. In 1860, he had been a candidate to assume the speakership of the House of Representatives, but was defeated by a coalition opposed to his moderate views on slavery and secession. McClernand's only previous military service had been three months as a private in 1832, during the Black Hawk War. Nevertheless, he was appointed to the rank of brigadier general of volunteers on May 17, 1861. The reason for this was that McClernand represented a portion of the state where Democrats and Southern sympathies were in the majority. Lincoln needed the support of area men like McClernand and John Logan to keep southern Illinois under the control of the Union, and patronage, in the form of generals' commissions, was the payment for their support. Other than his lack of military training, McClernand's main failing was a politician's need for self-promotion and advancement. The majority of his career was spent in criticizing and trying to supplant his superiors. Even so, he was promoted to the rank of major general on March 21, 1862. In January of 1863, McClernand mounted a successful campaign against Arkansas Post, before being given command of the XIII Corps in Grant's army, operating against Vicksburg, Mississippi.[23]

But his most important service to the administration came in the form of recruiting. In September of 1862 McClernand had approached Lincoln with a secret plan. He would make a recruiting sweep through the Northwest, bringing thousands of hesitating men into the army. In return, McClernand requested that he be put in command of this force, as a separate army, to operate independently against Vicksburg. In October of that year, Lincoln approved McClernand's plan and authorized him not only to raise new recruits, but also to organize all troops previously enrolled but not mobilized in Iowa, Illinois, and Indiana "to the end that when a sufficient force, not required by the operations of General Grant's command, shall be raised, an expedition may be organized under General McClernand's command against Vicksburg and to clear the Mississippi River and open navigation to New Orleans."[24] Lincoln presented him with orders marked "Private and Confidential," and sent him off on his detached mission to raise an army.

Over the course of the next two months, McClernand successfully organized thousands of troops and sent them forward. By the latter part of December, he was finally ready to end his recruiting and assume command of his new independent force. But when the general arrived at Cairo, Illinois, on December 23, there were no troops to take charge of. General Sherman had sailed for Vicksburg with the men four days earlier, leaving McClernand effectively without a command. The key phrase in Lincoln's orders was that McClernand would only be in charge of troops "not required by the operations of Grant's command." The insertion of this requirement meant that any troops McClernand raised could be viewed as being required for Grant's operations, and all of the troops intended for the independent army were swallowed up by Grant, with the approval of Halleck and the administration. McClernand exercised subordinate command during the Vicksburg Campaign, taking advantage of every opportunity to criticize Grant and promote himself. A statement to the press following a disastrous assault upon the Vicksburg fortifications, in which he overemphasized the role of his own troops, prompted Grant to relieve him and send him home. The following year, in 1864, McClernand would again command the XIII Corps, which was by then widely dispersed through Louisiana and Texas. He would continue to serve in this capacity until his resignation from the army on November 30, 1864.[24]

John McClernand was not a military man. He had precious little previous military experience, and no real qualifications to lead large bodies of men in battle, even though the record shows that he did an adequate job. He was ambitious and quarrelsome, and was a subversive element within General Grant's army. The fact that Grant relieved him and sent him home can be easily understood, and easily approved by anyone familiar with the general's personality and actions. The point of his inclusion in this chapter is not his own personal merits, but rather the manner in which his Democratic influence was used by the administration to raise the much-needed replacements for Grant's army. He was promised a command that the administration never intended to confer upon him in order to gain his influence with Democratic constituents. McClernand himself was a troublesome leader, but the administration manipulated and used him to accomplish its own goals, then cast him aside in a most unceremonious fashion.

General Ben Butler proved to be the most exasperating political general the administration was forced to deal with during the war. Butler was a powerful figure in the Democratic Party in New England, having served in the Massachusetts House of Representatives and Senate before becoming a delegate to the Democratic National Convention in 1860. At Charleston, Butler cast fifty-seven straight ballots to nominate Jefferson Davis as the Democratic candidate for president. Butler finally threw his influence behind John C. Breckinridge, and his extreme States' Rights platform. A brigadier general in the Massachusetts militia, Butler became the first major general of volunteers appointed by Lincoln on May 16, 1861. An energetic and aggressive leader, Butler rallied thousands of New England Democrats to support the administration by enlisting in the army. By virtue of the date of his commission, he ranked all other major generals of volunteers in the army for the rest of the war. For a period of time, the Democrats had the highest-ranking officer with a commission in the regular army, McClellan, and the highest-ranking officer with a commission in the volunteer service, Butler.

Butler's forces were defeated at the Battle of Big Bethel, while he was in command at Fortress Monroe, early in 1861. Later that year, he took part in the successful capture of Hatteras Inlet, North Carolina. In 1862, Butler's army accompanied Admiral David Farragut's fleet in the capture of New Orleans. While his qualities as a field commander are open to question, Butler, a former lawyer, proved to be an able administrator as the military governor of New Orleans. But his administration in New Orleans was as corrupt as it was effective, and Butler lined his own pockets, and those of his friends and family, while serving in that capacity. He was finally replaced by Nathaniel Banks in December of 1862. The next year found him appointed to command of the Army of the James, a force of two corps intended to cooperate with General Grant in his overall strategy for the campaign of 1864. When the Union armies marched out to begin the 1864 drive, Butler's Army of the James was assigned the task of operating against Petersburg, Virginia. Butler's management of the campaign was such that his army was defeated and bottled up at Bermuda Hundred by a vastly inferior Confederate force, under the command of General P.G.T. Beauregard.

Butler planned to parlay his military laurels into a bid for the presidency, but his performance in the Petersburg sector was a blotch on his record. Seeking to rectify that, and jump-start his postwar political career, Butler decided to take a personal interest in the combined army-navy expedition to capture Fort Fisher, North Carolina, and seal off the port of Wilmington. General Adelbert Ames had been appointed to lead the military portion of the expedition, but since Wilmington lay within the limits of Butler's department, Butler decided to personally accompany the expedition and take overall command of the troops. This action brought a storm of criticism on him from his superiors in the field and at the War Department, where it was felt that he was being derelict in leaving the bulk of his army to oversee a smaller operation. Butler weathered the storm, confident that the capture of Fort Fisher and the closing of the Confederacy's last major port in the East would win him more fame and praise than could be had back at Bermuda Hundred.

The first expedition against Fort Fisher, in December of 1865, proved to be a fiasco. The Naval flotilla, under the command of Admiral David Porter, failed miserably to silence any of the fort's guns, or to soften the way for the infantry to make an assault. Butler's personal scheme to blow up the fort with a ship loaded with gunpowder proved to be a waste of time. In all fairness, the powder boat failed in part due to the fact that the Navy detonated it beyond the range that had been called for in the plans. The powder that had been given to Butler was also of a damaged, inferior nature. When Butler's men waded ashore they were greeted by a determined enemy, unscathed by the Naval bombardment. The strength of Fort Fisher convinced Butler that it was suicide to make an assault in its present condition, and he called off the expedition and ordered those troops already landed to be taken back to their transports. The only problem was that Adelbert Ames had orders from General Grant to hold on under all circumstances if a landing was made. Should the fort prove too strong to be carried by assault, more troops would be sent. Butler had interfered with these orders, and had contradicted Grant's explicit instructions when he ordered the expedition to be abandoned.

Up to this time, the administration hesitated to deal with Butler because of his vast influence among Northern Democrats. Now, armed with his apparent bumbling of the Fort Fisher expedition, Lincoln was finally ready to rid himself of Butler. Executive Order 1 for 1865 officially removed Butler from command of the Army of the James. In doing so, Lincoln corrected a potential problem with army command that to most officers seemed unbelievable. According to his date of commission, Butler ranked second only to Grant among the officers in the Army of the Potomac and the Army of the James. If anything happened to Grant, Butler would assume top command of the Union's main military forces in the East. Butler's removal alleviated this potential catastrophe. At the same time, the disgrace caused to Butler by the failed campaign against Fort Fisher, and his subsequent removal from command, so tarnished the general's reputation that any aspirations for a run at the presidency were now out of the question.[25]

Butler resigned his commission on November 30, 1865. In the meantime, he switched his political affiliation to the Republican side and won a seat in Congress from Massachusetts. In 1868, he took a vigorous part in the effort to impeach Andrew Johnson, earning for himself the disdain of both Republicans and conservative Democrats. He was again elected to Congress in 1878, and was elected governor of Massachusetts in 1882. In 1884, Butler finally did make an insignificant run at the White House, but as a candidate of the little-known Greenbacker Party.[26]

The officers included in this chapter are but a sampling of the high-ranking Democrats in the Union army who suffered at the hands of the administration. It would require an entire volume to provide an in-depth examination of the officers listed above, not to mention those that time and space preclude from admission here. This chapter is intended merely to provide the reader with a glimpse of how the Republican Party used Democrats to gain their influence, then systematically eliminated them from top command. In most cases, such as with McClellan, Porter, and Buell, removal from command was not enough. Character assassination and ruined reputations were the reward for these officers who chose to stand with the Union and form an alliance with the Republicans. To this day, the reputations of McClellan, Porter, and Buell exist under a cloud of controversy that was first begun in the political propaganda of the Lincoln administration. The message was clear: Democrats were welcome to serve, but they were not allowed to command, especially if they posed a threat to the Republican Party in any way.

CHAPTER SEVEN

The Committee on
the Conduct of the War

During the Civil War, the Congressional Joint Committee on the Conduct of the War struck the same fear in the hearts of Americans that Senator Joseph McCarthy and his Red Scare committee did almost a century later. The Joint Committee on the Conduct of the War came about in the fall of 1861, when a group of Radical Republican Congressmen sought to establish both an investigatory agency and to bring pressure to bear against General McClellan. Many Republican Congressmen had become anxious with McClellan for not making an immediate push against the Confederates. They called for a drive on Richmond that would win the war before the before the year was ended.

On October 21, 1861, the debacle at Ball's Bluff aroused Congress to take action and form an official regulatory committee. General Charles P. Stone's division was assigned to the defense of Washington. A portion of Stone's division, under the immediate command of Colonel Edward D. Baker, was engaged by a superior Confederate force at Ball's Bluff, Virginia, along the Potomac River, some distance from the capitol. The engagement resulted in a humiliating defeat for Union arms, with 49 killed, 158 wounded, and 714 captured or missing. Colonel Baker, a personal friend of Lincoln and a former member of the Senate, was listed among the killed. Congress was in recess when the battle took place, but upon reconvening on December 2, 1861, the House of Representatives unanimously passed a resolution requesting the Secretary of War to make a full disclosure of the events at Ball's Bluff to that body. A second resolution was passed to create a Congressional committee "to inquire into the conduct of the present war." The joint committee was to consist of three senators and four members of the House of Representatives. Benjamin Wade of Ohio, Zachariah Chandler of Michigan, and Andrew Johnson of Tennessee formed the Senatorial portion of the committee. The House members were D.W. Gooch of Massachusetts, G.W. Julian of Indiana, John Covode of Pennsylvania, and Moses Odell of New York.[1]

The Committee on the Conduct of the War formed a distinctly partisan tribunal. As noted historian J.G. Randall stated in his book *The Civil War and Reconstruction*, "Not only did its members resent the importance given to Democratic generals; they labored to promote one flank of the Republican Party." By and large, the body was composed mainly of members of the radical portion of the party, and the Committee gave this faction an opportunity not only to repress the Democrats, but to assert a stronger influence within its own party as well.[2] Radical Republicans favored a severe prosecution of the war. Instead of mere reinstatement of the seceded states, they sought to punish the South for its part in the war. Thaddeus Stevens voiced the sentiment of this group when he stated, "[I]f the whole country [the South] must be laid waste, and made a desert, in order to save this Union from destruction, so let it be. I would rather, sir, reduce them to a condition where their whole country is to be repeopled by a band of freemen than to see them perpetuate the destruction of this people through our agency."[3]

Zachariah Chandler. This radical Republican senator was one of the leading members of the Congressional Committee on the Conduct of the War (Military History Institute, United States Army War College).

General Stone became the first victim of the Committee on the Conduct of the War when it focused its attention on investigating the Ball's Bluff incident. Stone was a graduate of the Military Academy in 1845, before seeing service in the war with Mexico as an ordnance officer in Winfield Scott's army. Following the war, he spent five years as ordnance officer of the Department of the Pacific before resigning his commission to accept employment by the Mexican government to survey the state of Sonora. When civil war seemed to be inevitable, Stone happened to be in Washington, and General Scott requested that he be commissioned to serve as inspector general for the District of Columbia to perform the vital tasks of raising, organizing and commanding troops for the defense of the capital. Stone was commissioned colonel of the 14th United States Infantry on May 14, 1861, and on August 6 he was promoted to the rank of brigadier general, with the commission dated May 17, 1861.

Following service in the field under General Robert Patterson during the Manassas Campaign, Stone commanded a division of three brigades charged with the observation of Confederate forces on the upper Potomac. Colonel Baker served as commander of one of these brigades, and showed rash behavior in bringing about the action at Ball's Bluff, but the Committee of the Conduct of the War used the incident to further its political goals by making Stone the scapegoat of the affair. The reason for Stone's being targeted was the fact that members of the Committee thought him "unsound" on the question of slavery. The Committee conducted an *ex parte* investigation of Stone, meaning that there was no opportunity for that officer to defend himself or tell his side of the story. The resulting investigation was filled with hearsay testimony and fabricated charges of Stone's alleged disloyalty and correspondence with Confederate officers. As historian T. Harry Williams states it, Benjamin Wade "conducted the inquiry in a manner that showed he had prejudged the case." All of the supposed evidence collected by the Committee was kept secret, and Stone was not made aware of any charges against him, or of the identities of any of his accusers. Stone demanded that a proper court-martial be held if there were any questions about his conduct, but the Committee refused. On the basis of unsubstantiated rumor and false testimony, Stone was ordered arrested on February 9, 1862, and was confined at Fort Lafayette, and then at Fort Hamilton, for a period of 189 days. This was done without Stone's ever receiving an official statement of the charges against him, and with no date ever being set for a trial, contrary to the existing Articles of War. Stone lashed out with heated eloquence: "This is a humiliation I had hoped I should never be subjected to. I thought there was one calumny that could not be brought against me.... This government has not a more faithful soldier; of poor capacity, it is true, but a more faithful soldier this government has not had.... If you want more faithful soldiers you must find them elsewhere. I have been as faithful as I can be."[5]

When McClellan learned of Stone's arrest he correctly ascertained, "They want a victim." Colonel J.H. Alen, an officer on his headquarters staff, said, "Yes, and when they have once tasted blood, got one victim, no one can tell who will be next."[6] It was not until February of 1863 that the Committee finally got around to presenting Stone with a copy of its charges against him. Stone was able to defend himself against all of the charges, and in so doing proved the Committee's case flimsy and groundless. As a result, he was reinstated to command in the Department of the Gulf under General Banks. Stone served at Port Hudson and in the Red River Campaign, but his reputation had been permanently ruined by the actions of the Committee. He was the victim of petty persecution by officers convinced that he was not innocent of the charges, but simply had gotten away with it, until his usefulness to the army had declined to the point that Stone resigned his commission on September 13, 1864. Charles Stone was to be the first Union officer to suffer the wrath of the Committee on the Conduct of the War. He would merely be the first in a long line of defamed and besmirched officers who found their careers and personal lives ruined by the quasi-judicial agenda of the Radical Republicans who formed the Committee.[7]

To be sure, the actions of the Committee were not limited to attacks on officers whom they felt to be uncommitted, or of the wrong political ideology, and it did perform a service to the war effort. Investigations of scandals involving government contractors, the treatment of the wounded, and illicit trade with the Confederates were a real boon to the military. It was in its self-appointed role as the conscience of the government that the Committee overshadowed the good it was doing in other areas, and set itself up as a tribunal to be feared. While the military was the main focus of the Committee, it also investigated private citizens engaged in government work who were thought to be disloyal. This was not limited to government contractors or suppliers. The reach of the Committee stretched into the offices of the Federal government, and to the offices and agencies of the individual states. Nothing more significant than a critical statement about the government, or a disclosure of political ideology that conflicted with the Republicans, was necessary to bring one under the watchful eye of the Committee.

Benjamin Wade. A leader of the radical Republican faction and member of the powerful Congressional Committee on the Conduct of the War (Military History Institute, United States Army War College).

The chairman of the Committee was Ben Wade, the 61-year-old Radical whose father had fought in the Revolutionary War. Wade had not always occupied a position of influence and power. Among his many previous vocations were a laborer on the Erie Canal, farm hand, cattle-driver, schoolteacher, prosecuting attorney of Ashtabula County, member of the Ohio legislature, and United States Senator. In 1851, he became one of the first antislavery men in the Senate to challenge the Southerners on broad policy. Wade held a particular hatred for George B. McClellan, and made his removal from command of the Army of the Potomac the number one objective of the Committee. On one occasion, Wade had walked into Lincoln's office to demand that the president dismiss McClellan immediately. Lincoln asked who the Senator thought could replace the general, to which Wade replied, "Anybody!" Lincoln ended the discussion by saying "Wade, anybody will do for you but I must have somebody." The chairman took special pride in his status as a radical leader. "Many seem still to be frightened by radicalism," he once said, "but I believe that all who have benefited the world, from Jesus Christ to Martin Luther and George Washington, have been branded as Radicals.... I am a Radical, and I glory in it!" Wade was described by one historian as having a "high, broad brow and cheekbones like marble slabs, burning eyes and a sledgehammer chin. It was like an Easter Island head on a living man's frame."[8]

Zachariah Chandler was another radical member of the Committee. A millionaire from Michigan who had made his fortune in business and land speculation, he was described by one historian as being restless to make history, and more money. Like Wade, he was an imposing man. He was tall, with a severe countenance, a nanny-goat beard, and piercing eyes that cast a baleful gaze on a world that he obviously disapproved of. Chandler had been among the throng of spectators who had driven out from Washington to witness the first battle at Bull Run. When he returned to the city, he immediately went to the White House to urge Lincoln to make a call for half a million more men to show to the country that the government was "just beginning to get mad." Chandler served as the liaison between the members of the Committee and Lincoln. Wade personally despised Abraham Lincoln. Chandler thought him to be a good man, but a weak one.[9]

Andrew Johnson was the only Southern representative on the Committee. In fact, he was the only Southerner to still hold a seat in Congress. He had been a Breckinridge Democrat in the 1860 election, but following the election of Lincoln had taken a firm stance against secession. His adherence to the Union was so unpopular in his home state of Tennessee that on several occasions he was compelled to draw a loaded pistol to back down crowds threatening to lynch him. At the outbreak of hostilities, Johnson became a War Democrat, eventually shifting his allegiance to the Republican Party. A self-educated man, he had never attended a single day of school in his life, and had taught himself to read while plying his trade as a tailor.[10]

Of the four members of the Committee from the House of Representatives, all were Radical Republicans with the exception of Moses Odell, a War Democrat from New York. Gooch, Julian, Covode, and Odell were very low profile in the Committee, with Wade assuming the lead, not only as chairman, but as the voice and face of the group. Senator Chandler was second to Wade, in terms of power and influence. None of the members had any previous military experience, except for a fleeting involvement with local militias, and all held professional military men with suspicion and contempt. The hostility of the Committee toward professional soldiers was especially severe in the case of West Point graduates. In fact, Wade attempted to garner Congressional support to close the academy, calling it "The hot bed from which rebellion was hatched."[11]

Wade's primary focus, and therefore the primary focus of the Committee, was the ousting of General McClellan from army command. All of the members of the Committee were convinced that Democratic generals had little or no loyalty to the cause, and the fact that most of the important commands were held by Democrats in the first eighteen months of the war presented a situation the Committee could not accept or condone. McClellan was the highest-ranking and most influential Democrat in the army, so Wade and the Committee devoted a major part of their attention toward securing his demise. Of the more than 4,000 pages of testimony published by the Committee, the main focus was on McClellan and the 1862 Peninsula Campaign. Wade made public the transcripts of the investigation in the hope of discrediting McClellan with the civilian population and reducing his popularity with his troops. During the Seven Days' Battles, when McClellan withdrew his army toward Harrison's Landing, Zachariah Chandler treated the guests of Willard's Hotel in Washington to a tirade, drunkenly denouncing McClellan as a coward. Chandler loudly proclaimed that McClellan, and not Lee, had defeated the Army of the Potomac, and stated that he ought to be condemned and shot for his failure.[12]

It was the Committee that had demanded that four corps be created in the army. This came not from any desire to establish better organization or command structure, as the members had little knowledge of such matters. Instead, it was the result of political posturing. The Committee sought to limit McClellan's influence by appointing older Republican corps commanders over the young, ambitious brigadiers who worshiped him. In doing so, McClellan was saddled with subordinate commanders hostile to both himself and his plans, and a wedge was driven between him and the army. The Committee encouraged subordinate officers to criticize their superiors, and insisted that commanders had no right to keep any information from Congress, even plans for future campaigns. McClellan's stingy disbursement of information infuriated Wade and the other members of the Committee, and fanned the fires of the charges of disloyalty they made against him.

In reality, the insistence of the Committee to be fully informed of commander's plans, and its ill-advised propensity to publish the information it received, gave immeasurable aide and comfort to the enemy. McClellan was quite correct in keeping his plans to himself, as the actions of the Committee were having an adverse effect on battles and campaigns. General Robert E. Lee claimed that the information he obtained from the published reports of the Committee on the Conduct of the War was worth as much to him as two additional divisions of Confederate troops.[13] McClellan was "very unwilling to develop his plans, always believing that in military matters the fewer persons that were knowing them the better." He consented to reveal his plans only if ordered to do so. When called before the Committee, McClellan gave a general outline of his proposed campaign on the Peninsula. After explaining a portion of his proposed movements, he was interrupted by Chandler, who snidely commented, "General McClellan, if I understand you correctly, before you strike at the rebels you want to be sure of plenty of room so that you can run in case they strike back." Wade chimed in, "Or in case you get scared." McClellan tried to explain the complexities of an army in the field, and the necessity for generals to have available lines of retreat as well as lines of communication and supply, but the members wanted none of it. The only thing they despised more than professional officers was the strategy and tactics espoused by professional officers.[14]

Though it was Lincoln who eventually was responsible for making the decision to remove McClellan from command, Ben Wade and the members of the Committee on the Conduct of the War had done more than their fair share to discredit and disgrace him. His removal caused jubilation among the members of the Committee. Their sentiments were best expressed by the editor of a radical newspaper who wrote of McClellan, "Stripped of his paint, feathers and tinsel, his little arts of urbanity no longer available, he stands pallid but subtle still, loaded with the reproaches of a nation he might have saved, but would not."[15]

Bruce Catton, possibly the nation's foremost Civil War historian, captured the essence of the dilemma faced by McClellan, one which refutes the accusations of the "slows" from which the general was said to have suffered. As the Radical Republicans gained an ever-increasing influence in the supervision of the war, the nation was brought to the brink of emancipation. The only way McClellan had to prevent abolition from becoming a war goal was through a speedy defeat of the Confederacy and a reunification of the divided country before that policy was set in place. "McClellan could best thwart them by doing exactly what they wanted him to do, a point which probably no one except Mr. Lincoln himself was subtle enough to grasp."[16] The Committee's claims of dilatory tactics against the general pale when one considers that McClellan was trying to negate their power by doing exactly what they wanted him to do. This would also lend credence to a circular that was supposed to have been read by several people in Washington while the army was fighting on the Peninsula. The document, signed by Stanton, stated that now was not the time to win the war, as its object had not yet become the abolition of slavery. McClellan claimed that his entire campaign on the Peninsula had been undermined and that he had not been given a chance for victory. These claims were ridiculed by the members of the Committee, who answered that McClellan's failure was due to his own fears and incompetence. Is it possible that Bruce Catton was wrong? Could it be that Lincoln was not the only one who understood that an early end of the war by McClellan would eliminate the opportunity to change the goals of the conflict from the mere reinstatement of the departed states to the abolition of slavery? When one considers the many obstacles placed in McClellan's way during the Peninsula Campaign, as covered in the previous chapter, it is easy to see how the general would feel that he had been forsaken by the very government he was attempting to defend.

The Committee targeted other Democrats whom it felt were not of the proper ideology to lead the nation's troops. Don Carlos Buell, Fitz John Porter, and William B. Franklin all shared in the fate suffered by McClellan and Stone when they became the focus of Committee investigations, and in each instance, their careers and reputations were ruined by the slanderous accusations made public by the members. Henry Halleck also felt the sting of the Committee's displeasure, as Wade had no respect for the West Point graduate Lincoln had appointed to be his general-in-chief. Halleck was constantly being privately undermined and publicly censured by the Committee. Senator Wade personally disliked Halleck and felt that he had no military ability. "Give Halleck 20,000 men," he had once said, "and he couldn't raise three sitting cows."[17]

Secretary of War Edwin Stanton had the complete support of the Committee, however, despite the fact that he was a Democrat. The reason for this was that Stanton was an avowed abolitionist, and though he supervised the Cabinet office entrusted to run the war, he was not a professional soldier. The members were delighted when Stanton replaced Simon Cameron in the War Department, and Wade, accompanied by the entire committee, paid him a personal visit to extend their congratulations. Stanton informed the members of his willingness to support their actions, stating, "We must strike hands and, uniting our strength and thought, double the power of the government to suppress its enemies and restore its integrity." From the day Stanton took office, Wade and Chandler met with him nearly every morning. Stanton used the coalition to have the Committee subpoena and question senior officers under oath, something he did not have the authority to do. He reciprocated by attending to military details that the Committee had no authority to oversee, such as the arrest and confinement of General Stone.[18]

Military incompetence alone did not ensure that one would be persecuted by the Committee. Political agenda was much more important than victories on the battlefield, and the proper political ideology was held in higher esteem than military expertise. The darling of the Committee was John C. Frémont, who despite his obvious ineptitude for high command was constantly being forwarded as a replacement for McClellan, and even Grant, by a Committee that placed his stance on abolition ahead of his capabilities as a commander. Ben Butler won the support of the Committee for the same reason. Butler's influence as a leading Democrat had made him difficult for the administration to remove, despite the fact that his performance in the field was less than desirable. His refusal to return runaway slaves while in command at Fortress Monroe, and his subsequent use of black troops while at New Orleans, caused the Committee to adopt him as one of their own, despite the difference in party lines. Following the debacle of the first expedition to capture Fort Fisher, Butler was called to testify before the Committee. Instead of the normal investigation, Butler was allowed to read a number of long, prepared statements. The Committee did not seek out other substantial evidence, and did not even cross-examine the general. It merely recorded his statements as fact in the transcript of the proceedings.[19] "Fighting" Joe Hooker was another Democrat whom the Committee deemed to be of the proper mindset on slavery, and to whom they delivered unbridled support, regardless of ineptness on the battlefield. Following the defeat of the Army of the Potomac at Chancellorsville, an affair that saw Hooker's army almost crushed, despite the fact that he enjoyed a superiority of 130,000 men with which to face Lee's 60,000 Confederates, Wade and Chandler hurried to the front to assure the general of their unwavering support.[20] One faction of the Republican Party sought to eliminate competent Democratic officers from the army, while another faction placed all of their influence behind incompetent ones, solely because of their stance on abolition. Either way, the army and the nation were the losers.

The Committee did not confine its activities solely to monitoring the actions of the Union army. One of its first investigations concerned accusations of Confederate cruelty to captured Union soldiers following the battle of First Manassas. Wild and unfounded rumors had made their way into Northern newspapers, and the Committee was determined to get to the bottom of it. The August 17, 1861, issue of *Harper's Weekly* had run an article entitled "Bayoneting Our Wounded," that claimed that horrid atrocities were committed by the Confederates against Union men falling into their hands. The paper even commissioned an artist to draw sketches of the dead being used for sport and the wounded being tortured for amusement.[21] After holding a kangaroo court in which the wildest fairy tales and gossip were entered into the official record as fact, Wade wrote a report of what he imagined to have taken place. He stated that wounded men had been operated on by inexperienced doctors who knew little of surgery but "seemed to delight in hacking and butchering" the defenseless soldiers. The Confederates were also accused of boiling the bodies of dead Union soldiers to make drumsticks out of their shinbones, drinking cups from their skulls, and rings from their thighbones.[22] Of course, nothing contained in the report was true, but that didn't bother the members of the Committee when they made their findings of the investigation public. Once more, political agenda became the most important feature, even if truth had to be sacrificed to attain it. Atrocity propaganda served the purpose of Wade, who not only hated slavery, but detested the South and all it represented as well. Wade was of the opinion that the North could never win victory over the Confederacy unless Northerners, and particularly Union soldiers, hated the South as much as he did. Most historians credit the period of the Spanish American War as being the beginning of yellow journalism in this country, but Wade pioneered it more than three decades before it was given a nickname.[23]

The Committee would employ the same sort of propaganda when it conducted its investigation of the battle of Fort Pillow, Tennessee. In his report, Wade asserted, "The rebels commenced an indiscriminate slaughter, sparing neither age nor sex, soldier or civilian.... [C]hildren not more than ten years old were forced to stand up and face their murderers while being shot; the sick and wounded were butchered without mercy, the rebels even entering the hospital and dragging them out to be shot." It even claimed that some of the prisoners were nailed to the floors and walls of buildings by the Confederates, who then set the structures on fire.[24] While it is certain that atrocities did take place at Fort Pillow, and that some Confederate soldiers were guilty of shooting black soldiers after they had surrendered or while they were trying to surrender, the Committee report amplified and exaggerated the horrors that had taken place in an effort to shock the nation. The resultant pressure brought to bear against President Lincoln caused him to suspend any further exchanges of prisoners until the Confederates agreed to treat black prisoners of war the same as whites. Political policy was once more being served.

Unable to bring the South to its knees on the battlefield, the administration had adopted a strategy of attrition to win the war. Grant's Overland Campaign of 1864 is a prime example of this thought process. In the three months that expired between the Battle of the Wilderness and the besiegement of Petersburg, Grant's army had lost more than 60,000 men as casualties. That was more than Lee had in his entire army at the commencement of the campaign. The logic was simple. The North had a vast superiority in population compared to the South. Such losses could easily be replaced by new conscription of Union troops, while the Confederates had no more men to put in the ranks. In a one-for-one, or even a two-for-one, tradeoff with the Confederates, the North would still have men in its army when the South was bled dry.

The policy of ending prisoner exchanges was a part of that overall strategy. Knowing that the South was starving and running short of everything, and that Union prisoners held in Southern camps were subjected to the most terrible privations the nation had ever seen, the administration still refused to broker an exchange that would secure their release. Why? Because to do so would have also released an equal number of Confederate prisoners who would then have been able to rejoin the Southern army and lengthen the time required to accomplish a war of attrition. To be sure, General Grant had stated his opinion that prisoner exchanges benefited the enemy more than they did the Union, and the number of exchanges taking place between the two sides had measurably decreased, but a curtailment of the process had not yet been made the policy of the administration. Pennsylvania Governor Andrew Curtin went to see Lincoln to plead for an exchange of the 30,000 Confederate soldiers being held by the North in the spring of 1864, but the president referred him to Secretary Stanton. Curtin did not understand that the sick and diseased Union captives were to be sacrificed in the name of overall victory. When he broached the subject with Stanton, the Secretary of War snapped at him, "Do you come here in support of the government and ask me to exchange thirty thousand skeletons for thirty thousand well-fed men?"[25] Stanton was well aware of the conditions in Southern prisoner of war camps, but was perfectly willing to allow the Union captives there to die a horrible death in order to further the agenda of the administration. The Committee had scored another victory in its quest for prosecuting a harsh and punishing war against the South, and in the process had condemned thousands of Union prisoners of war to death. It would score another victory once the war was concluded, when the government would hold the South accountable for those very same prison camp deaths. The accusations of Confederate barbarism would then be used to help justify a severe and punishing Reconstruction.

The Joint Committee on the Conduct of the War proved to be the hammer of the militant and radical abolitionist factions of the Republican Party. Granted broad powers from Congress, its members were men of relentless determination and unbridled zeal. The Committee carried out its own agenda of empowering the Republican Party in national affairs, and empowering the radical abolitionists within the Republican Party, and did its best to smash and ruin anyone who it felt stood in the way of accomplishing those goals. In its investigations, the Committee did not gather evidence, at least not in the form that any real lawyer could use in a court of law. Instead, it gathered testimony, much of which supported the preconceived judgment of the members as to the guilt or innocence of the person being investigated. According to J.G. Randall, "The committee's air of omniscience in military matters was matched only by the lack of military expertise on the part of its members. It dealt in partisanship and in the kind of 'flagrant wrong' of which, as Blaine has written, General Stone was a victim."[26] Geoffrey Perrett writes, "The committee never made any pretense of impartiality. Even in the middle of a nation's fight for survival, its hostility to the professional military was unrelenting.... The generals it praised were those who had been commissioned from civilian life, such as Butler and Frémont; those it disparaged were invariably West Pointers.... Committee members ridiculed entrenchments, advances in weapons technology, logistics and training. Their strategy was the application of brute force, applied by massive frontal assaults, wherever a Confederate army could be found, regardless of terrain, weather or defenses. This really was a strategy of 'hard, tough fighting.' No one despised 'strategy' more than the Committee on the Conduct of the War."[27]

The Committee was instrumental in helping to remove Democratic officers from high command, in promoting Republican officers to high command, and in sustaining abolitionist officers in command, regardless of their political affiliation. All in all, aside from its dealings with graft and corruption from government contractors, it did little to aid the war effort or the Lincoln administration. Its greatest accomplishment was the publication of thousands of pages of text about the officers and operations of the armies that proved more useful to the Confederate commanders at the time of their release than they are to the researcher and historian of today.

CHAPTER EIGHT

Riots in the North

The Conscription Act, combined with the ever-increasing casualty lists from the front, served create a mood of helplessness and hopelessness in parts of the North. The working class felt the effect most strongly, as they were the least able to control their own destiny. The provisions of the draft stated that a man could purchase his exemption from the service for a cost of $300.00, or he could hire a substitute, usually for around the same amount. On the surface, this sounds like a reasonable sum to those of us today who sometimes spend that much on a monthly cell phone bill. At the time of the Civil War, however, when the average income for a working man was ten dollars a month or less, three hundred dollars was an amount that only the wealthy could afford to pay. The sentiment that the conflict was a "rich man's war but a poor man's fight" permeated Northern society and magnified the class structure existing throughout the Union.

There was another factor that fired dissent among the poor and working classes, breeding resentment for the government and their more privileged fellow Americans. The nation, since its inception, had prided itself on the volunteer spirit of its citizens. The militia tradition had become deeply rooted in American psyche. All felt that it was their duty to defend the nation in times of crisis, but they clung to the volunteer system that had proved successful during the Colonial period, the Revolution, the War of 1812, and the Mexican War. The suffering and sacrifice that was Valley Forge was honored and memorialized by the nation because free men had, of their own free will, endured extreme hardships in the name of the cause they supported To a people accustomed to rising up against tyranny and despotism, the elimination of free will was tantamount to the elimination of free men. For people only eighty years removed from the Revolution, the idea that they could be forced to fight against their will sounded more like a monarchy or a dictatorship than a democratic form of government. The administration had included the ability to purchase one's exemption from the draft, but the exorbitant amount made it unrealistic for a large portion of the society and had the effect of creating animosity between the classes, as well as toward the government.

Resistance to the draft was such that anxious politicians scrambled to find alternative ways to fill the depleted ranks of the army. The bounty system proved to be a successful remedy. The Federal government employed a quota system in raising men for the army. When another call for troops was made, the total would be divided among the various states, and those states would then divide their portions among their own counties and districts. So long as the required number of men were raised, no draft would be imposed. If a state, or portion of that state, failed to meet its assigned quota, a draft would be held in that area to make up the difference.

States, counties, and towns began offering lump-sum payments to entice men to enlist, in order to avoid the necessity of invoking the draft. In the beginning, the sums offered were small. Bounties of $25 to $50 were enough to persuade men who would probably have enlisted anyway to sign up. As the war continued and the casualties increased, few thought that the sum offered was sufficient to compensate for the risk they would be taking. Bounty amounts increased, and at times, state bounties were augmented by ones offered by a county, a city, or both. Potential recruits could now expect to receive hundreds of dollars to enlist in the army. One of my great-great-grandfathers, John Secrist, enlisted in the 93rd Pennsylvania Infantry as a bounty man in 1864. The three hundred dollars he received was enough to pay for the family farm and have a little money left over besides. In some cases where multiple bounties were being offered, a man could be paid a thousand dollars or more to sign up. In such cases, the amount of money being offered for bounty men amounted to several years' pay. This brought about a sort of bidding war for potential volunteers, as men shopped around to get their best deal.

John M. Kelly of Huntington County, Pennsylvania, is an example of this. Though Kelly was from central Pennsylvania, he joined the 39th Illinois Infantry because the state of Illinois and the city of Chicago were paying the highest amount of bounty money at the time he enlisted. Kelly's combined bounty money was over one thousand dollars, and the total was so much that it was meted out in payments. At the time of his death, more than a year and a half after his enlistment, he was still owed $240.00 of his bounty money.[1]

Kelly was one of the honorable men who went into the service for bounty money. As the payment amounts increased, a new breed of flim-flam man appeared on the American scene: the bounty jumpers. A bounty jumper would enlist in the army to get the signing money, then desert at the first possible opportunity. He would then join another unit, collect that bounty, and desert again. The official record for bounty jumping belonged to John O'Connor, who enlisted and deserted 32 times before finally being caught by authorities and sentenced to four years in prison. O'Connor was lucky. As bounty jumpers became more prevalent in the military, the penalty increased until execution became common for those jumpers who were captured.[2]

The other way that politicians sought to ease the blow of conscription was by tapping into the flood of immigrants who were constantly arriving at Northern ports. Historians estimate that some 800,000 immigrants poured into the North every year during the war. This provided a constant and replenishable source of recruits to the army, and the government did not fail to avail itself of the manpower it offered. Recruiting officers set up shop at the docks and wharves of every major port city in the North and signed up men as soon they got off the ships. Immediate citizenship was promised to those who enlisted, as well as money for them to put in their pockets. Thousands of men, mostly Irish, were thus entered on the muster rolls of Northern regiments, creating an army of mercenaries.

Members of veteran regiments who had re-enlisted once their tour of duty expired took justifiable pride in the fact that they were making a supreme sacrifice to see the war through to the end. But the fact was that only a tiny fraction of those who had volunteered in the early days of the war were still around to witness the end. Even in the "veteran" regiments, the ranks were filled with conscripted and bounty men, much to the disdain of the actual veterans, who despised and distrusted those among them whose patriotism they felt to be for sale. The Union army in the second half of the war bore little resemblance to the army of patriotic volunteers that had begun the fight. Indeed, it more closely resembled the British army of the Revolution, with its regiments of hired Hessian mercenaries.

Recruiting officers enrolling immigrants often had to compete with substitute brokers to get men for the army. Substitute brokers dealt in finding low-cost replacements for drafted men, and their methods made them some of the most detestable individuals in the nation. Immigrants were a special target for the brokers. Foreigners were offered sums of money far below the $300 commonly required to hire a substitute. At times, when the monetary offering did not produce the desired results, men would be kidnapped right off the boats and offered up to enrolling officers. In Detroit, a ring of substitute brokers specialized in kidnapping Canadians, with the use of liquor and drugs. The brokers also paid men who were too old, and children who were too young, to become substitutes for them. A retarded youth from Troy, New York, was kidnapped and offered as a substitute. He was sent to the front and never heard from again, even though his mother met with President Lincoln in an effort to find him.[3]

These two methods of acquiring volunteers did succeed in funneling many thousands of men into the army and limiting the oppression of the draft. Shortfalls did occur, however, and at such times the deficient area would be compelled to impose conscription to make up the difference. In all cases, the compulsory draft was resisted by residents of the area in which it was implemented, sometimes with bloody results.

Perhaps the most famous disturbance to take place in the North was the 1863 draft riot in New York City. News of the impending draft in the city fomented resistance as early as the end of June 1863, when Governor Horatio Seymour was informed of an intended conspiracy to prevent the conscription. Seymour rushed to the city, where he received intelligence that some eighteen hundred deserters had banded together, joined by Copperheads, with the intended purpose of seizing the armory of the 7th New York Regiment. They had set the time for the raid at just after midnight on the night of July 3, when their actions would be covered by the noise of Independence Day celebrations. Guards were placed at the armory, but no insurrection took place. Even so, those "in the know" in the city braced for the clash of wills they knew would take place sooner rather than later.[4]

The city was severely divided along lines of class and politics. It was home to opulent mansions as well as deplorable slums. Wealthy bankers and merchants rode in fine carriages through a city that also contained some of the poorest people in America. New York City was truly a melting pot where the extremes of society were evident for all to see. New York politics exhibited this same collection of extremes. In the city, Mayor George Opdyke was a Lincoln Republican, devoted to the administration and its policies. The city council was dominated by antiwar Democrats, led by the notorious William Marcy "Boss" Tweed. Governor Seymour was himself an antiwar Democrat, while the state legislature was controlled by the Republican Party. While thousands of volunteers had marched from the city to defend the Union, thousands more denounced the war and the administration in mass meetings sponsored by the Democratic Party and the Society for the Diffusion of Political Knowledge, the latter being led by future presidential candidate Samuel J. Tilden. A large portion of the working class saw the war as a fight that would only benefit the wealthy and free blacks who would then migrate north to provide a cheap work force that would endanger their well-being. They viewed the Conscription Act to be an unconstitutional measure that "tyrannized the poor" and favored the rich. This sentiment was particularly strong among the Irish, who made up a quarter of the 814,000 total residents of the city.[5]

On the morning of Saturday, July 11, 1863, a large drum was filled with the names of all eligible males residing in the district at the draft office located at Third Avenue and 46th Street. The drum was rigged to spin, so as to mix up the names. A few turns of the handle was followed by the extraction of the first names of those to be drafted. Captain Charles Jenkins supervised the drawing, which by afternoon had selected 1,236 names of new draftees in what the public viewed as being akin to a death lottery. A crowd which had gathered to witness the proceedings dispersed at their conclusion on the afternoon of the 11th, but were prepared to assemble again when the draft resumed on the morning of Monday, July 13.[6]

On July 12, an instance of irony appeared in the newspapers of New York City when the names of the men drafted on Saturday appeared in the paper the same day that casualty lists from the Battle of Gettysburg were posted around the city. As the residents scanned the columns, first one, then the other, their anger intensified. The names of the draftees were viewed to be nothing more than a list of future casualties. Anger gave way to defiance as inflammatory speeches and threats of violence filled the otherwise quiet Sabbath.[7]

When Captain Jenkins arrived at the draft office on the morning of July 13, he was greeted by a mob of between 5,000 and 10,000 people, most of them Irish, and all in foul humor, with a will to retaliate against the injustice they felt was being perpetrated against them. The draft was resumed amid the boos and curses of the mob, prompting a police detachment to be posted outside the office. Suddenly, a shot rang out, quickly followed by a volley of stones thrown through the windows of the building. The mob surged toward the building, easily overpowering the police who stood in their way. Jenkins and the other members of the draft board beat a hasty retreat through a back door as angry rioters destroyed the office, paying special attention to the drum that contained the names of the potential draftees. Sixty policemen from the local precinct responded to quell the riot, but they were no match for the thousands of protesters who had taken to the street.[8]

Efforts of the police were hampered by the fact that the telegraph lines had been cut, making it necessary to use mounted messengers to communicate between precincts. John A. Kennedy, the police superintendent, hurried to the scene of unrest, where he was recognized by people in the mob. He was viciously attacked and beaten senseless before being dragged through the streets. The sight of his bruised and beaten body so infuriated Thomas Acton, the head of the board of police commissioners, that he ordered his men to crush the uprising without mercy. Knowing that he did not have enough men to deal with the mob head-on, Acton ordered detachments placed at places like City Hall, the police headquarters, banks, leading hotels, and department stores. Mayor Opdyke appealed to the government to release the 300 troops that were in the city, under the command of Brigadier General Harvey Brown, and the few companies of Marines and sailors in the Brooklyn Navy yard, to aid the police in restoring order. The request was immediately granted, but most of the troops were compelled to guard the various armories and arsenals in the city, leaving precious few available to fight the mob. One of the first units to do so, a detachment of fifty men from the Invalid Corps, was overrun and forced to flee for their lives. Two of their number were caught in their flight and beaten to death.[9]

The mob continued to grow until it had almost doubled in size by noon of the 13th. The area of the rioting had spread and now engulfed most of the East Side of the city, a space of thirty blocks between 16th and 46th Streets. Throughout this section of the city rioters attacked anything that symbolized government authority, wealth, or the Negro race. The Marston gun factory, a contractor of muskets for the army, was attacked by the mob, in hopes of better arming themselves from the 1,000 muskets stored there. The front door of the factory was smashed open with a sledgehammer before policemen fired into the crowd. But the police were too few and their rate of fire too slow to impede the intention of the mob, and they were forced to abandon the factory and flee for safety. The seizure of the factory did little to benefit the mob, however, as a fiery explosion tore it apart shortly after it had been captured.

It soon became evident that blacks were a particular target of the mob's wrath. Blacks were attacked wherever they were found, with many being beaten to death. George Templeton Strong, a native New Yorker, reported "a black man hanged ... for no offence but that of Nigritude." Strong telegraphed the president to ask for troops and to request martial law to be imposed. A black orphanage at Fifth Avenue and 43rd Street attracted the attention of the mob, and soon cries of "Burn the niggers' nest" were echoed through the crowd. The mob broke into the building, ransacked it, and set it on fire, but they were not able to lay hands on any of the 237 children who lived there. The orphans had been ushered out through a back door, where a group of Irish city firemen, who had come to fight the fire, formed a double line and protected the children with their axes and hook poles. Ann Derrickson, the wife of a black man, was beaten to death for defending her son, after the mob had soaked his clothes in kerosene, preparatory to setting him on fire.[10]

Several newspaper offices were also targeted by the rioters. Horace Greeley's *New York Tribune* office was sacked and the ground floor set ablaze. Greeley and his staff had escaped through the back door amid shouts from the mob to kill him. Henry Raymond took a different approach to guarding his office of the *New York Times.* He had armed his staff with rifles, and had borrowed three Gatling guns from the military that served as a deterrent to a mob armed mostly with stones and clubs. The rioters sacked and looted the homes of several prominent Republicans and abolitionists, and attacked any well-dressed men they happened to run across with shouts of, "There goes a $300 man!," alluding to the fact that they were obviously able to pay the amount to buy their way out of the draft.[11]

By evening, the streets were

Artist's depiction of the violence of the mob during the New York City draft riots in 1863. Opposition to the draft threatened to stall the Union war effort and became a major political issue in the elections held during the war (Military History Institute, United States Army War College).

littered with debris from the rioters' ransacking and the bodies of rioters and their victims. New York had become a war zone, just as frightening as any one of the battlefields several hundred miles south in Virginia. Edward Sanford of the United States Military Telegraph Service wired Edwin Stanton to report, "New York is tonight at the mercy of a mob."[12]

One of the first real checks administered to the mob took place after the sun went down. A large group of rioters marched on police headquarters, but were ambushed on Broadway by 200 police officers under the command of Sergeant Dan Carpenter. Obeying Acton's order to break up the mob and show no mercy, Carpenter led his men into the crowd, where an hour-long fight ensued. In the end, it was the mob that broke and ran, leaving a number of dead and wounded rioters lying in the street.[13]

Tuesday, July 14, proved to be even bloodier than the previous day, and confrontations between rioters and the police or military were common. On the Lower East Side, a detachment of soldiers turned back one group of rioters while a nearby detachment of Marines forced a second group to retreat. The mob tried to take possession of the Union Steam Works, where a number of government rifles were stored, but the weapons were saved by the police. At 19th Avenue and 34th Street police faced thousands of rioters who pelted them with stones and bricks from the rooftops of surrounding buildings, and shot at them from the upper floor windows. The officers fought their way to the rooftops, where they threw many of their assailants over the edge.[14]

Colonel Henry O'Brien and a detachment of 150 men of the 11th New York Volunteers held a group of rioters at bay by firing volleys over their heads. A two-year-old girl was accidentally killed by one of the volleys as she was watching the proceedings from an upper story window. Later in the day, a group of rioters recognized O'Brien as the officer in command when the little girl was killed, and the mob beat him and tortured him with fire until he was dead. O'Brien had made the mistake of traveling alone to his home to check on the safety of his family, and had been killed within sight of his house.[15]

By the night of the 13th, the mob had built barricades in many locations in an attempt to keep the soldiers and police out, but the authorities spent all of Tuesday night and Wednesday morning tearing down the obstructions. At Seventh Avenue and 32nd Street a mob of 5,000 rioters was driven to flight when artillery opened fire on them. A few hours later, a small infantry detachment under the command of Colonel Cleveland Winslow was overrun by the mob. A two-gun detachment of artillery, under the command of Colonel Edward Jardine, was also captured, and Colonel Jardine barely escaped with his life. The city seemed to be on the verge of complete anarchy. The rioters appeared to be gaining the upper hand, but unknown to the mob, the end of the disturbances was close at hand. Thirteen regiments of veteran infantry from the Army of the Potomac were on the way to the city, and would begin to arrive on Thursday the 15th. Twelve of the regiments were from the state of New York, and the remaining one hailed from Michigan. Heartened by this news, Mayor Opdyke vetoed a bill passed by the city council to give every drafted man the $300 needed to buy his way out of the service.

At sunrise on July 15 the Union troops marched up Broadway to confront the mob. The rioters had also heard of the arrival of the soldiers and attempted to counter this new development by procuring muskets stored in a Greenwich Street warehouse. The city police had been tipped off regarding this move, and were there to meet the mob and drive it off. That night, 5,000 rioters confronted 1,000 men from the 7th New York Infantry at Second Avenue and 28th Street. The soldiers opened fire with musketry and artillery, and the mob recoiled before the shock. The infantry followed up their volleys with a bayonet charge that scattered the mob and effectively ended the riots. Contemporary accounts listed fifteen soldiers and hundreds of rioters killed in the clash.[16]

Most contemporary accounts of the riots place the death toll between 1,000 and 1,200. Most modern historians feel these numbers to be greatly exaggerated, placing the number of dead at 105 to 119, and the number wounded at 306. Of the dead, eleven were blacks killed by the mob, eight were soldiers, and two were police officers. The rest were rioters in the mob. Property damage amounted to more than 1.5 million dollars. The draft was postponed until August 19, by which time forty-three regiments of troops were stationed in and around the city to protect against further violence. The equivalent of an entire Union army was sent to ensure a peaceful draft in New York, but by the time the second lottery was held not a single soldier would have been necessary. The city council had gotten the votes to override the veto and had approved the financial appropriation to pay the commutation fees of the men selected in the draft. In the end, the second draft in New York City was held mostly for appearances, as the administration felt it had to be carried out, lest other cities decide that the way to avoid conscription lay in the same sort of violent resistance that had taken place in New York City.[17]

The fear of the administration over similar outbreaks of rebellion was well founded. Resistance to the draft was evident all over the North. While most of the incidents were of a localized, small-scale nature compared to the New York City riots, all of them held the potential to escalate into blood baths. Smaller but bloody riots also took place in Boston and in Troy, New York. The anger shown toward enrollment officers erupted in acts of violence across the nation. In Rush County, Indiana, two enrollment officers were murdered as they made their rounds. In Chicago, two more were assaulted and seriously injured by a brick-hurling mob. In the Green Bay area of Wisconsin, threats of violence against enrolling officers were so numerous that no officers would take the post for fear of being killed. A small uprising in Holmes County, Ohio, was quickly put down, but a mob in Blackford County, Indiana, was successful in destroying all the records of the local draft board. A number of draft officers were attacked in Indiana and Illinois, and a few were killed. It became necessary in these strongholds of dissent for United States officials to be accompanied by armed guards. State authorities in Ohio and Indiana organized new militia units for the purpose of keeping the peace at home. By 1864, Ohio had raised a force of 40,000 men for this purpose, while Indiana's force was not quite that large. As can be seen by the armies stationed from New York City to the Old Northwest, almost as many soldiers were employed in quelling the disturbances in the North as were being used to put down the rebellion in the South.[18] Lincoln and the Republicans could hardly have been considered to have the consensus of the people in prosecuting the war.

Pennsylvania witnessed as much violence and resistance to the draft as any state in the Union. From the very start, Pennsylvanians exhibited open rebellion to conscription. A group of conscripted men brought suit against their local draft board because the conscription act infringed upon powers reserved to the states by making militiamen eligible for the draft. They won a ruling from the Pennsylvania Supreme Court in their favor, and for a period of time the draft was suspended in the state. When the Federal government chose to ignore the findings of the Pennsylvania Supreme Court and the draft was resumed, the method of resistance shifted from legal channels to acts of violence. Peter Kutz of Schuylkill County recounted an experience common to enrolling officers in the state when he told of being accosted by a mob of angry citizens carrying stones and threatening to kill him. Like more than half the enrolling officers in the state, Kutz resigned his position out of fear for his life. Violence was not limited to the enrolling officers, however. One mining company official was murdered in his home because he was thought to be providing enrollment officers with the names of his employees for the draft.[19]

In Fayette County, Pennsylvania, John Moats was drafted, but failed to report. When Federal authorities showed up at his home, Moats attempted to flee, but was shot dead by one of the officials, William Cooper. The Fayette County coroner's court found Cooper guilty of murder, but he was protected by Federal authorities and the case never came to trial. The outrage of men in Fayette County found expression when a large armed band took up a fortified position close to Camp Cross in Connellsville, Pennsylvania, with its garrison of 520 Union cavalry troopers. The troopers were not regular army men; they were nine-month militia, but they represented Federal authority to the residents of the county. A lively skirmish ensued as the opposing sides blazed away at one another from behind their fortifications. After a period of time, the civilians were forced to evacuate their position and retreat, though neither side reported any deaths in the incident. Edward Roddy, the editor of the local newspaper in Uniontown, was accused of inciting the violence because of editorials he had run in his paper opposing the draft. He was arrested for disloyalty and treason and confined in the Allegheny Penitentiary in Pittsburgh until influential Democrats were able to effect his release.[20]

An Irish group known as the Molly Maguires openly defied the authority of Federal draft officers in the coal fields of eastern Pennsylvania. The group had assumed the name of a secret society back in Ireland known for its acts of violence. The Irish coal miners of the region resented the fact that they could be drafted and forced to fight in the war despite the fact that they were still immigrants and not allowed to vote. It was rumored that the Molly Maguires had armed themselves, and that fully 1,000 of them carried firearms. When the number of enlisted men from the Cass Township area of Schuylkill County failed to meet the Federal quota, a draft was ordered to make up the difference. The Irish miners of the Molly Maguires immediately began to riot in protest. The miners openly confronted Federal authorities and used force and sabotage to try to prevent trains coming from Harrisburg, filled with draftees, from reaching Philadelphia. With this threat coming on the heels of the New York City riot, the administration sought to control the situation before it got out of hand and led to even more armed confrontations. Benjamin Bannan, the draft commissioner at the time, resolved to end the confrontation by crediting men enrolled in Philadelphia to the quota of Cass Township, thus alleviating the need for a draft in that area. The administration declined to enforce its own laws and manipulated the situation in order to appease the Molly Maguires and quiet the situation.

In the center of Pennsylvania, violence erupted in Clearfield County. This was a remote section of the state where lumbering was the primary source of income. In the early stages of the draft, many men came to Clearfield County to avoid conscription and lose themselves in the lumber camps. In a letter to Governor Curtin, one local official expressed concern for the developing situation: "The greatest drawback to the draft for the army is the lumber region. Every loose fellow who is or expects to be drafted runs off to the lumber shanties into the mountains and remote districts where he finds employment and high wages. In this way the vagrants hide and lay concealed from officers who find it impossible to catch or discover their den." As the war dragged on, however, the demand for lumber decreased, causing many lumber camps to go out of existence. The backwoods area of Clearfield County still provided men who sought to avoid the draft with a hiding place from Federal authorities charged with enforcing conscription.

In July of 1864, 660 Clearfield County residents were selected by the draft board. More than 400 of these failed to respond for enrollment. Colonel Cyrus Baker was sent to make arrests in the county. While in the process of serving notices in Lawrence Township, Col. Baker was shot dead by John Lounsberry, a deserter of two previous drafts. In response to the many acts of resistance in the county, Company C of the 16th Veteran Reserve Corps, under the command of Captain John M. Southworth, was ordered to the area to keep the peace and aid in enforcement of the draft. On the night of December 12, 1864, Captain Southworth marched 20 to 25 men into Knox Township and surrounded the cabin of Thomas Adams, where there was reported to have been a group of deserters and draft dodgers. An alarm was sounded from within the cabin, and Thomas Adams ran upstairs, took a musket from under a bed, and fired a shot at the troops, killing an 18-year-old soldier from New Hampshire by the name of Edgar L. Reed. Adams fired two more shots from a double-barrel shot gun before jumping from the attic to try to make good his escape. When soldiers ordered him to halt he failed to respond, drawing a volley of fire that resulted in Adams' being mortally wounded. The fire fight between the soldiers and those in the cabin was short-lived, as Captain Southworth broke into the structure to demand the surrender of those inside. Eighteen deserters and draft dodgers were captured.[21]

Small, isolated incidents, just like the one that took place in Knox Township, were being reenacted across the North, as resistance to the draft caused men to fight to protect what they felt to be their right not to fight in the army. In virtually all cases, the resistance ended in the same manner as it did in Knox Township, with the perpetrators being killed or captured. A lack of organization meant that all such protests were small, isolated affairs that could be easily dealt with by the Federal authorities. The fact that they continued to take place, with little or no chance of success, displays the resolve of the dissenters not to be forced to fight in a war many of them felt to be unjust.

The Conscription Act served to expand Federal control over the states. The Supreme Court of Pennsylvania was quite correct in asserting that the law was unconstitutional, and that it impinged upon the powers reserved to the individual states, but its institution was accomplished at the point of the bayonet by an administration already accustomed to trampling the Constitution whenever that suited its purposes. While the draft brought many thousands of men into the ranks of the army, either by means of the draft itself, or the bounty and substitute systems created to circumvent it, the quality of the men in the Union army suffered an obvious reduction from those who had previously served. The veteran troops who still remained in the army detested and distrusted the new levies who were brought in among them. The veterans had enlisted in the early days of the war out of patriotism and a desire to do their duty. They looked down on these men who had only enlisted for monetary gain, or because they were forced to do so. Veterans claimed that they could not be counted on in the field, often skulking on the march, or refusing to do their duty in battle, or, in the case of bounty jumpers, deserting at the first possible opportunity.

In the final years of the war, the Union army boasted a total strength of some 1,000,000 men, as opposed to the 200,000 to be counted in the Confederate army. Of these, only 46,347 came from the draft. Another 73,600 entered the service as substitutes. Some 210,000 were the result of the enlistment and formation of black regiments. These figures pale when compared to the number of men who came into the army for bounty payments. Though there are no accurate troop statistics available, due to faulty record keeping at local and

Cartoon showing Lincoln with a black Union soldier. The caption read, "Sambo, you are not handsome, any more than myself, but as to sending you back to your old master, I'm not the man to do it — and, what's more, I won't." The infusion of some 200,000 black volunteers into the Union Army helped to ease the demand for white soldiers and the upheaval caused by the draft (*Lincoln's Yarns and Stories*).

county levels, and to the untold numbers of bounty jumpers who would be listed several times in any accounting, it is known that the combined total spent by the states for bounties during the war was approximately $286,000,000. The Federal government expended more than $300,000,000 for bounty payments. It is easy to see that much more than half of the soldiers in the Federal army, during the final year of the war, were there because the had to be, or for reasons of monetary gain. The administration should have stuck to the system of volunteer enlistments, as these trusted and true soldiers were worth many times their numbers of draftees and bounty men on the field of battle.

CHAPTER NINE

Clement Vallandigham and the Copperhead Movement

The source of the most serious organized opposition to Lincoln's administration and the Republican Party came from a group known as the Copperheads. In reality, there was no group called the Copperheads. The term was used by Republicans as a derisive umbrella name to describe anyone thought to oppose the administration for any reason. The name was supposed to have come about in 1862 from lapel pins, made from the heads of Indian head pennies, worn by Midwestern opponents of the administration to identify them to one another.[1] But there is evidence that the term had already been applied to opponents of the administration as early as 1861. On August 17 of that year, The *Cincinnati Commercial* ran an editorial concerning Democratic complaints that they were being branded as secessionists, traitors, and Tories in the state because of their opposition to actions of the administration. "I see that some of the editors supporting the ticket lately nominated at Columbus are not pleased with the names suggested, as secessionists, traitors, or tories. The Confederacy at the outset symbolized itself in the figure of a rattlesnake. Would it not, therefore, be quite proper that its allies should select from the animal kingdom their heraldry and since the rattlesnake's mate, or copperhead, is in all respects a fitting representative we suggest that the term Copperhead be applied to the aforesaid party."[2]

Many people in the North were alarmed by the actions of the Republicans. Lincoln's unprecedented usurping of executive power, the suspension of the writ of habeas corpus, arbitrary arrests and imprisonment by the military, the first call for national conscription, and the unexpectedly high casualty lists of the war all combined to foment dissent. In the politically charged atmosphere that existed in the Union at that time, is was ill-advised to voice these concerns too openly, however, if one did not want to place himself in a position where he was ostracized, or possibly arrested, for his views. As a result, the nation saw a rise in secret societies, where like-minded citizens could gather together, discuss the topics of the day, and plan toward a common goal of unseating the Republicans.

One of the best known of these secret societies was the Knights of the Golden Circle. It was originally founded in 1854 by Dr. George W. Brickley for the purpose of gaining support for the forcible addition of Mexico to the Gulf States. Brickley developed a mysterious society, with rituals, passwords, and all the pomp and circumstance that would appeal to the minds of adventurous American expansionists. Brickley established his first lodge in his home town of Cincinnati, Ohio. He later set up lodges in Alabama, Kentucky, and Tennessee. Members were charged a ten-dollar membership fee that was supposed to go toward funding the activities of the group to make Mexico a part of the United States.[3]

When the Civil War broke out, Brickley, a Southern sympathizer, changed the ritual of the Knights of the Golden Circle from expansionism to secessionism, making the organization a secret society for secessionist sympathizers. Initially, there were few new members to the Knights, as citizens openly voiced their protests against the administration. The advent of Republican tyranny, in the form of arbitrary arrests for disloyalty, brought a sudden rise in membership, as opponents of the administration felt a need to go underground. The Knights of the Golden Circle became the subject of rumor and speculation with the Union press and the military, both of whom depicted the organization as a well-organized militant society, bent on the forcible overthrow of the duly elected government. The size, power, and goals of the group were greatly exaggerated by the administration, giving the military an excuse to investigate and confine all citizens suspected of being a subversive.

In 1863, Dr. Brickley, who had been serving as a medical officer on General Braxton Bragg's staff, was captured in Indiana. Authorities quickly learned that he was the founder and leader of the Knights of the Golden Circle, but they were disappointed during their interrogation to find that Brickley was a complete charlatan and the group he led was mostly bluff and bluster, and not a serious threat to the government. It was decided that a public trial would expose the fact that the Knights were nothing more than an insignificant bother, a revelation that would take the teeth out of the military's campaign to suppress opposition to the administration by means of their hunt for subversives. The decision was made to hold Brickley in solitary confinement for the duration of the war, so as to allow the legend of the Knights to continue. The administration created a bogie-man with which they could justify their extreme measures against suspected subversives. If the truth were known, then there would no longer be a legitimate reason, in the minds of the citizens, for the military tyranny to continue. Brickley had envisioned creating an organization to counter the power of the Republicans. Instead, his Knights simply provided the administration with the ammunition necessary to tighten its grip over anyone suspected of disloyalty to the current regime.[4]

The Democratic opposition had reached the height of its power during the winter of 1862-1863, after Peace Democrats made a good showing at the polls in the fall elections. In Illinois, they blocked every bill for the support of the war, and even prevented the passage of appropriations to support the state government. The lower house of the Illinois legislature passed legislation demanding an armistice to the war and called for a peace convention. The governors from the states in the Northwest feared the activities of the Copperheads and reported to Washington that they were kept in check only by the ever-increasing severity of oppressive measures. One Congressman stated, "The President tells me that he now fears the fire in the rear — meaning the Democracy, especially at the Northwest — more than our military chances." By the beginning of 1863, the Peace Democrats had captured the entire Democratic organization in the Northwest. A large part of their membership was in secret societies, and some of the secret societies were marshaled in quasi-military companies, arming and drilling themselves. In Iowa, the governor estimated as many as 33,000 disloyal men to be within the state, and the unrest became so prevalent as to cause him to bar any Iowan from granting asylum to any resident of Missouri who had fought against that state's Unionist government.[5]

Phineas Wright formed one of these militant secret societies, known as the Corps de Belgique, which, after Brickley's arrest, was later merged by Harrison Dodd with the remnants of the Knights of the Golden Circle to form the Order of American Knights. The greatest activity of the new Knights was in Ohio, Indiana, and Illinois, where dissension over Republican policies ran high. It was the Conscription Act and the suspension of the writ of habeas corpus that most inflamed those who would later join the Knights. In Wisconsin and Indiana, the state Supreme Courts had declared Lincoln's suspension of the writ of habeas corpus unconstitutional. Military authorities from Indiana invaded Illinois to arrest two deserters, and found themselves arrested by local authorities on the charge of kidnapping. Colonel Henry B. Carrrington, commander of the District of Indiana, forced his way into the courtroom with a detachment of troops, freed the military detainees and arrested the Illinois judge. One editor, outraged over administration attacks on Democrats, advised, "Matches are cheap. For every dime of property destroyed by political opponents, destroy a dollar's worth in return."[6]

Such extremist rhetoric caused many Democrats to abstain from lending their support to the Copperheads, not wanting to align themselves with traitors and rebels, as the administration was labeling them. Instead, they formed an alliance with Republicans under the Unionist banner, which helped the Republican ticket to take control of the New Hampshire legislature and executive mansion, to carry judicial and local elections in Michigan and Ohio, and to make serious inroads in Democratic strongholds in Indiana, Iowa, and Missouri. Once again, Democratic activism was backfiring and providing the Republicans the means with which they could consolidate control over the nation. It also meant that those who continued to oppose the administration must do so with increased secrecy, further adding to the propaganda effort of the Republicans to discredit anyone who spoke against them by keeping the public fearful over the threat of conspiracies.[7] Republicans were winning in every instance where public opinion was to be influenced. Every Copperhead who went to extremes in trying to voice opposition to the administration was painted as a traitor and conspirator, causing moderate Democrats to fall in line with the Republicans, regardless of their personal hatred of that party's policies and actions.

In some cases, conspiracies were more than just threats, as radical Copperhead leaders hatched grandiose plans to upset the Northern war effort, and even to take the Old Northwest out of the Union. Indiana was possibly the most active state for the Order of American Knights and its progeny, the Sons of Liberty. In 1864, the Sons of Liberty claimed 18,000 members in forty-four of the state's sixty-nine counties. Harrison Dodd, leader of the Order of American Knights, planned an operation for the groups to liberate the Confederate prisoners held at Camp Morton in Indianapolis. These freed prisoners would then be armed with weapons captured from the arsenal in the city. With this army, Dodd would begin an insurrection in conjunction with similar uprisings in other states to take control of the state governments to create a Northwest Confederacy. Dodd's plan was indicative of most of the extremist Copperhead operations during the war in that it was poorly organized and suffered from even poorer security. Dodd had no coordination with any members of the Order of American Knights or Sons of Liberty outside of his own county, and the plans for an organized uprising simply did not exist.

In addition, Dodd had revealed his plans to a government agent several weeks before his proposed date for the strike, on August 16. Colonel Henry Carrington and Governor Oliver Morton decided to prepare for the eventuality of an attack, but to take no preemptive action based on the information they had been given. August 16 came and went without any signs of disturbance from the Copperheads, as Dodd's plan never got off the ground. On August 20, military authorities received a tip that a shipment of weapons had just been delivered to Dodd from New York. The military investigated the tip to find four hundred revolvers at Dodd's place of business, along with a considerable amount of ammunition. Dodd was arrested in early September and tried for treason. During the trial, he escaped from prison and made his way to Canada. He was nonetheless pronounced guilty of the crime in absentia, and sentenced to be executed by hanging. Four of his accomplices were also tried, with three being sentenced to hang, and one to perform hard labor for the rest of the war.[8]

As with Brickley's case, the activities of Dodd proved to be far less threatening to the government than had been reported. True, Dodd had envisioned a forceful overthrow of the duly appointed governmental authorities in the Northwest, but he had been all boast and bluster, and showed complete ineptness in being able to accomplish any of the goals he had set for his group. As with Brickley, the administration was able to make significant propaganda usage of the Great Northwest Conspiracy, and the mere fact that such an operation had been planned allowed the military the latitude to expand and intensify its campaign against any and all opponents of the administration or its actions.

The acknowledged head of the Copperhead movement in the country was Clement Vallandigham, a two-term Congressman from the state of Ohio. Vallandigham has been described by a contemporary as "having one of those minds that instinctively fear innovation, whose eyes were on the past, whose faith clung to established institutions and time worn customs. The dogmatic assurance and inflexible purpose of his kind were entrenched in a cold and selfish personality. As a man he stood apart from others, set off by an arrogance and egotism which would neither take council of man or God." Despite these negative qualities, he "possessed grace of bearing and powers of address which captivated those who came within his sphere. College education, legal studies and practice in the courts, and editorial experience on the *Dayton Empire* failed to liberalize his ways of thinking, but from their training he developed a power of expression, the eloquence of political platform, in which few of his generation surpassed him."[9]

During the debates over compromise Vallandigham had argued in Congress:

> We of the Northwest have a deeper interest in the preservation of this government in its present form than any other section of the Union. Hemmed in, isolated, cut off from the seaboard upon every side; a thousand miles and more from the mouth of the Mississippi, the free navigation of which under the law of nations we demand, and will have at every cost; with nothing but our great island seas, the lakes—and their outlet, too, through a foreign country—what is to be our destiny? Sir, we have fifteen hundred miles of southern frontier, and but a little narrow strip of eighty miles or less from Virginia to Lake Erie bounding us upon the east. Ohio is the isthmus that connects the South with the British possessions, and the East with the West. The Rocky Mountains separate us from the Pacific. Where is to be our outlet? What are we to do when we have broken up and destroyed this Government? We are seven States now, ... and a population of nine millions. We have an empire equal in area to the third of all Europe, and we do not mean to be a dependency or province either of the east or of the South; nor yet an interior or second-rate power upon this continent; and if we cannot secure a maritime boundary upon other terms, we will cleave our way to the sea-coast with the sword. A nation of warriors we may be; a tribe of shepherds never."[10]

On February 20, 1861, Vallandigham forwarded a proposal to his fellow Congressmen for Federal reconstruction in the hope of peacefully bringing the already seceded states back into the fold. Vallandigham's plan called for a Constitutional amendment restructuring the country into four sections—a North, a West, a Pacific, and a South. Under his system, the assent of a majority of legislatures from each section would be required to pass national laws. The Electoral College would likewise be restructured, making it necessary for a majority of electors from each of the four sections to elect a president and vice-president. Secession would be recognized as a legal right, but regulated, as the act would only be valid if it had the sanction of all the legislatures in the section in which the individual state was a part. The potential problems with Vallandigham's proposed restructuring are readily apparent, and his proposal received nothing more than passing consideration in Congress. Failing to effect any sort of positive change in the government, he then resorted to becoming an obstructionist to the Lincoln administration until he was defeated for reelection in 1863.[11]

The eloquence of Vallandigham's oratory in Congress propelled him to national prominence in the Democratic Party, despite the fact that he was, at the core, a proponent of his own section, who sought to raise the consciousness of the people of the Northwest. His message, however sectional, had appeal for Republican opponents throughout the North, and was echoed in the editorial pages of newspapers across the Union. In all cases, Vallandigham and his followers firmly placed the blame for the war on the shoulders of Lincoln and the Republicans. When Lincoln made his initial call for 75,000 volunteers, the *Ashland Union* replied, "Fight your own battles. We have only to say to you, gentlemen, this is not our fight; you have followed your own councils, you must do your own fighting.... The Administration leaders have succeeded in their unhallowed work of destroying the Government and Union. They have robbed us of our National Union — and shall we (the Democracy) give our blood to their service to consecrate the crime?" *The Old Guard*, published in New York, asserted: "Had Lincoln confined his acts within constitutional limits, and attempted no deed not authorized by that sacred instrument, not only should we have been spared all their bloodshed and debt, but the Union would have been saved."[12]

The Democrats set new lyrics to the tune of the song "America" and asked all patriotic Americans to sing it every night.

> God save our wretched land.
> From Lincoln's traitor band,
> From woe and blight;
> Make all the people brave,
> To shout o'er land and wave,
> Arise our homes to save,
> In freedom's might.[13]

The ultimate defeat of the administration, unnecessary bloodshed, and the upheaval of society echoed through the pages of a collection of Democratic poems and songs, published in pamphlet form, and distributed for the use of the faithful.

> We are coming, Abraham Lincoln,
> From mountain, wood, and glen;

We are coming, Abraham Lincoln,
With the ghosts of murdered men.
Yes! we're coming, Abraham Lincoln,
With curses loud and deep,
That will haunt you in your waking,
And disturb you in your sleep.

There's blood upon your garments,
There's guilt upon your soul;
For the lust of ruthless soldiers
You let loose without control;
Your dark and wicked doings
A God of mercy sees;
And the wail of homeless children
Is heard on every breeze.[14]

Vallandigham endeavored to accomplish what neither Douglas nor Calhoun had been able to achieve: a united West and South, and the subsequent end of the war. On January 14, before his term in Congress had come to an end, he began his campaign to capture the leadership of the Democratic Party by stating, "My Lords, you cannot conquer America. And you never will. The war for the Union is a bloody and costly failure. The President confessed it on the 22nd of September [the date Lincoln issued the Emancipation Proclamation]. War for the Union was abandoned and the war for the Negro begun. Stop fighting. Make an armistice, withdraw your army from the seceded states!"[15]

During the following weeks, Vallandigham fanned the flames of discontent by warning that the war would never end if the people consented to conscription. He advised that men refuse to be drafted, so that the Confederates would outnumber the Federal troops, warning that abolitionists had taken over the Republican Party, and that their prosecution of the war would erase American civil liberties forever. Vallandigham's public addresses spurred Democrats to action across the nation. Emboldened by his words, Democratic newspapers and politicians increased their condemnation of the administration and its policies, and membership flourished in secret societies like the Order of American Knights.

In March of 1863, when Vallandigham left Washington to return to his home in Dayton, Ohio, he was already being anointed as being the unofficial leader of the Democratic Party. Once home, he continued to blast Lincoln and the administration at every opportunity. General Ambrose Burnside, commander of the Department of the Ohio, became concerned that Vallandigham's actions were supporting resistance to the draft and increasing desertions and sabotage within his district. He therefore issued General Order No. 38 on April 13, 1863, stating that those who committed acts for the benefit of the enemy would be tried as spies and traitors. He further stated that "the habit of declaring sympathy for the enemy" would be considered to be the same as taking action on their behalf. "Persons committing such offenses will at once be arrested, with a view to being tried as above stated or sent beyond our lines into the lines of their friends." This was an open challenge to Vallandigham and the Copperheads, who claimed that like the Alien and Sedition Act of 1798, this was a violation of the right of free speech.

Vallandigham decided to challenge Burnside's order on May 1, 1863, when he made two speeches to a mass meeting of Democrats at Mt. Vernon, Ohio. Vallandigham made a point of being as inflammatory as possible, even though he knew that plainclothes military authorities were in the audience to report on his words. He told the crowd that the war was "wicked and cruel" and was "not being waged for the preservation of the Union," but "for the purpose of crushing out liberty and erecting a despotism," as "a war for the freedom of the blacks and the enslavement of the whites." He urged his followers to inform "the minions of usurped power that they will not submit to such restrictions on their liberties" as were stated in the order issued by General Burnside, which he described as "a base usurpation of arbitrary authority." He charged that the Republicans were attempting "to build up a monarchy upon the ruins of our free government."[16]

Burnside hesitated to enforce his own order for four days, but at 3 o'clock in the morning of May 5, more than one hundred soldiers surrounded Vallandigham's home in Dayton. His door was broken down, and the soldiers seized him out of bed to inform him of his arrest. Friends of Vallandigham rang bells to announce the intrusion, and an angry mob gathered to denounce the action. The mob did not attempt to interfere with the arrest, satisfying its anger by instead burning down the office of the local Republican newspaper. Vallandigham was allowed time to dress, and was then taken to Cincinnati to face trial by a military tribunal. On May 16, Vallandigham was found guilty of disloyal and treasonable acts, and was sentenced to be confined at Fort Warren, in Boston Harbor, for the duration of the war.[17]

By all accounts, Burnside had acted on his own in arresting and prosecuting Vallandigham, and his actions now placed the administration in an unenviable position. Lincoln knew that if he held Vallandigham in prison, he would be creating a martyr for the Copperhead movement, and would only serve to intensify their opposition by giving them a central object to focus their attention upon. If Lincoln ordered Vallandigham's release, he would be publicly stating that his arrest had been in error, and would be adding to the influence and stature he already held within certain sections of the Democratic Party. Therefore, Lincoln settled upon a plan intended to defuse the situation by taking Vallandigham out of circulation without confining him to prison. He was to be sent into exile in the Confederacy, with instructions that the original sentence would be carried out if he returned to Union lines. General Braxton Bragg described the events of the banishment. "On the 25 inst. the Hon. C.L. Vallandigham of Ohio U.S. was brought by an armed guard of the enemy, to the neutral ground between our pickets, on the road from Murfreesboro to this place [Shelbyville]; and was there abandoned by them — I have admitted him within my lines, and received him with the courtesy due any unfortunate exile seeking a refuge from tyranny — He desires to go to the state of Georgia, and I have granted him permission for that purpose."[18]

Back in Ohio, Burnside was once more attempting to suppress the Copperheads within his department. On June 1, he closed the *Chicago Times* for publishing criticisms of the administration. Lincoln reversed Burnside's order and reopened the paper a few days later. Burnside later advised Secretary of War Stanton of his intention to arrest a Kentucky judge for making public statements against the war. Stanton voiced the administration's desire not to create martyrs for the Democrats when he replied: "If Mr. Trimble is found encouraging desertion from your army, or in any way interfering with or endangering your military operations you will be authorized to place him under arrest; the mere declaration of his opposition to the war or that if elected he will oppose furnishing supplies of any kind is a good reason why loyal men should not vote for him but is not sufficient ground for military arrest."[19]

Vallandigham's placement in the South was uncomfortable for him as well as for his hosts. The Congressman was not a Southern sympathizer and held no support for the rebellion. Though Vallandigham's agitation of the administration had been widely reported in the Southern press, gaining him the admiration of a number of Confederates, Southerners knew that he did not support secession or rebellion, and was, therefore, not one of them. He could best serve the Confederacy if he were in a position to continue weakening the Union cause. The South wanted no part of the peace and reconciliation platform advocated by the Copperhead movement, and did not want to appear to the world that they were making any sort of alliance with Vallandigham or his followers. In an official game of passing the buck, it was determined to adopt Vallandigham's own suggestion that he be conveyed to a neutral site and released. Accordingly, on June 17, 1863, a blockade runner transported the exile to Bermuda, where he arranged passage to Canada. By July 15, Vallandigham had set up shop at Niagara, just across the New York border from the United States. In the meantime, the Democratic Party of Ohio had held their convention on June 11, for the purpose of nominating a candidate for the fall gubernatorial election. Vallandigham was chosen to represent the party, even though he was, under threat of imprisonment, no longer a citizen of the state.[20]

Vallandigham accepted his nomination as Ohio's gubernatorial candidate on the day he arrived in Niagara. He also issued a manifesto for the Democrats of Ohio that contained a description of his exile intended to incite outrage among his constituents. "Arrested and confined for three weeks in the United States, a prisoner of state; banished thence to the Confederate States, and there held as an alien enemy and prisoner of war, though on parole, fairly and honorably dealt with and given leave to depart, — an act possible only by running the blockade at the hazard of being fired on by ships flying the flag of my own country, — I find myself first a freeman when on British soil. And today, under the protection of the British flag, I am here to enjoy and in part to exercise, the privileges and rights which usurpers insolently deny me at home." Vallandigham outlined his party program. He went on to intentionally misconstrue the facts when he avowed that he had not heard one person in the South "who did not declare his readiness, when the war shall have been ceased and invading armies been withdrawn, to consider and discuss the question of reunion."[21]

In August of 1863, Vallandigham moved his residence to Windsor, opposite Detroit, so that he could be closer to the strongholds of his party in the Northwest. His imprisonment and subsequent release had emboldened the Democratic press in that sector, as had the actions of several Northwest judges in blunting the Conscription Act by issuing habeas corpus to the draftees. Lincoln decided to turn his attention to the judges, and leave Vallandigham to his own devices. The president had suspended the writ of habeas corpus several times thus far in the war, but always as an executive order, without the approval of Congress. In March of 1863, Congress had passed a law granting Lincoln the power to suspend the writ wherever public safety demanded it. On September 15, 1863, Lincoln used this approval of Congress when he suspended the writ of habeas corpus for the duration of the war throughout the United States in cases where "spies, or aiders or abettors of the enemy" were held by the military. By doing so, he crushed the efforts of the Northwest judges to circumvent the draft by use of the writ.[22]

So far as Vallandigham was concerned, Lincoln's decision to exile the activist proved to be the wisest course. After the initial outrage over his arrest and trial had subsided, Vallandigham's influence within the party went on the decline. His bid for the Ohio governor's mansion proved unsuccessful, and by 1864, with the presidential election looming, he had been replaced as the party's darling by George B. McClellan. The Copperhead movement suffered the same fate as its self-appointed leader. After an initial bluster of threats and condemnations most of its members simply faded away. The movement was once more revived in 1864, for the presidential election, at which time the Sons of Liberty elected Clement Vallandigham to be their national commander. The leaders of the militant portion of the movement planned to mount a nation-wide insurrection to take place during the Democratic convention, but, as with all of their previous enterprises, nothing ever resulted from their plans. This militant faction was further weakened by the fact that McClellan, the party's new face, wanted nothing to do with them and considered their actions hurtful to the Democratic Party's chances for winning the fall election.

In the end, all that the various militant factions of the Democratic Party were able to accomplish was to further the suppression by the administration of the individual states. The Copperhead movement provided Lincoln and the

Republicans with an opportunity to discredit the Democratic Party as a whole, and to lump anyone who disagreed with the government under the heading of being disloyal or a traitor. The fact that elements of the movement had planned armed insurrections against the government gave the administration license to clamp down its grip on all who voiced opposition to its actions and policies, even though those insurrections turned out to exist more in the minds of their fomentors than in reality. In fact, the administration perpetuated the mystery of the Great Northwestern Conspiracy for its own advantage, and imprisoned the founder of the Knights of the Golden Circle without trial, so that the ineptitude of the movement could not be universally known. The poor organization and poorer security of the so-called secret societies eventually caused them to become outcasts within their own party, as they were seen as being too militant by the masses, and their reputation was so soiled that the Democratic Party, under McClellan, sought to distance itself from them. A common Republican saying of the time stated that while not all Democrats were traitors, all traitors were Democrats. The militant faction of the Democratic Party had assisted the Republicans in casting all Democrats in the worst possible light, and through the skillful political manipulations of Abraham Lincoln, their blunders had been used against them to increase Republican power and control over the government.

CHAPTER TEN

Ordered to Vote for Lincoln: The Election of 1864

The presidential election of 1864 was one of the most hotly contested in American history, even though the vast majority of the Democrats living in the country never cast a vote due to the fact they no longer lived in the Union. For a period of time it appeared that Lincoln would lose his bid for reelection. In fact, Lincoln himself was convinced that would be the case. The war had not been going well for the North. Though it seemed to the folks back home that the Union armies definitely had the Confederates on the defensive, they just couldn't deliver the knockout punch that would decide the conflict. The South doggedly persevered, resisting all pressure brought against it, and the casualty rolls continued to increase.

In the spring of 1864, General Ulysses S. Grant's campaign to end the war gave hope to the citizens on the home front. For the first time in the war, all Union armies were to act in concert to engage the Confederate forces in their respective theaters of operation. This would effectively pin down the Confederates and prevent them from using interior lines of supply and communication to shift men and supplies to face isolated Union threats, as had been done in the past. This strategy would allow the Union army to take full advantage of its superior numbers in a way that had never before been employed in the conflict. The intention was to wear the Confederacy down, to fight like a bulldog: latch on and don't let go until the enemy is bled dry. According to Grant's orders, every commander was to do his part by keeping the Confederates in his front occupied. As Grant put it, those who couldn't skin could hold a leg for those who did.

Grant would accompany the Army of the Potomac and engage Robert E. Lee's Army of Northern Virginia. Major General William T. Sherman, with his army at Chattanooga, Tennessee, was to launch an offensive to capture Atlanta and occupy the heart of the Confederacy. Major General Franz Sigel was assigned the task of conquering the Shenandoah Valley, a major source of supplies, and an important line of march and maneuver for the Army of Northern Virginia. General Benjamin Butler was given the task of capturing the important transportation and supply hub of Petersburg, in the rear of Lee's army. In May of 1864, the various fingers of Grant's combined fist began their march to end the war in one nationwide campaign. But Grant's strategy was in trouble right from the start. Franz Sigel was defeated by John C. Breckinridge at the Battle of New Market, Virginia, and when Sigel retreated he left the Confederates in control of the valley. Ben Butler met unexpected opposition from P.G.T. Beauregard's forces, who drove Butler's Army of the James back and bottled them up at Bermuda Hundred, Virginia, despite the fact that Butler had Beauregard significantly outnumbered. Grant, with the Army of the Potomac, numbering between 120,000 and 130,000 men, marched into the Wilderness, where Lee was able to soundly defeat him in a two-day battle, even though the Army of Northern Virginia numbered only about 60,000 effectives. Sherman's drive to Atlanta was blunted by General Joseph E. Johnston's Army of Tennessee. Two drives had been turned back, and the other two had run into a brick wall. Union casualties at the Wilderness amounted to 37,737. In the month of May alone, the various Union armies added more than 76,000 names to the casualty rolls nationwide, and appeared to be no closer to victory than they had been when the campaign began. During that same period of time, the Confederate armies lost just over 33,000. Grant and Sherman seemed to be no closer to Richmond or Atlanta.[1]

War weariness permeated the North. After three years of the bloodiest fighting ever seen on the North American continent, the Southern Confederacy still defiantly resisted all efforts of the government to force them back into the Union. The Northern populace was beginning to believe that this was a war that could not be won. Then there were the casualties. In the previous years of the war, the armies would come together to fight a great battle, and then they would separate, lick their wounds, reorganize, and plan for the next campaign. Grant's strategy called for constant pressure on the Southern armies, meaning that there was no time between the battles. Every day was spent in contact with the enemy, and every day saw more and more men added to the casualty lists. The Northern public had become accustomed to extreme casualties from battles like Shiloh, Antietam, Fredericksburg, Chancellorsville, Gettysburg, Chickamauga, and more, but they had always had a chance to catch their breath after the latest bloodletting. Not so with Grant's campaign. Every day, Northern papers published the names of the fallen, as Grant held onto Lee's army like a bulldog. It was the war of attrition that the administration had adopted, and in U.S. Grant it found a willing accomplice. From May 5 to July 31, 1864, the Union armies operating in Virginia lost just under 71,000 men.[2] Grant alone lost more men in Virginia than Lee had in his entire army at the beginning of the campaign.

The apparent failure of the Lincoln administration to bring about an end to the war, combined with casualty rates that made the draft almost a death sentence, created a wave of resentment in the North that was all focused upon Lincoln and his party. With the presidential election looming in the fall, it was clear to all that the Republicans would be ushered out of office unless some great deed could be performed to give heart to the people and strengthen their will to continue. By the end of July, Grant was besieging Richmond and Petersburg, but he could not crack Lee's defenses nor break his line of supply. Thousands upon thousands more names would be added to the casualty rolls from this bloody trench warfare, occasionally accented by desperate forays attempting to break the Southern lines. In Georgia, Johnston had countered all of Sherman's thrusts, and though the two armies had fought and maneuvered through half the state, Atlanta, the Gate City of the South, was still in Confederate hands, and the objective of the campaign remained unaccomplished.

Their victory at New Market even gave the Confederates the opportunity of mounting an offensive campaign of their own from the Shenandoah Valley. Major General Jubal Early made a third invasion of Maryland, and took his army to the very outskirts of Washington, striking fear into the hearts of the residents, before being forced to withdraw from the formidable defenses. This was followed by another, smaller invasion of the North by a large raiding party, under the command of Brigadier General John McCausland, which culminated its foray with the ransom and burning of Chambersburg, Pennsylvania. The prospect that the great deed the Republicans were searching for would come from the battlefield seemed remote indeed.

Back in Washington, the Republicans were not quite sure exactly who would even be running for president in the fall. Lincoln was an obvious frontrunner, but his nomination for a second term was far from being a foregone conclusion. His administration assumed most of the blame for the static condition of the war effort. He was also being charged with violating the Constitution for the heavy-handed means employed to snuff out detractors at home. The Emancipation Proclamation had alienated most Democrats and some conservative Republicans. But the draft was possibly the single most damaging point of contention for the voters, who felt that the government was forcing them to go and uselessly die in a war they could not win. Then there was the aspect of breaking tradition. No president had served two terms in office since Andrew Jackson, some three decades before, and it had come to be accepted that one term was sufficient for any president. Lincoln would be breaking with tradition to even seek a second term. There was also opposition coming from within the Republican Party itself. Salmon P. Chase and John C. Frémont both enjoyed the backing of the abolitionist faction of the party, and threatened to unseat Lincoln from even being the Republican candidate in the election. Even Ben Butler, Ulysses S. Grant, and Hannibal Hamlin were gaining support and being forwarded for possible nomination.

As early as September of 1863, a movement was undertaken to supplant Lincoln with Salmon Chase as the Republican candidate in the next election.

Chase had courted the support of the radical Republicans. In November of 1863, Chase wrote a letter to William Sprague, the former governor of Rhode Island. "I think a man of different qualities from those the President has will be needed for the next four years. I am not anxious to be regarded as that man; and am quite willing to leave that question to the decision of those who agree in thinking that some such man should be chosen."[3]

Salmon P. Chase. Lincoln's Secretary of the Treasury and a competitor for the Republican nomination in the 1864 election (Military History Institute, United States Army War College).

Chase found many prominent Unionists who felt as he did in regard to Lincoln. William Cullen Bryant, Theodore Tilton, Horace Greeley, and John Sherman all felt that there were better men than Lincoln to serve as president. A group of congressmen initiated what came to be known as the Chase Boom, sponsored by Senator S.C. Pomeroy of Kansas. The group distributed a paper called the "Pomeroy Circular," with Chase's approval, that declared Lincoln's reelection was almost an impossibility. It suggested that Chase was the best possible candidate for the Republicans to nominate. Thus, Lincoln faced his first competition for the nomination from within his own Cabinet.[4]

The emergence of Chase as a contender prompted Lincoln to undertake one of the most unbelievable actions of the war: a military campaign to gain votes. Lincoln had recently unveiled his Ten Percent Plan for reconstruction, and he thought that Florida would be a suitable candidate in which to try it out. Lincoln had been approached by several Florida men, including Judge Philip Fraser, an exiled Floridian who had been a Republican officeholder before the war, and who informed him that "if forces are to be sent to Florida to be used as tools for political wire-pullers and speculators it were better not to send them at all. We want bold and earnest men to go down inspired by true purpose — the restoration of Florida to the Union as a free state, Political maneuvers may come after that but not before."[5]

On December 22, 1863, a number of exiled Florida men sailed from Port Royal, South Carolina, to St. Augustine, Florida, to hold a meeting to discuss the reorganization of the Florida state government, preparatory to re-entering the United States. They declared the Articles of Secession to be null and void, and called for the election of congressmen to a "loyal" legislature and the abolition of slavery within the borders of the state. The conferees drafted a petition to be sent to Lincoln that requested the immediate "armed occupation" of the entire state. It was signed "many Union men."[6] Lincoln had received the promise of political support from these organizers should Florida be occupied by military force. He was told that Florida, once readmitted to the Union, would commit its delegation to Lincoln in his bid for renomination at the Republican Convention.

The prospect of a military expedition to the state interested Lincoln on several levels. The administration was in need of a victory on the battlefield, and the capture and occupation of a Southern state could be made to serve the purpose of bolstering public opinion and improving the reputation of the government. The state was also known to have a large population of slaves within its borders, and this could prove to be a fruitful recruiting ground for enlistments in the army. Lincoln was looking for any advantage he could get in staving off the challenge posed by Chase and the Radicals, and the promise of Florida's backing at the convention, and its electoral votes in the election to follow, was a prime motivator in his decision to mount a military campaign to capture a large enough portion of the state to administer his Ten Percent Plan and declare Florida reconstructed. Should the state be reconstructed, it would also constitute the fourth new Republican state to come into the Union since the 1860 election, the others being Kansas, West Virginia, and Nevada. The additional electoral votes from these Republican states would come in handy in the general election, and might be needed in a close election against the Democrats. One important item of note here is that West Virginia was still a slave state when it was granted statehood in 1863, providing more evidence that slavery might have been a catalyst to bring about the war, but it was certainly not the cause. If it were, why would a slave-holding state be admitted to the Union two years into the conflict?

On January 13, 1864, Lincoln wrote to Major General Quincy Gillmore in Charleston, "I Understand an effort is being made by some worthy gentlemen to reconstruct a loyal state government in Florida. Florida is in your department, and it is not unlikely that you may be there in person. I have given Mr. Hay a commission book and other blanks to aid in the reconstruction. He will explain as to the manner of using these blanks, and also my general views on the subject. It is desirable for all to cooperate; but if irreconcilable differences of opinion shall arise, you are master. I wish the thing done in the speediest way possible, so that when done it will be within the range of the late proclamation on the subject. The detail labor, of course, will have to be done by others, but I shall be greatly obliged if you will give it such general supervision as you can find convenient with your more strictly military duties."[7]

Gillmore was receiving his orders directly from the president. The plan to mount an expedition against Florida had not been sanctioned by the War Department or any other of Gillmore's military superiors. Stanton was opposed to the operation, feeling Florida's insignificance as a military target made it nothing more than a waste of manpower badly needed in other theaters. The "Mr. Hay" referred to in Lincoln's message to Gillmore was John Hay, the president's personal secretary. Hay had been commissioned a major in the army especially for this expedition. One of the most trusted of Lincoln's political family, Hay carried with him record books and certificates to be given to all who took the oath of allegiance to the Union. He also bore an address from the president to convince the citizens of Florida to give their support to the Federal government once the Union army had seized control of the area.[8]

Brigadier General Truman Seymour was selected to command the expedition, and he would have an army of about 5,000 men. His force put to sea on February 5, and landed at Jacksonville on the morning of February 7. Once the city was occupied, Seymour began his drive inland in an effort to capture the area of central Florida. Initially, his campaign went according to schedule, and there was little enemy opposition. At the time of his landing, the Confederates had but a few hundred soldiers with which to defend the region, under the command of Brigadier General Joseph Finegan, and could do little to stop Seymour's advance. General P.G.T. Beauregard, commander of the Confederate forces at Charleston, ordered reinforcements from Charleston and Savannah to be sent to bolster Finegan's defense.

Brigadier General Truman Seymour. Seymour commanded the Federal expedition to Florida in 1864, designed to bring a reconstructed government back into the Union in time to throw its support behind Abraham Lincoln's campaign for a second term in office. The Federal expedition culminated in failure as a result of the Confederate victory at the Battle of Olustee in February of 1864 (Military History Institute, United States Army War College).

When Seymour's army closed with Finegan at Ocean Pond, otherwise known as Olustee, in the center of the state, the two armies were evenly matched. Seymour's forces were badly defeated in a four-hour battle that cost his army 1,861 casualties.[9] Seymour retreated back to Jacksonville, and the expedition was brought to a close. Florida was not to be reconstructed, and would not reenter the Union as a supporter of Lincoln. In fact, the area fought over by Seymour and Finegan was the largest single section of Confederate territory still in Southern hands at the end of the war. The Battle of Olustee was the largest land engagement to be fought in Florida during the war, and its 1,861 Union casualties were the cost of this endeavor to gain the delegates of the state for Lincoln in the coming election. It was a military operation undertaken for the purpose of political advancement, but it turned out to be nothing more than another embarrassment to the administration. If military successes were to alter the public opinion of Lincoln or the administration, they would have to come from another sector. The only significant accomplishment of the expedition was that Salmon Chase withdrew himself from consideration for the nomination shortly after the Battle of Olustee.

On May 31, 1864, barely a week before the Republican National Convention was held in Baltimore, Maryland, a group of radical Republicans met in Cleveland to nominate John Frémont as a third-party candidate for the presidency. Frémont's nomination was heartily supported by Wendell Phillips and Horace Greeley. His base of support came mainly from German immigrants, strict abolitionists, War Democrats, and Copperhead Democrats, with the latter backing Frémont only from a wish to embarrass their opponents in the fall. Those present at the convention took the name of the Radical Democracy for their party, signifying the coalition of radical Republicans and Democrats it was supposed to attract.[10]

On June 7, the Republicans held their scheduled convention in Baltimore. There had been concern among Lincoln's managers, following the Cleveland convention, that the radical faction of the party might be able to block his nomination, so they immediately set to work making sure that there were no surprises. Lincoln's managers had the advantage of controlling the regular portion of the Republican Party. They controlled the patronage of provost marshals, postmasters, and Federal employees throughout the nation, and exercised the distribution of Federal contracts. At state conventions, where the delegates to the national convention were being selected, the managers exerted influence to make sure that only Lincoln men were being sent to Baltimore. It is a testimony to the efficiency of Lincoln's campaign managers, and the power of patronage, that despite all of the opposition to both Lincoln and his administration, he was elected to be the Republican nominee by a large margin. Ulysses S. Grant received 22 dissenting votes, even though he was not a candidate for the nomination.[11]

Lincoln did not personally attend the convention. Instead, he sent his personal secretary, John Nicolay, to monitor the proceedings for him. Nicolay was instructed to make sure that nothing was adopted in the party platform that was distasteful to the president. He was also to express Lincoln's thoughts and preferences in regard to the selection of a vice-presidential candidate. The platform adopted by the convention was influenced by the radicals, but included no radical planks. It appealed to the patriotism of the voters by calling for unified action to put down the rebellion, blamed slavery as the cause of the war and demanded complete extermination of the institution, thanked soldiers and citizens for their many sacrifices, promised a system of soldier relief, stated that only supporters of the administration were worthy of confidence (a slam against all Copperheads), called for protection for black troops against violations of the rules of war, encouraged immigration, and supported the construction of a railroad to the Pacific.

So far as the vice-presidential nomination was concerned, historians disagree as to whether or not Lincoln expressed a desire to replace Hannibal Hamlin as his running mate, or if the delegates acted on their own initiative. There would seem to be evidence to support either side. What is known for certain is that Henry Raymond forwarded Andrew Johnson's name at precisely the right time in the proceedings, and that his unanimous selection was approved by thunderous applause. All in attendance felt that his inclusion on the ticket strengthened Lincoln's chance for reelection because Johnson represented both the War Democrats and Southerners.[12] Johnson had been selected in an attempt to draw War Democrats into the fold. The Republicans endeavored to entice more War Democrats by dropping the title of Republicans, and assuming the name of the National Union Party. Republicans they were in 1860, and Republicans they would be again in 1868, but in 1864 the party was pulling out all the stops to counter the formidable opposition they anticipated from the Democrats in the fall. The adoption of the name National Union Party also lent itself to the already popular campaign dogma that all who were opposed to the Republicans were traitors and Southern sympathizers. It cast the Republicans, and their War Democrat supporters, as the defenders of the nation, while the Democrats were portrayed as seeking to destroy the country through disunion.

Following close on the heels of Lincoln's nomination there arose a fresh outbreak of opposition within the Republican Party caused by the Wade-Davis Reconstruction Bill. The bill, drafted by Senators Ben Wade and Henry Davis, called for a severe and punitive reconstruction of the South once the war was ended. Lincoln disagreed with the severity of the bill, feeling that it would obstruct restoration by perpetuating wartime resentment. He decided to veto the bill, but, not wanting to give Congress an opportunity to override him, he used the pocket veto, which required no veto message to Congress. Both Wade and Davis unleashed a barrage of public denunciations against Lincoln. A second outcome of Lincoln's pocket veto of the Wade-Davis Bill was the resignation of Secretary Chase from his cabinet. Orville Browning joined in the recriminations of Lincoln, even though he was a close personal friend. In a diary entry, Browning wrote that the "nation's great need is a competent leader at the head of affairs."[13]

Meanwhile, the Democratic Party delayed holding its national convention, taking advantage of the split in the Republican ranks to further their claims that the administration was not suited to running either the country or the war. Democratic delegates held their convention in Chicago on August 29.

George B. McClellan was nominated to be their presidential candidate, with George Pendleton of Ohio receiving the nod to be his vice-presidential running mate. McClellan's nomination pleased the War Democrat faction of the party. The platform of the campaign, adopted with a view of appeasing the Peace Democrats of the party, called for an immediate cessation of hostilities. Reunion was set as the condition for peace, so this was not by any means a peace-at-any-cost proposal. The end of the war would only be attained if the Confederacy agreed to lay down their arms and assume their place back in the Union.

As such, this plank of the platform was poorly thought out. Why would the Southern states, victorious thus far in defending their liberty, agree to give up the fight and rejoin the Union when the prevailing conditions existing in that Union were unchanged from those that had caused secession in the first place? The South would never consent to such a proposition so long as it still had an army in the field with which to fight. In August of 1864, the peace platform of the Democratic Party appealed to a majority of the war-weary voters of the North. The situations at the front, in Virginia and Georgia, seemed static, and victory appeared out of reach. Public opinion was such that Lincoln despaired of being reelected, and took steps to meet with McClellan for the purpose of planning for a transition of the administration in the hope of winning the war before the Democrats took power. Just prior to the Democrats' holding their convention, Lincoln had put down his feelings on paper: "This morning ... it seems exceedingly probable that this Administration will not be re-elected. Then it will be my duty to so cooperate with the President elect, as to save the Union between the election and the inauguration; as he will have secured his election on such ground that he can not possibly save it afterwards."[14]

Lincoln did indeed despair over the chances of his reelection, but the wording of this memorandum was also intended to serve as political propaganda. Yes, there was a peace plank in the Democratic platform, but the restoration of the Union was the overriding sentiment of their campaign. If that objective could be peacefully attained, then that was the strategy Democrats would adopt. But if war was the only method of achieving the goal, so be it. McClellan was embarrassed that there was even a peace plank in the platform, and in his letter accepting the nomination expressed his convictions that the preservation of the Union was the object of the war. Democrats campaigned against Lincoln's policies, his usurping of power, and the inability of Republicans to end the war and restore the Union. On the other hand, Republicans portrayed the Democratic platform as one that intended to end the war, with or without the restoration of the seceded states. The Republicans claimed that the election of McClellan would bring peace, but it would be tantamount to giving up, to making all of the sacrifices of the Northern people and all of the lives thus far lost an act of futility. This was certainly not what the Democrats had in mind, but it was an effective ploy that helped the Republicans create a mindset with the public that would pay dividends later that fall.

In the beginning of September it seemed as if the Democrats would certainly sweep the elections, so much so that on September 2, Horace Greeley, Theodore Tilton, and Parke Goodwin, all editors of New York newspapers, contacted the governors of the Northern states to see if there could not be a movement to replace Lincoln on the ticket. A second convention was proposed, to be held at Cincinnati, to act on the suggestion, but events quickly transpired that altered the political landscape.[15] The resignation of Montgomery Blair from the Cabinet appeased the radical faction of the Republican Party and led to the withdrawal of John Frémont as a third-party candidate. Sherman's fortuitous capturing of Atlanta inspired the electorate at home with hope that the war could be won, and Republicans swept state elections in Maine and Vermont. Talk of a second convention was dropped, and, seeing that Lincoln was not to be replaced, even Senators Wade and Davis ended their personal campaigns against Lincoln and tendered him their support.[16]

No one did more to help ensure Lincoln's reelection than General William T. Sherman. By capturing Atlanta and staging his celebrated March to the Sea, he demonstrated that the Confederacy could be beaten, and that the end of the war was at hand. The capture of Atlanta was the proverbial straw that broke the camel's back for the Democratic Party. For the voters in the North, the fall of the Gate City gave promise that the final victory was near. Sherman's planned march across Georgia, though it came after the election, served as a sort of exclamation point to the Republican victory at the polls. The March to the Sea was a spectacular campaign, but it initially caused fear and apprehension on the part of the government. Sherman was going to do what had not been done before. He proposed to march his army from Atlanta to the sea, through enemy country, with no lines of supply or communication. His men would live off the land. They would become a Union island, moving freely in the heart of the Confederacy. The danger was evident. It was feared that Sherman's army would be swallowed up, embattled on all sides by a swarming enemy that could annihilate the Union's major army in the west. But Sherman believed that the Confederate army was near its end, and he convinced his superiors in the military and government to allow him to make the march. By moving his army through the heart of enemy territory he would prove that the Confederacy was losing the ability to defend itself.

Sherman's capture of Atlanta and subsequent March to the Sea filled the Northern electorate with renewed confidence that a military solution to reuniting the country was feasible, and fostered a desire to see the thing through to the end. Major General Phil Sheridan's crushing victory at Cedar Creek in the Shenandoah Valley in October added emphasis to Sherman's deeds at Atlanta, and showed positive movement on the Virginia front, adding to the feeling that the war could be won. Lincoln's campaign made the most of this sentiment by portraying the Democrats as being defeatists, who were not only willing to end the war when victory was in sight, but were also willing to allow all those who had already died in pursuit of that goal to have died in vain. Indeed, Sherman and Sheridan gave Lincoln the victories he so sorely needed to be able to influence the Northern psyche and effect a change in popular opinion.

The Republicans were not content to allow shifting popular sentiment to take its course, however. True, they had made up considerable ground on the Democrats, and the election might have even been considered to be too close to call by the beginning of November. That being the case, the administration decided to employ tactics used in the 1862 and 1863 elections, as well as a new wrinkle or two, to try to tip the balance of power in its favor. Just as in the two previous elections, military presence was to be evident at polling places in Democratic strongholds, particularly in border states. New York City was also targeted for the special attention of the War Department. Secretary Stanton threw the full power of his department behind the operation, and requested troops from Grant's Army, ostensibly to guard against any disturbances by Democrats. He also assigned General Ben Butler to command those troops. Butler had already shown himself to be a capable martinet in his administration of martial law in New Orleans, and could be counted on to make the greatest show of military power with the troops at his disposal. The object of having armed soldiers at the polling places was to dissuade Democrats from turning out to vote, and it is certain that the tactic achieved some measure of success.

In his memoirs, Butler recalled the meeting with Stanton, in which the War Secretary presented him with exaggerated reports of political unrest in the city. "I carefully read the papers.... In substance they stated that there was an organization of troops to be placed under the command of Fitz John Porter; that there was to be inaugurated in New York a far more widely extended and far better-organized riot than the draft riot in July 1863; that the whole vote of the city was to be deposited for McClellan ... that Republicans were to be driven from the polls; that there were several thousand rebels in New York who were to aid in the movement; and that Brigadier General John A. Green, who was known to be the confidential friend of the governor was to be present, bringing some forces from the interior of the State to take part in the movement." After reading the report, Butler asked Stanton what he wanted him to do. The Secretary replied, "I want you to go down there and take command of the Department of the East, relieving General Dix, and I will have sent to you from the front, a sufficient force to put down any insurrection." When asked what force he required to accomplish his mission, Butler stated, "About 3,000 men will be enough, but a larger force may be better for over-awing an outbreak."[17]

Of course the contents of the report Butler had read were little more than rumor and fabrication. General Fitz John Porter was never implicated in a plot to seize the polls or capture the election by military force. That part of the report was merely another defaming slander against an already disgraced officer who was known to be one of McClellan's top supporters. The allegations that there were several thousand Confederate "rebels" in New York, preparing to act in concert with the New York State Militia, was an attempt to show that Governor Seymour and his administration were disloyal, in hopes of aiding Reuben Fenton's Republican campaign to depose the incumbent. Both claims were preposterous, and were nothing more than political propaganda used to legitimize the strong-armed military tactics that Butler was authorized to enforce.

General Butler arrived in New York City on November 4, four days prior to the election. On that day, he was visited by Major General Edward Sanford, commander of the New York State Militia. Sanford "called upon me and said that he proposed on the day of the election to call his divisions of militia to preserve the peace. I told him that could not be done without his reporting to me as his superior officer.... He could not agree to that. I then told him that I did not need his divisions, and that I did not think it would be advisable to have the militia called out; that if they were called out they would be under arms, and in case of difficulty it was not quite certain which way all of them would shoot.... He was very obstinate about it, and said he should call out the militia.... 'Well,' said I, 'If there are to be armed forces here that do not report to me, and are not under my orders, I shall treat them as enemies.'... And from the reported doings of Governor Seymour in the center of the State in organizing new companies of militia, which I believe to be a rebellious organization, I may find it necessary to act promptly in arresting all those whom I know are proposing to disturb the peace here on election day."[18] Butler followed up his interview with Sanford by issuing a proclamation threatening immediate arrest for any citizen felt to be conspiring against the administration or the elections. In substance, he was issuing a warning to all members of the Democratic opposition that they were under observation, and that their political affiliation might land them in jail. Governor Seymour protested against the presence of Butler's Union army in the city, asserting, "The power of this state is ample to protect all classes in the free exercise of their political duties." He directed sheriffs and other state officials to see that "no military or other organized force shall be allowed to show themselves in the vicinity of the places where the elections are held, with any view of menacing or intimidating citizens attending thereon. Against such interference they must exercise the full force of the law."[19]

Butler gave little attention to Governor Seymour's proclamation. Instead, he prepared for the armed invasion of New York City, should the state authorities attempt to exercise their right to hold their own elections. In addition to the several thousand troops already in the city and assigned to duty at the polls, Butler had at his disposal some 15,000 men at Jersey City. He commandeered several dozen ferry boats, loaded the troops aboard, and prepared for an amphibious landing across the Hudson River at any point in the city where protest to the Union military presence might occur. Union gunboats flanked the entire attack route, as a not-so-subtle reminder to the residents that the Federal government, and not the citizens of New York, was in charge of the state's election. Butler intended to enforce his own personal sentiments regarding persons opposed to the administration or its policies. It was his opinion that any voter who supported the Democratic ticket was acting in a way "more detrimental to the country and beneficial to the rebellion than if they placed themselves actively in arms, side-by-side with the rebels in the field." When criticized for his brutal tactics, he once responded, "I have not erred too much in harshness.... There is no middle ground between loyalty and treason."[20] Butler's intimidation of New York City voters paid dividends, as many voters were cowed into staying home and not casting a ballot for McClellan, out of fear of retribution from the army of occupation within their city. As Lincoln biographer David Donald put it, "Under the protection of Federal bayonets, New York went Republican by seven thousand votes."

In the end, New York City in fact went for Lincoln by some 9,000 votes. The same scene was being played out in Maryland, Delaware, Kentucky, Illinois, Indiana, Pennsylvania, and other places, as the administration flexed its muscles to subdue the opposition at the ballot box. But this show of force on election day was merely the final phase of a campaign within the military to ensure Lincoln's reelection. Most historians credit the soldier vote as being the deciding factor in the 1864 election, and point to the 78 percent who cast their ballots for Lincoln as proof positive that the Republicans enjoyed strong support within the army. This would appear to be a correct analysis, but it provides only superficial insight. Few historians examine how the administration manipulated these numbers, or controlled the voting process within the army, and that is the real meat behind the story of the soldier vote of 1864.

Stanton used his office to conduct a smear campaign on McClellan's reputation when he ordered Brigadier General John G. Barnard to write unflattering histories of the Peninsula Campaign, to be distributed to Northern newspapers. Stanton exercised editorial control over Barnard's work, frequently inserting his own derogatory comments. He also encouraged Major General John E. Wool to pen a few articles of his own, to augment those being submitted by Barnard, as well as to add credibility through substantiation.[21] The War Department's mudslinging was highly successful in creating a negative impression of McClellan's contributions to the war effort, as well as his abilities as a military leader. These virulent attacks not only impaired the general's reputation during the political campaign of 1864, they have been credited and perpetuated by subsequent historians until McClellan has come to be viewed by most students of the period to be just short of incompetent. But during the campaign, as the failure of the Lincoln administration to end the war became a main issue of the election, McClellan's own failures were brought the forefront, complete with enhancements and exaggerations.

The Civil War witnessed the first time in American history that soldiers in the field during wartime were permitted to vote in a national election. The Republicans had instituted voting in the field, as well as liberal furloughs so that troops could return to their home states to vote, during the state elections of 1863. Now, they were eager to put the machinery in place to take advantage of soldier ballots to reelect Lincoln. Democrats, fearing possible election fraud, attempted to block soldiers from voting in the field. The Republicans used this to their advantage by flaunting Democratic opposition as proof that they were not only against the war, but prejudiced against the soldiers who were fighting it as well. Of the twenty-four states participating in the 1864 election, nineteen passed legislation to provide for soldier voting in the field. The method of voting varied from place to place, with some soldiers casting proxy ballots that would be voted on their behalf by a third party, some being furloughed to go home and vote, and others sending their absentee ballots directly to their voting precincts.

The case of the of the election commissioners from New York State is indicative of the actions of the War Department throughout the 1864 election. The commissioners, led by Chauncy Depew, Secretary of State for New York,

Edwin Stanton. Abraham Lincoln's Secretary of War. Stanton used the military to help sway the vote in the 1864 election, both through soldier ballots and by placing soldiers at the polls in various places to intimidate opposition voters (Military History Institute, United States Army War College).

visited Stanton's office several times for the purpose of obtaining information concerning the whereabouts of New York regiments, but the War Secretary refused to provide the data, claiming that to do so would be tantamount to giving the information to the enemy. It was only through Lincoln's personal intervention that the commissioners were provided the location of the various units. But the listing of locations would do the commissioners little good. The commission contained both Republican and Democratic members, and Stanton instructed high-ranking army officers to aid Republican state agents in every way, while placing any and all obstacles they could in the path of Democratic agents. General Marsena Patrick, the Provost Marshal General of the Army of the Potomac, himself a native New Yorker and Democrat, violently protested Stanton's actions, stating, "The insolence of the Secretary and of the Administration generally, is intolerable." His protests only served to bring upon him the criticism of the War Department, and he was personally charged with favoring Democratic agents.

When the New York commissioners reached Baltimore on their way to the front, the three Democrats among them found themselves under arrest by the Union military, charged with "gross frauds and forgeries." They were imprisoned without charges, while the Republican members of the commission were allowed to continue on to the army to collect their votes for Lincoln. General Patrick tried to influence Major General George G. Meade to intervene and lodge a protest against the high-handed methods being employed by the administration, but Meade declined to become involved. Patrick then contacted New York's members of Congress, but when the Congressmen went to discuss the matter with Stanton they were not even granted an interview. Complaining of the "Systematic abuse" he was suffering from the War Department because of his efforts to correct the inequality of the situation, Patrick decided to give up the contest, "for it was clear that army officers who supported McClellan were not going to get a fair hearing from the Department."[22]

Within the army, efforts to garner support for McClellan met with varied results, all designed to obstruct and limit the ability of the organizers. McClellan rallies, when they were even allowed to be held, were systematically broken up by Lincoln supporters. Strong-arm tactics, akin to those used by the strike-breakers of later decades, were employed to scatter and disperse those who had gathered in McClellan's behalf. Officers were instructed to "influence" their men to vote the right way, and the message was abundantly clear to those in the ranks. The account of a New Hampshire officer is indicative of the sort of pressure exerted in Lincoln's favor. This captain influenced potential voters in a subtle manner he described as not being "undue": "I read aloud and as impressively as I could, the following lines of poetry printed on the back of the Republican ticket, while they listened attentively:

> What! hoist the white flag when our triumph is nigh!
> What! crouch before treason — make freedom a lie!
> What! spike our guns when the foe is at bay,
> With his flags and black banners fast dropping away!"[23]

Soldiers were pressured by being told that voting for McClellan was the same as siding with the enemy, and all who openly voiced their support of the Democratic ticket found themselves the victims of persecution and recrimination. The Army of the Potomac was composed largely of men from the North and East, and subsequently contained a large number of Democratic voters. Sherman's western army was mostly made up of men from the Midwest, where the Republican Party enjoyed its strongest support. This fact would play prominently in the handling of the soldier vote.

An example of the support to be found for the Republicans can be found in the reenlistment statistics of the Union army. As a whole, only 6.5 percent of all Union soldiers reenlisted when their term of service was complete. In Sherman's army, the rate of reenlistment was an unbelievable 50 percent. Non-commissioned officers in the western army reenlisted at a rate of 98 percent, while company-grade officers reenlisted 99 percent of the time. Of all the men in Sherman's army, some 78 percent had originally enlisted in 1861 or 1862.[24] These were largely men who were in the army because they chose to be, unlike the draftees, substitutes, and bounty men who made up the majority of the rest of the Union military. They were also largely Republicans, from Midwestern Republican strongholds, and could be counted on to support the administration in any way in the coming election.

This might go a long way toward explaining the differing attitudes apparent from the commanders with the two primary Union armies in the field. Ulysses S. Grant, while publicly supportive of the soldier vote, issued a statement calling for "No political meetings, no harangues ... no canvassing of camps or regiments" for votes. Sherman, on the other hand, exhibited enthusiastic support for the administration, furloughing thousands of men to go home and vote. Indiana was a particular source of concern for the administration. Initial indications pointed to a Democratic victory in the state, increasing the importance of soldiers voting in their home election. In the days before the election, the railway system was flooded almost to the breaking point with troops being sent home from the western army to vote, with many thousands of them destined for Indiana. Being a citizen of the state did not seem to be of particular concern to Sherman, as many men from other states were sent to Indiana to cast their votes for Lincoln. The most glaring example of this was the 9th Vermont Infantry, who were sent to Indiana en masse to cast their ballots for the Republicans.

This scene was repeated in Baltimore and other major cities of loyal states, as soldiers were funneled into critical areas to help swing the vote in favor of Lincoln. "Soldiers in the field gave Lincoln 119,754 votes to 34,291 for McClellan. When soldiers voted at home their ballots were not segregated, but the ratio must have been approximately the same. Without their ballots, Lincoln might have lost New York, Connecticut, Maryland and Pennsylvania, and the arrest of New York's Democratic agents had helped to take that state. Furloughed troops swelled Republican totals in Illinois and Indiana, where soldiers also guarded the polls. All together these six states contributed 101 electoral votes, enough to elect Lincoln."[25] The problem with these statements becomes evident when one considers that the Union army numbered some one million men at the time of the election. Historians estimate that soldiers accounted for some 4 percent of the total vote cast in the 1864 election, translating to some 160,000 votes of the more than 4,000,000 cast. That means some 840,000 Union soldiers never got to cast a ballot. Overall voter turn out for the election was 78 percent, while the soldier vote was only 16 percent. If the same percentages are applied to the army as to the overall populace, then 780,000 votes would have been the result, minus the approximately 180,000 black troops who had not yet been given the vote. This would mean that 440,000 soldiers did not have the opportunity to exercise their franchise in the 1864 election. Voting in Sherman's predominantly Republican/pro-war army was excessive, while votes from the rest of the Union military, where Democrats and antiwar sentiments were much higher, was exceedingly small. As in the case of the 9th Vermont Infantry, soldier votes were often transferred to where they were most needed, and not to their home districts.

A total electoral vote of 117 was needed to win the election, and it can be easily seen that the 101 electoral votes in the contested states of Indiana, Illinois, Maryland, New York, Pennsylvania, and Connecticut were to be the margin of victory for either candidate. Had McClellan been able to carry those states his electoral total would have been 122 to Lincoln's 111, and would have won the White House for the Democrats. Northern Democrats complained bitterly about the way in which the military had interfered with state elections. Claims of Democratic editors, like Edward Roddy of the *Genius of Liberty*, were echoed throughout the North. Roddy noted that soldiers from Fayette County, Pennsylvania, had cast 56.6 percent of their votes for Lincoln, but that only 659 soldiers actually voted in the election. Fayette County had twenty-one companies of men serving in the army, and their numbers should have far exceeded the 659 ballots actually cast. The county enjoyed a Democratic majority, with 57.4 percent of the local vote going for McClellan in the election, and it can be assumed that a full accounting of the soldier vote from that county would have mirrored the vote of the county as a whole. But only a portion of the Fayette County men were allowed to vote, prompting Roddy to level allegations of election fraud against the administration.[26]

This charge was echoed throughout the nation, as Democrats pointed to obvious inconsistencies in the election. Who could condemn the Democrats for complaining when the Republicans themselves admitted to manipulation? Take into account the statements of Thurlow Weed, reporting to Lincoln about the soldier vote in New York. Weed thought that the election in the state would go in favor of Lincoln, though he was "sorry to see so many returning soldiers against us. They obtained furloughs under false pretenses." The false pretenses were that they intended to vote for Lincoln. They were granted furloughs to come home and vote solely for that reason, but had double-crossed the military by voting their preference instead. Weed's statement was a glaring and arrogant admission to a particular instance of voter tampering. Similar instances throughout the North led to cries of outrage from the Democratic community.[27] The administration responded to the charges by ending any investigations before they could be undertaken, claiming Federal jurisdiction over any and all such investigations and proceedings. By doing such, they effectively precluded what would normally have been a process of the individual states, conducted in state courts. In another example of despotism, the administration forbade the states the authority to conduct their own affairs in investigating election fraud.[28]

But the military was not the only group charged with manipulation the election, and it was not the only group protected by the administration proclaiming Federal jurisdiction in cases of fraud. The administration itself had been complicit in extorting support from within the government, as well as from others who owed their jobs to the government. The executive committee of the party deducted $250 from the salary of each of the members of Lincoln's Cabinet, and assessed every employee of the War, Treasury, and Post Office Departments with a five percent deduction from their pay to fund the campaign. Secretary of the Navy Gideon Welles spoke out against this policy. "To a great extent," he claimed, "the money so raised is misused and misapplied, and perverted and prostituted." Welles went on to charge, "A set of harpies and adventurers pocket a large portion of the money extorted." Forced financial support of the administration was but a part of the Republican campaign to exert force over government employees. Another example can be found in the case of the workers at the Brooklyn Navy Yard, where any workman who voiced sentiments in favor of McClellan, or the Democrats, found his employment immediately terminated. The message was clear: vote for Lincoln or find another job.[29]

The most effective form of Republican bullying came from the quasi-military ranks of the Union League. These Republican "clubs" formed themselves into vigilante groups and militia companies, assuming the role of the party's secret police among the populace. Members reported directly to the War Department the names of all those considered to be disloyal, to be picked up by the military and held under suspicion of Southern sympathies. Supporters of McClellan and the Democratic ticket headed the list of the supposed disloyal and received the special attention of the League, in an effort to suppress all opposition to the Republicans. Armed bands of League members regularly patrolled the streets of major cities in the North, confronting and dispersing Democratic rallies wherever they might be found. Their organizers oftentimes found themselves accused of disloyalty and imprisoned without charges. The efforts of the League were highly effective in obstructing the Democrats' ability to organize and campaign, and in convincing many Democrats to abstain from voting at all. James Edmonds, the national president of the Union League, contacted Lincoln concerning the propriety of showing military force on a larger scale in Maryland and New York, where the Republicans were doubtful of victory. "I trust there will be no hesitation," he wrote. "There is power behind a bold hand at this time." Subsequent actions of the military in Baltimore and New York City suggest that the administration agreed with this assessment. Many Democrats interested in self-preservation simply faded into obscurity rather than face the retribution of the League. Those who did stand up for their

Cartoon showing Lincoln sitting on the chest of a slumbering Jefferson Davis. Davis asks, "Is that you, still there, Long Abe?," to which Lincoln replies, "Yes! And I'm going to be four years longer." Lincoln's reelection ensured that the war would continue and that there would be no negotiated peace with the Confederacy (*Lincoln's Yarns and Stories*).

convictions were subjected to severe recrimination, even after the election had already been decided. Supporters of McClellan faced reprisals for their political affiliation up to and including acts of violence and destruction. Newspaper editors were especially targeted by the League, with a large number of offices being mobbed and destroyed because of their support of McClellan or attacks on the administration.[30]

In the end, soldier activity did swing the vote in Lincoln's favor, whether by the casting of ballots or by the show of force at polling places across the nation. The question became not who voted, but who did not, and why. It is clear that the Republicans manipulated the soldier vote to their best advantage, be it by the exclusion of dissenting votes, or by the application of soldier votes to areas where the election was in doubt, such as in the cases of Indiana and Maryland. The complete power of the War Department was brought to bear on Lincoln's behalf, which, at the very least, created an unfair advantage for the incumbent. At the most, it assured Lincoln's reelection even before the votes were tallied. Alan Pinkerton is alleged to have informed McClellan, following the war, that the outcome had been settled before election day. The actual vote was just a formality, the tabulation of results already predetermined. Indeed, the soldier vote was crucial to Lincoln's obtaining a second term in office, but the evidence would seem to indicate that the army was ordered to vote for Lincoln or not to vote at all.

CHAPTER ELEVEN

Lincoln: The First Modern President

To most people reading this book, it might seem that I am a serious detractor of Lincoln, and that the intention of this work is to discredit his actions and the reputation he enjoys in American history. Such an assumption would be incorrect. I am not attempting to defame Lincoln. Instead, I am trying to give the reader a more comprehensive insight into his life, and the way in which he and his supporters influenced the events of his time. It is my intention to offer information that will dispel the traditional legends and myths associated with our 16th president, and to show him in a more factual manner. We have come to view Lincoln in such simplistic terms that our depiction of the man is what causes him dishonor. Lincoln is portrayed as the self-made, self-educated rustic who rose above his social condition to occupy the highest office. Indeed, he is the epitome of the old saying that anyone can grow up to be president. He is touted as an example of all that is good in American society. He is the common man, possessed of common sense, who guided the country through its most perilous period armed with little more than frontier values and grim determination. He is the kind-hearted patriarch who was more at home telling humorous stories than conducting the affairs of state. Hogwash!

For all those who hold to these beliefs, let me wash them away with one simple observation. This common man, this lowly and self-educated rail splitter from Illinois, was the very same person who penned the Gettysburg Address, the Emancipation Proclamation, and both of his inaugural addresses. Lincoln served during a time when people actually got to hear what the president thought about the issues of the day. There were no speech writers, no spin doctors to prepare the words the public would hear. When the president spoke, the people heard his words, not those of a ghost writer. These addresses are four of the most eloquent, well-written documents to be found in American history, and rank among the leading documents ever drafted in the history of the English-speaking people. The mind that conceived them was both brilliant and polished. Cast aside your convictions that Abraham Lincoln was a log cabin man of the people. He was one of the most supremely intelligent men of his era, and possibly the greatest political strategist in American history. The log cabin image got him votes and endeared him to the masses of American voters. As such, it was an extremely successful political ploy. The real Lincoln was as complex as his image was simplistic. He was the first "modern" president, and the trailblazer for all American chief executives who were to follow.

The legacy of Lincoln is to be found in every facet of society. The truth is, Lincoln sells. A recent poll determined that a majority of Americans consider him the greatest president in the history of the nation, followed by Bill Clinton, Ronald Reagan, John F. Kennedy, and Franklin D. Roosevelt. George Washington and Thomas Jefferson, two of my

A contemporary broadside of Lincoln's Emancipation Proclamation. Lincoln's freeing of the slaves aplied only to those in bondage who resided within Confederate-held territory. It freed no slaves in the border states or in any portion of Confederate states that were under Union control (Military History Institute, United States Army War College).

personal favorites, did not even make the top five. Why do most Americans feel that way? Lincoln is everywhere! His face adorns the penny and the five-dollar bill. His birthday, once a national holiday, was merged with Washington's to create Presidents' Day. His memory has been invoked by both political parties, and has been used to sell everything from cars to sleep medicine. Most cities have a Lincoln Avenue, a Lincoln school, or some other landmark in his honor. For most of the time since his death, even historians have been caught up in the myth that is Lincoln by giving the public what it wanted, a hero for the ages.

Lincoln's humanity was displayed in the movie *Saving Private Ryan* when General George Marshall read a copy of the letter written to Lydia Bixby, a Boston lady who had lost five sons who were fighting for the Union. The letter, which has become a fixture of Lincoln lore, expressed the compassionate sentiment that has come to epitomize the man:

I have been shown in the files of the War Department a statement of the Adjutant General of Massachusetts, that you are the mother of five sons who have died gloriously on the field of battle.

I feel how weak and fruitless must be any words of mine which should attempt to beguile you from the grief of a loss so overwhelming. But I cannot refrain from tendering to you the consolation that may be found in the thanks of the Republic they died to save.

I pray that our Heavenly Father may assuage the anguish of your bereavement and leave you only the cherished memory of the loved and lost, and the solemn pride that must be yours, to have laid so costly a sacrifice upon the altar of Freedom.[1]

The problem is that almost everything about the "Bixby Letter" is a fraud. Lydia Bixby did have five sons who served in the Union army, but only two of them were killed in battle. Of the remaining three sons, one was honorably discharged, and the other two deserted, with one or possibly both of them going over to the enemy. Given the fact that Lydia Bixby was a Southern sympathizer herself, it would not have been odd for two of her sons to change sides. In an apparent attempt to receive money, Mrs. Bixby approached William Schouler, the adjutant general of Massachusetts, with five different letters detailing the deaths of her sons. The letters were all written by different commanding officers, but pertained only to the two sons that had actually been killed. Mrs. Bixby successfully duped Schouler into believing that all five of her sons had lost their lives, and, in a spirit of humane sympathy, that officer laid the matter before Governor John Andrew, stating that Lydia was "the best specimen of a true-hearted Union woman I have yet seen."

The adjutant general had been completely taken in by Lydia Bixby. His "best specimen of a true-hearted Union woman" was actually the matron of a house of ill repute in Boston. Sarah Cabot Wheelwright, a resident of Boston, had made her acquaintance during the war, and had considered hiring her before the Boston police, "on finding out that we were helping this woman ... told [a friend of Wheelwright's] that she kept a house of ill-fame, was perfectly untrustworthy and as bad as she could be." Schouler, somehow unaware of this information, published an appeal in the *Boston Traveller* in November of 1864, seeking contributions to assist New England families with loved ones in the service to have "good New England Thanksgiving dinners." He made a special plea for "a poor but most worthy widow lady ... who sent five sons into this war, all the children she had, every one of whom has fallen nobly in battle." A few days later the *Traveller* reported that "a considerable amount of money was received for soldiers' families, and some was sent especially for the lady to whom allusion was made. General Schouler visited her and left the money, and called yesterday to see that she had everything comfortable for Thanksgiving." Governor Andrew contacted Lincoln, to lay the matter before him, which resulted in the issuance of the now-famous letter. Richard N. Current and James G.

Randall felt that the letter stood "with the Gettysburg Address as a masterpiece in the English language." Dr. J. Herbert Claiborne thought it to be superior to the Gettysburg Address, stating, "It is cleaner English, better constructed and shows a heartful of emotion and sympathy." Henry Watterson believed it to be "the most sublime letter ever penned by the hand of man." Lydia Bixby held a different impression of the importance of the letter. Mrs. Bixby was a long-time detractor of Lincoln and the Republican Party. Her daughter related how she "resented" the letter and "destroyed it shortly after receipt without realizing its value."[2]

But the next question is what hand of what man actually wrote the letter. A growing number of historians now believe that Lincoln never wrote the Bixby letter, though evidence of that fact has been around almost since the time of its release. The evidence points to John Hay, Lincoln's personal secretary, as being the true author of the letter. Hay took pains never to publicly claim authorship, but he is on record as having confided the fact to a number of individuals, including W.C. Brownell, Walter Hines Page, and the Rev. G.A. Jackson. Jackson published the following letter in the *New York Times*: "When I lived at Knebworth, Cora, Lady Stratfford — an American — occupied for a time Knebworth House, Lord Lytton's place, and the late Mr. Page ... used to spend weekends there. On one occasion, Lady Stratfford told me, he noticed a copy — framed, I think — of Lincoln's letter [to Mrs. Bixby] and asked her if she knew the true history of it. He then related that John Hay had told him that when the news of the mother's bereavement was given to Lincoln he instructed Hay to write a suitable reply of condolence. This Hay did, and handed it to Lincoln [who] was so surprised that Hay had so perfectly captured his style of composition that he had the letter exactly as Hay wrote it sent to the mother as coming from himself." In 1866, Hay told Lincoln's old law partner, William Herndon, that Lincoln had actually written "very few letters" while he was president. "He did not read one in fifty that he received. At first we tried to bring them to his notice, but at last he gave the whole thing over to me, and signed without reading them the letters I wrote in his name." On another occasion, John Morely, while a guest of President Theodore Roosevelt at the White House, went to see John Hay, then Secretary of State. Morely expressed to Hay his admiration for the Bixby letter, and after he had concluded, Hay sat briefly in silence before proclaiming that he was, in fact, the one that had written it. Hay asked Morely to "treat this information as strictly confidential until after his [Hay's] death," and Morely did not break that trust. There were literally dozens of people who had been taken into Hay's confidence, and to whom he had divulged the fact that he had authored the famous epistle.[3]

Despite the fact that many contemporaries of both Lincoln and Hay believed Hay's story of the letter, historians refused to attribute it to anyone but Lincoln. Any and all attempts to credit it to Hay were derided as gossip and hearsay. Most of the Lincoln biographers of the late 19th and early 20th centuries refused to even mention the possibility that anyone but Lincoln had penned the letter. It would appear as if they adhered to an old principle of Western dime novelists: "When the fact interferes with the legend, print the legend." The Bixby letter is but one example of the way in which any controversy concerning Lincoln was ignored by historians and biographers for decades following Lincoln's death, beginning with the eulogies and memorial works that appeared soon after the assassination.

In May of 1865, one month after the fateful shooting, Josiah Holland, editor of a Republican newspaper, interviewed William Herndon, Lincoln's old law partner, for the purpose of eulogizing the martyred president in a book. When the subject of religion came up, Herndon told Holland that Lincoln doubted the divinity of Jesus and the infallibility of the Bible. "Oh, never mind. I'll fix that," Holland responded, and in his book he portrayed Lincoln as a pious, model Christian. Alexander McClure, a close, intimate friend of Lincoln's, stated that Holland was not alone in "fixing" Lincoln. McClure said, "Those who have spoken most confidently of his personal qualities are, as a rule, those who saw least of them below the surface."

When William Herndon attempted to provide people with a more complete biography of Lincoln in 1889, his book was met with marked opposition and ridicule. Herndon had included his own memories, augmented by interviews held with a number of Lincoln intimates. His book dealt with such things as Lincoln's mother being born out of wedlock, and the former president's nearly fatal bouts of depression. When the book came out, a Chicago newspaper editor asserted, "It vilely distorts the image of the ideal statesman, patriot, and martyr.... It clothes him in vulgarity and grossness. Its indecencies are spread like a curtain to hide the colossal proportions and the splendid purity of his character." Herndon's biography was a marketing fiasco, as readers refused to purchase any work that damaged or impugned the stainless Lincoln reputation they had come to accept as the truth.[4] It was not until the middle of the 20th century that any historians dared to forward criticisms of Lincoln, and even then, their work was viewed more as extremist propaganda than historic investigation. As the nation awaits the 200th anniversary of Lincoln's birth in 2009, a new corps of historians are once again reviewing the facts about Lincoln, and this time, it appears that the public is more open to a true accounting of the man.

Historian William Marvel captures the essence of the Lincoln legend when he states that once John Wilkes Booth pulled the trigger that made Lincoln the first assassinated President in American history, "Political associates, personal friends, a scattering of shirttail relatives and a host of casual acquaintances started recording or relating their memories and impressions of the first national martyr in an atmosphere of profound grief and exaggerated reverence, and the most sincere of those recollections absorbed the adoring tenor of the moment. Time failed to diminish that tendency, so that outside of Lincoln's own written words historians have found little more than loving gospel on which to base their treatment of him."[5]

But grief-stricken homage was but a part of building the Lincoln legend. Republicans saw his assassination as having political value, particularly among the radical element of the party, as that faction pressed for punitive measures against the South at the end of the war. General Ben Butler, in a speech to a New York City audience following Lincoln's death, attempted to fan the fires of retribution. "If the rebels can do this to the kind, generous, tender-hearted ruler, whose every thought was purity," he said, "whose every desire a yearning for forgiveness and peace, what shall be done to them in high places who guided the assassin's knife?" The crowd promptly responded, "Hang them! Hang them!" It mattered not that Booth and his conspirators acted on their own, or that Confederate officials had no knowledge of their activities, and had certainly not sanctioned their actions. It didn't even matter that Butler mistakenly cites a knife to have been the murder weapon instead of the small derringer Booth used. The president had been murdered, and the nation demanded its pound of flesh in return. A caucus of Republican Congressmen quickly seized on the mood of the country regarding Lincoln's murder and noted, "His death is a godsend to our cause."[6]

Republican leaders built upon the incendiary tone of General Butler's sentiments as they transformed Lincoln into an emblem for the party. As one historian explains it, "In the wake of his assassination, his every act and utterance underwent so deliberate and comprehensive a process of purification and glorification that no mere mortal could satisfy the idealized image of Lincoln we have inherited."[7] Lincoln's radical opponents in his own party glorified his name as they passed reconstruction legislation contrary to that supported by the fallen president. Lincoln's death was used to transform most Northern voters into advocates of a vengeful policy of reconstruction that would punish the South for its part in the war, giving the radicals control over the reunification process that they would not otherwise have enjoyed. The created image of Lincoln was used to circumvent the very spirit of Lincoln, who had advocated that both sides had shared equally in the guilt of the war, and that both must also share in the peace. In his second Inaugural Address, he had promoted a policy of "malice toward none ... charity for all." Upon his death, his wishes were cast aside, as Republicans used Lincoln's symbolic murder to rally support for the very measures he had fought against.

With historians, politicians, religious leaders, and marketing directors all combining to memorialize and mold Lincoln for almost a century and a half, how does one sift through the legend and the hype to gain a true perspective of the man who guided the country through its most trying and turbulent era? For starters, the historian must attempt to look beyond the created image. The humorous stories and humane actions of the sixteenth president have become the bane of our interpretation of him, but they do not tell the entire story. For instance, Lincoln is idolized for his compassion for soldiers sentenced to death for indiscretions such as falling asleep on guard duty. There are several stories concerning how Lincoln interceded on the soldier's behalf to stay the execution, in some cases during tearful heartbroken requests, made in person, by the boys' mothers. It may stun the casual Lincoln reader to learn that these instances were but a minuscule fraction of the executions that took place in the army for similar offences. Lincoln could have interceded in all of them. Instead, he chose to do so only in isolated cases, allowing execution of the sentences in the vast majority of the instances. Most of the stories of Lincoln's clemency were widely reported in Republican newspapers during the war. Whether or not Lincoln himself was involved, these stories were used to political advantage to combat the dictatorial and usurping image with which many people of the North viewed him. This is not to suggest that Lincoln was not a caring or humane man, for he surely was, as attested to by many first-hand accounts of how easily he could be moved to the verge of tears by piteous stories. However, this example shows the tendency of Lincoln biographers to tell only part of the story.

To understand Abraham Lincoln, and the importance he holds in American history, one must first discard the image of a simplistic, easily defined man. Lincoln, the man, was as complex as any leader in history, and possessed of many of the same faults and frailties that define us all. Lincoln was plagued throughout his life by bouts of depression of almost paralyzing proportion. At the ages of 26 and 32, he broke down so completely that he came near taking his own life. This depression continued through his middle years, and was the source of both feelings of doom and determination during his presidency. "I am the most miserable man living," he once wrote, and he believed that his melancholy was a "misfortune, not a fault." His famous humor was a result of his depression, and his personal attempts to control it. He once stated that without his jokes he would surely die, for they "are the vents of my moods and gloom." His ability to find the absurd in otherwise deadly serious events enabled Lincoln to deal with situations that would otherwise have emotionally crippled him.[8]

Lincoln's early life was marked by the death of his much-beloved mother. The writings of his childhood and later life display an adoration for her memory, in stark contrast to the feelings expressed for his father, which were deep-seated rage that bordered on hatred. It is little wonder then that he struck out on his own as early as possible to make a life for himself apart from the influence of his father.

Lincoln developed a skill in storytelling and debate at an early age. Though possessed of substantial physical strength, Lincoln presented a gangly and uncoordinated appearance such as would probably have left him open to derisive comments and insults from the frontiersmen who were his friends and neighbors. It is probable that Lincoln cultivated his oratory abilities in much the same manner as most local wits, to ensure that his peers were laughing with him, and not at him. Education only expanded upon his natural wit and intelligence, giving him the ability to be eloquent, as well as burlesque, and to play as effectively to men of culture as to frontier rubes. The study of the law also served to sharpen his wits, as he became a master of satire and rejoinder.

An example of Lincoln's prowess as a debater can be found during his campaign for the Illinois state legislature in 1836. Lincoln's opponent was George Forquer, a long-time Whig who had recently changed his affiliation to the Democratic Party, in order to maintain his political office. Forquer was many years Lincoln's senior, was a socially accepted member of Springfield's finest circles, and had attained a level of financial comfort. He lived in a fine house, adorned with the first lightning rod that the residents of Springfield had ever seen. Forquer considered himself to be Lincoln's superior in every way, and when the two men met for a campaign rally, he endeavored to demonstrate the difference between them to the crowd. Lincoln had made his initial speech, and when Forquer stood to speak he told the assembly that "the young man will have to be taken down." He then proceeded to recount all of the ways in which he was superior to Lincoln, citing Abe's youth, his lack of political experience, and the low stature of his social prestige. When it was Lincoln's turn to respond, he launched an attack that was both calculated and brilliant. "The gentleman has seen fit to allude to my being a young man; but he forgets that I am older in years than I am in the tricks and trades of politicians. I desire to live, and I desire place and distinction; but I would rather die now than, like the gentleman, live to see the day that I would change my politics for an office worth three thousand dollars a year, and then feel compelled to erect a lightning rod to protect a guilty conscience from an offended God."[9]

On another occasion, Lincoln squared off against Jesse B. Thomas during the electoral canvass of 1840. Lincoln did an impersonation of Thomas for the crowd "in gesture and voice, at times caricaturing his walk and the very motion of his body." The audience found the performance to be hilarious, and roared with approval, at the same time giving a thumbs down to Thomas, who was so disturbed by Lincoln's antics that he retreated from the platform in tears, all but ending his political career.[10] Lincoln's ability to use words to influence potential voters and bring about desired results continued to improve through the decade of the forties, and by the time of the Lincoln-Douglas Debates, he had come to be known as one of the greatest stump speakers in Illinois.

Lincoln also understood the power of public sentiment as well as any politician of his era. During the debates with Douglas, he was quoted as saying, "In this and like communities, public sentiment is everything. With public sentiment, nothing can fail; without it nothing can succeed. Consequently he who moulds public sentiment, goes deeper than he who enacts statutes or pronounces decisions. He makes statutes and decisions possible or impossible to be executed."[11] It was this understanding of public sentiment, combined with

his powers of oration, that made Lincoln the most dangerous political opponent of his time. During his first debate with Senator Douglas, he had charged
that his opponent had conspired with Presidents Pierce and Buchanan and
Supreme Court Chief Justice Roger Taney to spread slavery over all the states
of the Union, and that the Dred Scott decision and the Kansas-Nebraska Act
were merely precursors to that eventual event. There was no basis for the charge,
and Lincoln possessed no evidence that justified its being made, but he correctly ascertained that "a man cannot prove a negative," and by placing the
burden of proof on Douglas, cast him in a negative light to the voters.[12]

He also planted the seeds of political and sectional discontent that would
lead to a divided nation. Most Republicans felt slavery to be a moral wrong.
Those who sought abolition, however, were a small minority within the party,
and were viewed by the masses to be extremists. By asserting that Douglas and
his fellow Democrats sought to extend slavery into all the territories and states
of the nation, Lincoln established slavery to be a main focus of his party, while
he carefully avoided aligning himself with the abolitionist faction, a move that
would have caused him to be viewed as being too radical to be considered for
any national office. While most Northerners thought slavery to be a moral
wrong, the majority felt it to be a Southern problem, to be dealt with by the
states within whose borders it existed. Lincoln created the fear of a Southern
slave conspiracy that took root with the otherwise conservative and moderate
members of the Republican Party. Most people, North and South, believed that
slavery was in its final phases, and that the institution was destined to die out
from economic necessity in the foreseeable future. Now, in the North, these
same citizens had been given cause to anticipate that before that event should
take place, Southern Democrats would use the Federal government to force an
encroachment of the institution upon the free states of the Union. Northern
Republicans might have been willing to live with slavery, and allow it to die a
slow death from its own weight, but they were not about to stand still for its
expansion, particularly into their own towns and states.

It mattered not that Lincoln's accusations against Douglas were unfounded.
He had struck a chord with public sentiment, and altered the very way in which
Northerners viewed an issue they had been dealing with for several decades.
Though Douglas offered forth a mountain of evidence and testimony to refute
the claim that he was part or party to any slave conspiracy, the accusation made
by Lincoln cast him under a cloud of suspicion from which he was never fully
able to extricate himself. In attempting to explain his actions to Northern voters, he merely perpetuated the controversy. At the same time, he lessened his
influence in the South, where many voters felt that he was abandoning his
stance on states' rights to pander for Northern votes. In one stroke of genius,
Lincoln had succeeded in alienating Douglas from many voters who would otherwise have supported him in both sections of the country. He had neutralized
the most influential member of the Democratic Party, and though Douglas pre-

vailed in winning the contested Senate seat in 1858, his national stature had been diminished in the process. Lincoln's powers of oration were used to their fullest capabilities because of his acute perception of how to influence public opinion. The debates with Douglas provided him with an opportunity to showcase these talents on a national stage, and thrust him into a leadership role in the new Republican Party that would eventually lead to his nomination for President in 1860.

But it is Lincoln the President that is to be the focus of this chapter. We have already discussed the campaign of 1860, and many of the events leading up to the firing on Fort Sumter, but now we will examine Lincoln's performance as chief executive of the United States. Such an analysis must begin on February 11, 1861, prior to the inauguration, when the president-elect was making his journey from Springfield to Washington. On that date, at Indianapolis, Indiana, Lincoln spoke about the secession crisis to the crowd that had gathered, saying, "I ... am but an accidental instrument, temporary, and to serve for a limited time." He asserted that the people, not the politicians, president, or office-seekers, should determine "the question 'Shall the Union and shall the liberties of this country be preserved to the latest generation?'" At Lawrenceburg, Indiana, he stated, "I have been selected to fill an important office for a brief period, and am now, in your eyes, invested with an influence which will soon pass away." He reflected that his administration would prove incidental if the people were but "true to yourselves and to the Constitution, there is but little harm that I can do, thank God!" On February 15, at Pittsburgh, Pennsylvania, he acknowledged that the secession of the Southern states "fills the mind of every patriot with anxiety and solicitude," but avowed that "there is really no crisis, springing from anything in the government itself.... In plain words, there is really no crisis except an artificial one ... such a one as may be gotten up at any time by designing politicians." He acknowledged the "very great responsibility" invested in him, but insisted that "there is nothing wrong ... nothing that really hurts anybody." He pointed out that "nobody is suffering anything," and counseled that "time, patience, and a reliance on that God who has never forsaken this people" was all that was needed to weather the storm and restore normalcy to the nation. Lincoln deliberately avoided any pointed statements about the secession of the cotton states, preferring instead to cast himself as a statesman in the impending crisis. This was a stretch, considering the fact that he was the ambitious leader of a new political party, "whose sectional constituency placed in question its claim to represent the good of the country as a whole."[13]

Once Lincoln reached Washington, he was no longer able to duck the issue of secession, and set about addressing it in his inaugural speech. Even then, he skirted the issue as best he could by offering conciliatory rhetoric to the departed states, in the form of assurances of noninterference in the institution of slavery by the Federal government. He asserted the perpetuity of the Union and forwarded his belief that no state could lawfully get out of the Union. He acknowledged and intensified fears of secessionist violence against Union authority, and vowed that any such moves would be treated as "insurrectionary or revolutionary, according to circumstances." He also laid down the foundation that it was his duty to "take care, as the Constitution itself expressly enjoins upon me, that the laws of the Union be faithfully executed in all the States," while at the same time pledging that "there will be no invasion — no using of force against, or among the people anywhere." In states or sections where opposition to the authority of the United States was such as to prevent its citizens from holding Federal offices, no such appointments would be made.[14]

In all of his public statements, Lincoln was bowing to the weight of public opinion, and the majority of the electorate who believed that the Southern states had the right to withdraw from the Union. To have done otherwise would have placed him in the light of being an antagonist in the sectional strife and won deeper sympathy for the South. Therefore, Lincoln publicly portrayed himself as being the peacemaker, attempting to avoid conflict unless it was forced upon him without another viable alternative. His words belied the fact that from the time he assumed office he was actively manipulating the situation at Fort Sumter to coerce the Confederacy into the position of being the aggressor in the crisis. When the South fired on the flag of the United States, it caused exactly the shift in public sentiment that Lincoln anticipated, and allowed his administration to conduct its affairs under the guise of the aggrieved party. Self-righteous indignation filled the hearts of the citizens of the North, who now called upon the administration to take the very action that would have caused its demise only a day before. Just as with the issue of the slave state conspiracy, Lincoln had orchestrated public opinion to suit his own initiatives, and his subtle manipulation had paid dividends on both occasions. Republicans had refused to participate in any of the compromise offers that had been forwarded to defuse the present difficulties of the nation. The tone of their negotiations, or lack thereof, is evidence that the party wished to plunge the nation into civil conflict, but were prevented in doing so by the voices of the very people who had elected them to office. Lincoln's skilled manipulation of events presented the Republicans with a public mandate to embark on a mission that they had contemplated all along. It also provided Lincoln with an opportunity to expand the authority of the executive branch of the government beyond anything that had previously been dreamed of by any American president. By Lincoln's hand, many of the fundamental beliefs of the old Federalist and Whig parties would come to fruition, as the power of the centralized Federal government was expanded and entrenched until it exercised absolute control over the nation, its will and actions placed above the interdiction of those it was designed to represent.

Though Abraham Lincoln won political distinction and everlasting fame as the standard-bearer of the Republican Party, he was first, last, and always a

Whig in his political beliefs. Some twenty years of membership in the Whig Party had left its indelible mark, and provided the foundations for all that Lincoln would subsequently stand for and support politically. Lincoln himself acknowledged as much in 1859 in an autobiographical fragment in which he stated that he was "always a Whig in politics."[15] As such, Lincoln held true to the doctrines of the old Whig Party, including Federally financed internal improvements, a strong protective tariff, a national bank, and national currency. Strong central government was a fundamental plank in the Whig platform, just as it had been for the Federalist Party before them.

Lincoln and the Republicans supported the construction of a transcontinental railroad as part of their program for internal improvements. This went hand in hand with the settlement of the West and the expansion of markets and goods throughout the nation. Accordingly, Lincoln signed the Homestead Act into law on May 20, 1862. For a small registration fee and a commitment to live on the land for a period of five years, the head of a family could obtain a 160-acre parcel. This offer was valid for all American citizens, as well as all foreigners who desired to become citizens. The bill was proclaimed as being an effort to enable poor families to own their own farms, and as such was heartily supported by the segment of the party that had previously been members of the Free-Soilers. In reality, the law benefited few of the people it was supposed to have helped. Most poor families simply did not have the resources necessary to relocate themselves to where the land was available, to say nothing of the money to then construct a house, purchase farming implements and seed, or set in the needed stores to subsist on until a crop could be harvested. Some 15,000 claims were filed before the end of the war, mostly by poor Eastern and Midwestern families. A majority of these were forced by economic hardships to give up their farms before the five-year residency condition could be met. In the end, the primary beneficiaries of the Homestead Act were land speculators, closely aligned with the railroad interests, to which Lincoln himself had personal ties. Internal improvements, including the transcontinental railroad, would definitely benefit the people as a whole, but that benefit would be derived in a trickle-down effect, and not in the instant and personal manner which the Homestead Act was intended to provide.

The issue of funding the war effort gave Lincoln the opportunity of instituting another of the old Whig platforms when he signed into law the Legal Tender Act of 1862. This bill allowed the government to print greenbacks, or paper currency, not backed by gold or silver, to be circulated as legal tender throughout the nation. One of the first propositions concerning the issuance of paper currency was forwarded by David Taylor of Ohio. Taylor presented his plan directly to Lincoln, who sent him to Treasury Secretary Chase with the statement, "He is running that end of the machine, and has time to consider your proposition." But Taylor's project found little support in the Treasury Department. Chase listened coldly as Taylor explained his proposal, and

Cartoon of Lincoln as the American Phoenix, rising from the ashes caused by the destruction of states' rights, free press, the Federal Constitution, national credit, the writ of habeas corpus, and free commerce (*Lincoln's Yarns and Stories*).

when he had finished dismissed the entire thing by saying, "That is very well, Mr. Taylor; but there is one little obstacle in the way that makes the plan impracticable, and that is the Constitution." Taylor returned to Lincoln to report his failure with Chase. "Taylor!" Lincoln exclaimed, "Go back to Chase and tell him not to bother himself about the Constitution. Say that I have that sacred instrument here at the White House, and I am guarding it with great care." The President then took a card from his table and wrote upon it: "The Secretary of the Treasury will please consider Mr. Taylor's proposition. We must have money, and I think this a good way to get it. A. Lincoln."[16] As with the suspension of the writ of habeas corpus, Lincoln circumvented the Constitution whenever it was in his best interests to do so.

Another means of financing the war came in the form of the first national income tax, signed into law by Lincoln in 1863. The provisions of the law dictated that all people earning incomes of more than $800 a year would have to pay a tax of three percent. Income tax became a favorite method of the government to acquire the funding needed to support an ever-increasing Federal bureaucracy, and is one of the many legacies of the Lincoln administration that has, with some discontinuity, been handed down to the current time. The income tax law resurrected the call for a chartering of national banks. Legislation established these institutions, and empowered them to issue 90 percent of the value of the United States bonds they held in the form of bank notes. The institution of a national bank system forced most of the existing private and state banks to buy government bonds and enter the fold in order to avoid failing. By doing so, the Federal government achieved control over the financial structure of the nation, and would eventually enjoy a complete monopoly in that field.

The Lincoln administration also planted the seeds of Federal government domination in the field of education with the passing of the Morrill Land Grant Act of 1862. This bill, sponsored by Senator Justin S. Morrill, gave some seventeen million acres to the states for the purpose of establishing land-grant agricultural colleges. The Act demonstrated the desire of the government to be an important force in higher education, one that would ensure its democratization. Many of these schools went on to become important state universities, like Penn State and Purdue. The Morrill Land Grant Act of 1862 opened the door for a more proactive approach by the Federal government in education. Today's Federal guidelines concerning curricula taught in the public schools of the nation can trace their beginnings directly to the establishment of the land-grant colleges.

By exerting government influence in the fields of transportation, finance, and education, Lincoln's administration was fulfilling the dream of the old Whig Party, as well as those of its predecessor, the Federalists. The central government was involving itself in sectors that Jeffersonian and Jacksonian Democrats believed reserved for the private sector, or for state and local government. By his interpretation of the War Powers accorded to the president by the Constitution, Lincoln was expanding the Federal government to an extent that Whigs and Federalists could only have hoped for. He was also converting the office of the presidency from the mere administrator of legislative action to the catalyst of governmental change.

The biography of Lincoln included in the *Historical Times Encyclopedia of the Civil War* describes him as being generally "an inefficient administrator, running his office like a large law firm, with a staff of 2 male secretaries, John Hay and John Nicolay." The sketch goes on to state that Lincoln was "a superb leader," but "made himself needlessly accessible to office seekers and special pleaders." It is my contention that this assessment is both grossly inaccurate and unfair. I believe that Lincoln's greatest achievement during his presidency was not Union victory in the Civil War, but instead was his ability to hold together the varied factions of the Republican Party. So long as there were no splits in the ranks of the Republicans, and so long as they continued to control the government and commit the resources of the North to the war effort, final victory was somewhat of a foregone conclusion. Keeping the divergent factions of the party working together was quite another matter. Lincoln was forced to be free with his time with the "office seekers and special pleaders" who came to call in an effort to bind together the coalition party he represented. Patronage and appeasement were only a part of the process. Each segment of the party had its own specific agenda, whether it be the abolitionists, or previous members of the Whig, Free-Soiler, or Know-Nothing parties. Lincoln was able to hold the factions together, even though he rarely satisfied the desires of any one of them. His political skill and savvy were brought to bear in the fact that while he completely satisfied very few members of his own party, he alienated even fewer. Everyone got something, and was therefore kept in the fold.

A prime example of this would be the Emancipation Proclamation. The wording of the document meant that it actually freed no one, as it granted emancipation only for those slaves residing in states or parts of states which were then in open rebellion against the Union. In other words, it freed only those slaves who lived within the Confederacy, and over which the Federal government held no jurisdiction. This greatly angered the radical abolitionists of the party, who sought immediate and universal emancipation, and Lincoln was condemned by this faction for what was seen as a half-measure. Still, by issuing the proclamation, Lincoln had placed the issue of emancipation on the front burner, and brought the sentiments of the abolitionists to the forefront. While they were not pleased with the final result, abolitionists contented themselves that at least they were moving in the right direction. Lincoln's wording of the Emancipation Proclamation also pacified the much larger moderate and conservative portions of the party by the absence of radical measures or policies. In a stroke of genius, Lincoln gave both factions a policy that was not exactly what they wanted, but something they could live with. At the same time, he placed the war on a moral footing, that made it increasingly difficult for England or France to intercede on behalf of the Confederacy.

Everybody got something from the Lincoln administration. For the old-line Whigs, there was the revival of the national bank. The Free-Soilers could point to the Homestead Act, and the Know-Nothings could take solace in the president's proposals for colonization for the emancipated slaves. Through appeasement and partial measures, Lincoln was able to hold together the party as he forwarded his own agenda of expanding the size and scope of the government. The followers of Jeffersonian and Jacksonian principles were cast aside as the followers of Hamilton created the all-powerful central government the Federalists could have only dreamed of. The nation was no longer to be a league of willing partners. Instead, it would become a Union bound together by mandate, with its states subservient to the authority and policy of the central government.

Lincoln also expanded the power and influence of the executive office. Prior to his administration, the presidency was largely an administrative position. The president was charged with making sure that the laws of the land were being observed, but he had very little power in effecting political change. It could be said that prior to Lincoln, the executive was the weakest of any of the branches of government. By a liberal interpretation of the War Powers reserved to the president in the Constitution, Lincoln changed all that. He transformed the office of the president into a position that rivaled, and at times eclipsed, the other two branches of government. All of the presidents who have succeeded Lincoln can trace the source of the power and influence they have wielded directly to his term in office and the manner in which he governed and not merely administrated.

Lincoln's approach to the presidency was much akin to the way he described his feeling about emancipation to Horace Greeley, prior to the issuance of the Emancipation Proclamation. He told Greeley he would free all the slaves if it would preserve the Union to do so. If the nation could be saved by keeping them all in bondage, he would do that as well. If freeing some, while leaving others in slavery, would ensure the continuance of the nation, then that is what he would do. Lincoln brought this same philosophy to his dealings with matters concerning the Constitution. If holding it up as a sacred document and enforcing a rigid adherence to the letter of its wording provided the desired result, then that is what he did. If using the Constitution only as a guide, enforcing what he felt to be the spirit of the document, provided the objective, that course was adopted. If making a loose and liberal interpretation of Constitution was what was needed to effect the change he sought, then Lincoln could twist and alter words with the best of them.

Abraham Lincoln was a superb administrator, and one of the most cunning and savvy politicians to be found in American history. In the end, he achieved his goal of transforming the Federal government into the central authority of the land. He provided the death knell for states' rights and popular sovereignty, and paved the way for Jefferson's yeoman farmer and craftsman classes to become the factory workers of the 20th century. It is for each individual reader, according to his personal values and convictions, to determine if the end justifies the means used by Lincoln to attain it. The bottom line is that he did attain the end he sought, personally holding together the fragmented parts of his own party, and all the while embroiled in the bloodiest war

this nation has ever known. It was an administrative, political, and psycholog-
ical challenge that would have ruined most men, including many in his own
party who felt themselves his superior.

Lincoln's greatest accomplishment in life may have been holding the
Republican Party together, and it is certain that he was the glue that kept the
pieces in place. Coming from several different political parties and ideologies,
Republicans shared few goals in common, and those they did were held with
unequal ardor by the factions. Lincoln's assassination provided the party with
a symbolic and unifying common ground that it had not before known. In
death he would become the foundation upon which would be built the future
prominence of the party. The shot fired by John Wilkes Booth transformed
critics into eulogists, and forever cast Lincoln as a symbol of the bloodshed and
loss that had been suffered by the nation as a whole. Spectators who lined the
route of the funeral train taking Lincoln's body from Washington to Springfield, hoping to get a glimpse of the black-draped car that bore his body, did
so in tribute to Lincoln the man. They were also reflecting on the significance
and mourning the loss of the leader who had guided the country through a
period of its history that witnessed the death of national innocence, and the
ascendancy to becoming a world power.

CHAPTER TWELVE

Reconstruction and Consolidation

The era known as Reconstruction ranks as possibly the saddest chapter in the history of the United States. Many in the South viewed it to be a second Civil War, while most Northerners felt it was suitable recompense for four years of bloody war and the assassination of President Lincoln. However one views it, the twelve years of Reconstruction mark the first and only time in American history that a portion of its citizens were forced to live under the rule of a conquering power.

Abraham Lincoln, as previously noted, felt that both sides shared in the guilt that had brought about the Civil War, and therefore felt that both sides must share in the peace. Lincoln's plans for reconstructing the South showed a pragmatic appreciation of the most expedient manner in which to heal the nation and move forward as a reunified country, with all sides represented. In December of 1863, Lincoln had unveiled his Ten Percent Plan as a means of reconstructing states, or portions of states, that were expected to come within the control of the Union. The Florida expedition that culminated in the failed Olustee Campaign was to be the first test of this plan. Lincoln called for a lenient program that allowed a state to set up a government, which he would recognize, once ten percent of its eligible voters in 1860 swore an oath of allegiance to the Union, and pledged to abide by the Emancipation Proclamation and all Congressional acts concerning slavery. The measure was another example of Lincoln's political genius, as all sides seemed to be satisfied with the wording it contained. Republican radicals took heart in the fact that the plan safeguarded the Emancipation Proclamation and promised that no freed slaves would be returned to bondage. Conservatives and moderates praised it for acknowledging the prewar boundaries and laws of the seceded states, excepting those regarding slavery, and offering a gradual adjustment in moving the freed slaves into the mainstream of American society.[1]

The president's Ten Percent Plan was a far cry from the punitive measures set out in the Wade-Davis Bill that Lincoln had so fiercely opposed. Though the public lauded the administration's policy, their support for leniency vanished with Lincoln's assassination, and was replaced by vindictive cries for retribution against the South as a whole. The hanging of the four alleged conspirators in the assassination plot, on July 7, 1865, served to placate the mood of the North toward revenge, but the majority still approved of adopting punitive measures toward the South that were in direct conflict with those forwarded by the man they sought to honor.[2]

In order to study the period of Reconstruction, it is necessary to break down the twelve years into the three distinct phases that define it: Presidential Reconstruction, Congressional Reconstruction, and Redemption. Presidential Reconstruction is generally regarded as taking place from 1865 to 1866, during which time Presidents Abraham Lincoln and Andrew Johnson presided over the return of the Confederate states into the Union. Lincoln had planned for reconstruction as early as 1863, as evidenced by his proposal of the Ten Percent Plan, but the ability to put widespread reunification policies into action did not present itself until the surrender of the Confederacy's primary armies and the fall of its government offices With the ascension of Andrew Johnson to the presidency following Lincoln's death, radical Republicans found that the White House was home to a courageous man of intellectual honesty. Johnson was as firm in his beliefs as Lincoln had been, maybe more so, but he lacked the latter's political savvy, and his ability to defend or attain his agenda without alienating his constituency.

Andrew Johnson. Added to the ticket to replace Hannibal Hamlin for Lincoln's second run at the White House, Johnson found himself the primary target of the radical Republicans following Lincoln's assassination and narrowly survived being impeached (Military History Institute, United States Army War College).

A former Democrat turned Unionist, Johnson was viewed with skepticism by the power brokers in the Republican Party. It was stated by his detractors that he was both a Catholic and an atheist. Neither assertion was correct. Johnson believed in both the Bible and in Jesus Christ, but there was enough of the social revolutionary in him to protest the discrimination he found practiced in the churches of the day regarding the different treatment of rich and poor. For this reason, he refused to affiliate himself with any specific church, instead attending worship services among several different denominations, including the Catholic Church. He also entered one of his sons in a Catholic school, giving credence to the claims of his Catholic bonds, however unfounded they might have been.

Johnson stood in solid opposition to discrimination against the Irish. When a member of the House of Representatives had made a slanderous statement about them, Johnson arose to take up the gauntlet. "Are the bloodhounds of proscription and persecution to be let loose on the Irish? Is the guillotine to be set up in a republican form of government?" He showed a defiance against the platforms and policies of the Know-Nothings that often brought him into open conflict with all supporters of the nativist program. "Show me a Know-Nothing," he once shouted to a group of bigots, amid the sound of cocking pistols, "and I will show you a loathsome reptile on whose neck every honest man should set his heel." This defense of freedom for Irish and Catholics set Johnson at odds with all current Know-Nothings, as well as with those nativists who had affiliated themselves with the Republican Party.[3]

The question of slavery similarly became a point of contention between Johnson and the radical portion of the party. Like Lincoln, Johnson felt slavery to be a moral wrong. Also like Lincoln, he felt that the institution was protected by the Constitution, and was not himself a supporter of the abolitionists. He had sided with the administration for the purpose of preserving the Union and protecting the Constitution, and believed that the restoration of the disaffected states should "preserve the Union with all the dignity, equality, and rights of the several States unimpaired." While never a proponent of radical manumission, Johnson was perceptive enough to realize that all segments of the country were injured by slavery, particularly the poor white working class. In response to the issuance of the Emancipation Proclamation, Johnson stated that "the emancipation of the slaves will break down an odious and dangerous aristocracy," and will "free more whites than blacks in Tennessee." His lack of support for radical abolitionists, combined with the fact that he was a Southerner from Tennessee, brought charges that Johnson intended to interfere with the civil rights programs that Congress intended to implement in the South. No evidence of this intention has ever been forwarded, however.[4]

Johnson also stood for the common man in regard to the distribution of the wealth of the nation, taking issue with the enormous land holdings of the few, while multitudes were unable to own the roofs over their heads. "I am no agrarian," he once stated, "but if through an iniquitous system a vast amount of land has been accumulated in the hands of one man ... then that result is wrong." He denounced the landed aristocracy as "inflated and heartless." In Congress, he asked, "If you can grant public lands as gratuities to men who go out and fight the battles of the country ... is it not passing strange that you cannot grant land to those who till the soil and make provision to sustain your army?" "Do you want cities to take control of the government?" he asked. Johnson's stance on public lands brought him the support of the Free-Soiler faction of the Republican Party, but it set him against the more numerous and powerful industrial and railroad interests.[5]

Initially, Johnson found his support among the moderate members of the Republican Party. As the radical portion of the party gained greater control of the government, the influence of the moderates began to wane, and Johnson broke ties with the party altogether before reverting to his prior ideological alignment with the Democrats. The Republicans could not condone having a Democratic idealist in the White House again, even if he had been elected on the Republican ticket, particularly one that saw it as his duty to defend the rights of the individual and to uphold a constitutional administration of the government and its laws. Johnson became a target for members of the Republican Party who sought to eliminate his influence on the government in general, and the reconstruction of the Southern states in particular.

The final straw came when Johnson vetoed both the Freedman's Bureau Act and the Civil Rights Act. His veto message regarding the latter stated his opposition to a measure that conferred citizenship on the freedmen at a time when eleven out of thirty-six states were unrepresented in Congress. He went on to cite that the bill sought to fix, by Federal law, "a perfect equality of the white and black races in every State of the Union." Johnson viewed this to be an invasion of Federal authority on the rights of the states, and cited that there was no provision in the Constitution that allowed it. Johnson saw the bill as a "stride toward centralization and the concentration of all legislative power in the national government."[6] He felt that all should be represented in the reconstructed governments of the South, and opposed giving freed slaves the franchise when thousands upon thousands of whites had been stripped of their voting rights because of their participation in the military or civil government of the Confederacy. Jefferson Davis had been imprisoned in the casemate at Fortress Monroe, as radical Republicans pondered the possibility of trying and executing him for treason. Johnson saw the ramifications of elevating the social stature of Southern blacks at a time when Southern whites were being punished and excluded from participation in self-rule.

The Bureau of Refugees, Freedmen and Abandoned Lands was established by Congress in March of 1865. It was to be part of the Department of War and headed by General Oliver O. Howard. The intention of the bureau was to serve as a bridge between slavery and freedom by aiding Southern blacks in adjusting to their new conditions. The Bureau was to supervise labor contracts, set up work opportunities, provide education, and distribute abandoned lands. By 1866, however, it had become a foundation for Republican political mobilization in the South. In all fairness, the Bureau did accomplish a number of its humanitarian goals. Some 4,000 schools and 100 hospitals were established

Above: Artist's rendering of General Oliver O. Howard, head of the Freedman's Bureau, defending recently freed blacks from a mob of angry white Southerners. *Below:* Major General Oliver O. Howard. Appointed to head the Freedman's Bureau after the war, Howard's agency was used to cultivate support for the Republican Party among the newly freed blacks in the South, creating a voting bloc that helped the party remain in power for twenty years after the end of the war (both photographs Military Hitory Institute, United States Army War College).

because of its efforts, 15 million food rations were distributed, and $350,000 was set aside to help employers feed the black workers they hired. However, the opportunity to form a Republican voting bloc from among the ex-slaves was not lost upon the radicals. The slogan of "forty acres and a mule" became a watchword of the Republican Party, and blacks were instructed that they needed to cast their votes for the Republicans who had effected their escape from bondage and were now taking care of them. Some unscrupulous Bureau agents promised that the plantation lands of their former owners would be divided between the slaves if they voted Republican. Blacks were told that Southern white Democrats had been responsible for their enslavement, and that these same men would seek to take away their newly won freedoms if they came to power again. The policy worked to perfection, as millions of newly franchised freedmen flocked to the Republican banner.

Johnson viewed the establishment of the Freedmen's Bureau as creating an unfair advantage for blacks that would hamper the process of reunification, and when Congress attempted to increase powers of the agency in 1866, the president vetoed the bill. In doing so, he had the backing of many conservative Republicans in the party, but the radicals had swept the 1866 fall elections, making his conservative backing a moot point. Johnson was opposing what he felt to be an unfair system. What he failed to realize is that the radical Republicans intended for the system to be slanted against the white Democrats in the South. Reunification would be accomplished only when Republican control of these Democratic strongholds of the South had been achieved.

Radicals, like Thaddeus Stevens, attempted to prevent all white ex–Confederates from voting for a period of five years, by imposing an oath stating that the individual had never supported the Confederacy, nor taken part in the military or any Confederate civil agency. White Southerners countered this by imposing voting codes on the ex-slaves, attempting to allow only those who were free men before the war to vote. Congress reacted to these "Black Codes" by enacting the Civil Rights Act of 1866, proposed by Senator Lyman Trumbull.[7] Johnson also opposed the enactment of the Civil Rights Act, greeting the bill with a veto, just as he had the Freedmen's Bureau Act. With the increased power their victories in the 1866 elections afforded them, the radicals were able to gather the votes needed in Congress to enact both pieces of legislation over Johnson's veto, however.

By September of 1866, the breach between Johnson and the radical faction of the Republican Party had become such that prominent members of the latter were already calling for impeachment proceedings against him. Zack Chandler, Wendell Phillips, and Ben Butler were among the leaders of the movement. The *New York World* published a statement from Ben Butler to "'Impeach him and remove him now.' And how? Let the Senate sergeant at arms place him under arrest and tell him that unless he does as told 'the boys in blue will make him.' More; if Johnson dare call on the standing army, these 'boys in blue' will sweep it away 'like cobwebs before the sun.'"[8] Thus was Johnson to be brought into line with the policies of the ruling radical faction of the Republican Party. What Butler proposed boiled down to nothing less than having Congress assume all power in the Federal government, and he threatened that if Johnson attempted to resist, Congress should call forth the recently discharged Union volunteers to force him into line, even if that meant they would have to fight against the standing regular army of the nation. In effect, Butler was proposing another civil war if Johnson sought to invoke any executive powers to deal with Congress or their actions. Zachariah Chandler attacked Johnson's character when he addressed his shift from Unionist back to his Democratic roots by saying that "every man who murdered and stole and poisoned was a Democrat" and making accusations that Johnson was a tool of the rebels.[9]

The radical Republicans went so far as to try to implicate Johnson as a conspirator in Lincoln's assassination. A convicted perjurer and prison inmate by the name of Sanford Conover (whose real last name was Dunham) became part of a plot to frame Johnson when he was visited in jail by Ben Butler and J.M. Ashley. The two Republicans wanted Conover to provide them with names of witnesses who could connect Johnson with the assassination, and they were very specific about the sort of people and information they required. In particular, they wanted a "witness" who would testify that John Wilkes Booth had told others that Johnson was connected to the plot. Conover provided names of people who would be willing to testify to the President's supposed connivance, and Butler and Ashley promised each of them that they would be "splendidly rewarded" for their services. Their testimony was collected, and Butler added to it, or detracted from it, creating as damaging material as he could. As with the former Congressional Committee of the Conduct of the War, testimony was all that Butler and Ashley sought. No effort was given to collecting and evaluating evidence. But the conspiracy to defame Johnson came unraveled when Conover refused to proceed further without a full pardon. The story found its way to the press, prompting Ashley to distance himself by claiming that he had never accused Johnson of having any part in the murder conspiracy. Though the plot failed to bear fruit, it was an example of just how far the radical Republicans would go to try to remove Johnson from office, and served as a warning to the president.[10]

But Johnson failed to heed the warning and continued to use what influence he could muster to oppose the radicals, leading to impeachment proceedings which eventually failed, ever so slightly, to remove him from office. Though Johnson survived the effort to impeach him by a single vote, his power and influence as the nation's Chief Executive were injured to the point that his final years in office were served as a lame duck, and Congress assumed the leading role in the reconstruction of the South. Johnson had been circumvented. His refusal to support the radical Republicans in their reconstruction agenda had cost him his influence, his power, and his good name, and all of them had been lost for nothing. His opposition to the radicals had proved to be little more than a temporary inconvenience, and with him now slandered and stifled, they could now push forward to accomplish all of their goals.

The years of 1866 to 1873 are known as Congressional Reconstruction, also called Radical Reconstruction. During this period of time, the 13th, 14th and 15th Amendments to the Constitution were passed. These years also witnessed the readmission to the Union of all eleven of the former states of the Confederacy, starting with Tennessee in 1866, and ending with Georgia in 1870. Under

18. *How the President went into the excursion.*   *How he came out of the excursion.*
          N. B.—*This is meant Allegorical.*

Cartoon of the radical Republicans showing an ever-diminishing Andrew Johnson as he faced continued political pressure because of his refusal to align himself with the extreme portion of the war (Military History Institute, United States Army War College).

the Reconstruction Act, ten of the Southern states had been banded together into military districts, with Tennessee being the only exclusion from the military rule that followed. Martial law was enacted throughout the South, with the military closely supervising local elections and local government. The military even took upon itself the responsibility of registering voters, and of excluding those it deemed ineligible. An example of the tampering involved in this registration can be found in the actions of General Phil Sheridan in Texas. "The Reconstruction Acts called for registering all adult males, white and black, except those who had ever sworn an oath to uphold the Constitution of the United States and then engaged in rebellion.... Sheridan interpreted these restrictions stringently, barring from registration not only all pre–1861 officials of state and local governments who had supported the Confederacy but also all city officeholders and even minor functionaries such as sextons of cemeteries. In May [Charles] Griffin ... appointed a three-man board of registrars for each county, making his choices on the advice of known Unionists and local Freedmen's Bureau agents. In every county where practicable a freedman served as one of the three registrars.... Final registration amounted to approximately 59,633 whites and 49,479 blacks. It is impossible to say how many whites were rejected or refused to register (estimates vary from 7,500 to 12,000), but blacks, who constituted only about 30 percent of the state's population, were significantly over represented at 45 percent of all voters."[11] Using methods like this all across the South, the central government, through the military, was able to shift the balance of power in local, state, and national elections by controlling the vote. By doing so, they were also able to ensure that Republican candidates would occupy the vast majority of those offices.

Radical Republicans not only attempted to manipulate political power in the cities and states of the South, they also endeavored to do so within the hallowed halls of Congress. The radicals embarked on a campaign intended to seize complete control of both houses, affording them the chance to enact their pet legislation without fear of serious opposition, now that Johnson was effectively silenced. In 1867, Congress refused to seat any of the officials from the state of Kentucky who had been elected to that body on the grounds that "loyal voters" in Kentucky had been "overawed," and that the "elections were carried by ... returned rebels." The radicals further charged that several Kentucky legislators were disloyal. Daniel Vorhees, a Democrat from Indiana, John Stockton of New Jersey, and several other Democratic Congressmen were similarly removed from their seats under various trumped-up charges, all of which, upon investigation, were found to be untrue. All of the unseated Congressmen were eventually returned to their elected offices, but not before the radicals achieved the majority they sought and were able to push through their legislative agenda.[12]

Among the measures adopted by the radical-controlled Congress was legislation that dictated that no Southern state could have its representatives seated in Congress until that body determined that such state was entitled to do so. In essence, Congress had removed presidential influence altogether from the process of reconstruction, and had set itself up as the authority of the land in dealing with the question of reunification. The radicals then turned their attention to taking control of the military through passage of the Army Appropriations Act, which stated that all orders of the president or War Department had to go through the general of the army. It also dictated that the general of the army must be permanently stationed in Washington, and that the president did not have the authority to remove him without the consent of Congress. The act further ordered that it was forbidden to organize militias in the former states of the Confederacy.[13]

The radicals also took steps to control Congress's own sessions by creating an additional term, to begin in March of 1867 with the 40th Congress. Though the attorney general of the United States charged that the action was unconstitutional, it nevertheless went forward without formal opposition. The actions of the attorney general, as well as the other members of the Cabinet, were also being addressed by the radicals, who brought the presidential body under its control through the passage of the Tenure-of-Office Acts. The Supreme Court was brought under the control of the Congress through the passage of legislation that limited the jurisdiction of the high court, forbidding it to rule in the South, where the states were not considered to be entitled to judicial review, owing to the fact that they were not yet reconstructed, or thereby recognized as being a represented part of the United States. By doing so, Congress ensured that the Supreme Court would not have the opportunity to interfere with any legislation passed in regard to the occupied South. In reality, a congressional dictatorship had been created with all real power in national government resting in the hands of the legislative body.

The unconstitutional actions of the Congress troubled many Americans, who feared that it might spark an uprising among the people that would lead to a revolution more terrible than the Civil War had been. Indeed, Congressional Reconstruction is an appropriate label for the period that began in 1866, as Congress was in control of all facets pertaining to the conditions for readmitting the Southern states. Congress was able to dictate that such terms as Negro suffrage and disqualification of ex–Confederate officials must be written into the new state constitutions in order for a state to even be considered for readmittance. It further trampled the Constitution by its mandate that reconstructed Southern states could only gain admittance to the Union through ratification of the Fourteenth Amendment, an edict that eliminated the aspect of the free will of the people in adopting constitutional change, and demoted white Southerners to the status of being subjects, and not citizens.[14]

Though Congressional influence and tyranny ebbed and flowed during the seven years from 1866 to 1873, along with the fortunes of the radical Republicans, Reconstruction at the state level was an almost constant example of graft and corruption. The case of Georgia can be used to show the sort of carpetbagging government that controlled the South during this time. Rufus Bullock, the appointed governor, was assisted in looting the treasury of the state through the efforts of his assistant, H.I. Kimball. Kimball was so successful in his con-man endeavors, and his payoffs were so lucrative, that local and state politicians became eager to do his bidding. Kimball became a partner

Contemporary newspaper cartoon showing a Northern carpetbagger on his way South to make his fortune at the hands of the defeated Confederates (Military History Institute, United States Army War College).

in the Tennessee Car Company, whereupon he purchased railroad cars from himself out of the state treasury, then forgot to deliver them. In the matter of railroad construction, which was Kimball's specialty, large sums were appropriated with the stipulation that a certain number of miles of track be completed prior to payment. Kimball often bypassed the stipulation and took payment for jobs where no track had been laid at all. The case of the Brunswick and Albany Railroad typifies his management of the railroads in the state. Prior to the war, the line had contributed twenty-five thousand dollars a month to the state coffers. Under Kimball's management, it plunged the state three-quarters of a million dollars into debt, with a large portion of that amount going into the pockets of Kimball and his cronies. But Kimball did not limit himself to railroads. Thinking that the capital needed a new hotel, he constructed the Kimball House, funded through a state bond issue. Kimball had complete control over the construction, which meant that he was not compelled to make any reports to justify the gross cost overruns of the project, which was the money that was being skimmed off the top for graft. He bought a partially constructed opera house in Atlanta, remodeled it, and sold it to the state as a State House at a huge profit to himself. So complete was the system of corruption that forty-two newspapers in the state received payoffs from the carpetbagger government to buy their patronage and support. In 1870, the state legislature investigated supposed wrongdoing in the government, but, being a Republican-controlled body, the incidents of graft and corruption were swept under the carpet and Bullock's administration was given a clean bill of health.[15]

Widespread corruption, soaring taxes, the ascendancy of the newly freed blacks to a position of superiority over the whites of the area, the exclusion of many of those same whites from the democratic process, and the outlawing of state militias combined to make many Southerners feel as if they were not only unrepresented, but were virtually prisoners in a land that used to be their home. One response to this was the creation of the Ku Klux Klan. The Klan's initial purpose was to serve as a force to influence political affairs in the South, to provide white Southerners with a way to have a voice in determining their own affairs. Nathan Bedford Forrest, the famed Confederate cavalry commander, was approached with the offer of becoming the first Grand Imperial Wizard of the organization, and he quickly accepted. Secret meetings and clandestine forays became the normal order of business for the Klan, as intimidation was its chief weapon in countering the actions of the carpetbaggers. But the Klan proved hard to control, and intimidation quickly transcended into violence and murder, as members took the opportunity to settle old blood-feuds and hatreds. Blacks became the main target of Klan violence, and reports of atrocities against them reached an epidemic proportion. General Forrest, appalled by the wanton killing, officially called for the disbandment of the Klan, and resigned as its leader. But local groups refused to obey his orders and continued to visit atrocities upon blacks. In the end, this violence only served to give the Federal government reason to increase its military hold on the former Confederate states, as it pointed to the disturbances as proof positive that those same states were still unworthy of being readmitted to the Union.

The graft, corruption, and violence would continue throughout the Reconstruction years, and would only come to an end in 1877, when President Rutherford B. Hayes recalled all Federal troops and declared the process complete. With self-determination came a decline in Republican control and a resurgence of the Democratic Party in the South. Though Republicans would continue to control the national government for more than a decade following the end of Reconstruction, their era of control over the government was coming to a close.

From 1873 to 1877, the South experienced the period called Redemption, which witnessed white Democrats gain an ever-increasing control over their state and local institutions. All of the former Confederate states had been readmitted to the Union, and while Federal troops still occupied the region, and Republicans exerted unfair influence over the affairs of state and local government, white Southern Democrats were gaining in power and increasingly threatening Republican domination. By the conclusion of Redemption, the South had cast off the Republican yoke and once more become the Democratic stronghold of the nation. The presidential elections of 1876 and 1880 would show that Southern Democrats were poised to once more assume a leadership role in national affairs, as the Republicans narrowly clung to the reins of power.

CHAPTER THIRTEEN

Twenty-Four Years in Charge

Though Andrew Johnson's time in the White House was a period of controversy and contention for the Republican Party, the reconstruction of the former Confederate states was providing Republicans with the means to perpetuate their dominance of the national government. The 1868 election promised to be a referendum on Reconstruction. A great deal had taken place since the last presidential contest. The Civil War had ended, Lincoln had been assassinated, and Johnson had narrowly survived impeachment. Social upheaval had become the norm, and Reconstruction promised to continue that trend for many years into the future.

Of particular interest was the ratification of the 14th Amendment, which granted blacks citizenship and prohibited state governments from denying those rights in any way. With citizenship came voting privilege, and it was upon this point that controversy arose within the party. Many Republicans in the North were opposed to Negro suffrage, threatening to cause a rift that might have given the Democrats an opportunity to capture the fall election. Republican leadership headed off the impending trouble through an inequitable enforcement of their own platforms and policies. Southern states were required to adopt Negro suffrage as a prerequisite for readmission to the Union, while Northern states were allowed to decide their course of action on an individual basis, not bound by the edicts of Congress. A second major point of contention between the Republicans and Democrats arose over specie. Republicans had introduced paper money during the war. Following the end of the war, Republicans continued to advocate the printing of paper money to spur inflation in an effort to ease the burden on people having war debts. Democrats supported "hard money," money tied to the gold standard, and charged that the paper-money policy damaged the economy while it benefited Republican cronies.

The state elections of 1866 had resulted in decisive victories for the radical faction of the Republican Party, causing most to feel that a leader from this group would secure the nomination in 1868. Salmon P. Chase and Benjamin

Wade were the front-runners. But radical fortunes were reversed in the 1867 state elections, when Democratic control was attained in New York, Pennsylvania, and Ohio, and black suffrage was rejected in Kansas and Ohio. Moderate Republicans lacked a potential candidate with the national recognition necessary to secure the nomination, causing them to turn to Ulysses S. Grant. A nominal Democrat, Grant had also been approached by Democratic leaders, including party chair August Belmont, in an effort to persuade him to accept their nomination. Democrats felt that Grant would be able to unite the party, while at the same time erasing the stigma of being a party of traitors, as the Republicans alleged. Grant declined any affiliation with the Democratic Party, however, and once the Republicans began to give serious consideration to his nomination, the Democrats decided to focus their attention elsewhere.

On May 20, 1868, the Republicans met in Chicago to hold their national convention. The platform they adopted supported Congressional Reconstruction, denounced President Johnson, called for veterans' pensions for those who had served in the Union army during the war, encouraged immigration, and officially mourned the death of Abraham Lincoln. The denouncement of Andrew Johnson was particularly significant as the convention was being held during a recess of the proceedings that were being held in the Senate to try to impeach him. John Logan, Congressman from Illinois and former Union general, forwarded Grant's name for the nomination amid thunderous applause. He received unanimous approval on the first ballot. The leading candidates for vice president were Benjamin Wade, Henry Wilson, and Schuyler Colfax, with Colfax receiving the nod on the 6th ballot. Grant, who had been waiting at his home at Galena, Illinois, received the news of his nomination with the same restraint that had typified his command of the Union army during the war. One observer noted, "There was no shade of exultation or agitation on his face, not a flush on his cheek, nor a flash in his eye."[1]

The Democrats held their convention in July in New York City. Ironically, among the leading candidates for the nomination was Salmon P. Chase. Chase had courted the party for its nomination following the Republican convention, and appeared to be the front-runner in May and June, even though his stand on black suffrage made him unpopular with the mainstream of the party. By the time the convention convened, Chase's chances for the nomination were fading. Winfield S. Hancock and George Pendleton became serious contenders, with Pendleton receiving the largest number of votes on the first ballot, though not enough to secure the nomination. Twenty-one ballots were taken without any candidate acquiring the necessary margin of victory, and on the twenty-second ballot General George McCook nominated Horatio Seymour, who neither sought nor wanted the nomination. Seymour respectfully declined the honor, but the delegates ignored his wishes and voted unanimously to make him their candidate. Francis P. Blair, Jr., was given the nod as Seymour's running mate, with the delegates making his nomination unanimous as well.

General Grant, following the custom in presidential elections, remained at his home in Galena and declined to campaign. He left that part of the election to others, including the numerous pro–Grant clubs like the Tanners and the Boys in Blue. His support among former veterans of the Union army was particularly strong, with torchlight parades and barbeques being held in his support all over the nation. Grant's supporters portrayed the Democrats as having supported slavery, secession, and attempts to thwart the Union war effort. They alleged that Horatio Seymour had been one of the instigators of the New York City draft riots, and insinuated that his prior affiliation with the Peace Democrats made him akin to being a traitor. The Republicans further claimed that Frank Blair was a drunkard, partly in an effort to counter talk of Grant's own drinking problems.

Democrats avowed that theirs was the only party that could heal the nation's wounds and bring about a peaceful reconciliation of the states. Grant was depicted as a drunken, Negro-loving tyrant, and Colfax's prior affiliation with the Nativist Party was used to claim that he was an anti–Catholic bigot. Unlike Grant, Seymour broke with American political tradition and made a series of campaign stops in Buffalo, Philadelphia, Pittsburgh, Cleveland, Columbus, Detroit, Indianapolis, and Chicago.

In the November election, Seymour showed unexpected strength, capturing the electoral votes of Georgia, Louisiana, Kentucky, Maryland, Delaware, New Jersey, New York, and Oregon, and losing in California by only 500 votes. Nevertheless, he was soundly defeated by Grant, who won 53 percent of the popular vote and secured 214 electoral votes to Seymour's 80.

Grant's first presidency was basically uneventful, with the only significant event being the passage of the 15th Amendment, which guaranteed suffrage regardless of "race, color, or previous condition of servitude." Grant enjoyed the status of being a war hero, and his approval with the masses remained strong as the election of 1872 loomed on the horizon. During his first term, all of the former Confederate states were reorganized with new state governments and given Congressional representation. The Amnesty Act pardoned nearly all of the former Confederates. The nation's economy was strong, and the national debt had been significantly reduced. The Enforcement Act and the Ku Klux Klan Act gave the president the power to protect black rights. Grant had even nominally taken on the practice of political patronage by establishing the first federal civil service commission. All in all, the nation appeared to be coming together and enjoying prosperity, and Grant received the lion's share of the credit. The only black mark against his record had been a failed and ill-advised attempt to annex Santo Domingo to the Union.

The election of 1872 was one of the strangest in American history. The Republican Party was in the midst of a rift in which the liberal faction, headed by men like Horace Greeley, Francis Adams, and Carl Schurz, advocated a break with the main party, and held a convention to nominate their own candidate for president. Liberal Republicans advocated an immediate removal of troops from the South, a return to the gold standard, elimination of political patronage, public education, and national expansion. In May of 1872, the Liberal Republicans met at Cincinnati, where Horace Greeley was nominated on the 6th ballot, with Gratz Brown being chosen as his running mate. The liberals had created a third party, which threatened to endanger Grant's chances for reelection, but all that was due to change in July when the Democrats held their national convention in Baltimore. Lacking a strong national candidate of their own, the Democrats unbelievably nominated the Greeley-Brown ticket to run for them and adopted the Liberal Republican platform in its entirety. In reality, there were no Democrats running in the 1872 election. Greeley had been one of the founders of the Republican Party. He and his Liberal Republican supporters accepted the Democratic nomination because they believed that they were going to take over the Democratic Party.

The Republicans had held their convention in Philadelphia in June, where Grant was renominated by acclamation. Senator Henry Wilson of Massachusetts replaced Colfax as the vice-presidential candidate, owing to a rift that had taken place between the latter and President Grant. The Republicans adopted a platform including amnesty for former Confederates, Union veterans' benefits, enforcement of the 14th and 15th amendments, and a lower tariff.

As he had done in 1868, Grant declined to campaign for himself. Greeley followed the precedent set by Seymour in the previous election. From September 19 to September 29, he set out on a grueling speaking tour through New Jersey, Pennsylvania, Ohio, Kentucky, and Indiana, giving more than 200 speeches during that ten-day span. Greeley's efforts were somewhat diminished by the antics of his running mate, who was also in the midst of a campaign tour. Brown was drunk when he gave a talk at Yale University, and fainted during a speech in New York City. Brown's actions, and not the speeches of Greeley, were what the newspapers of the nation concentrated on in their reporting. The partisans of the respective candidates engaged in a mudslinging campaign that was one of the dirtiest in American history, so much so that Greeley was led to comment, "I have been assailed so bitterly that I hardly knew whether I was running for the presidency or the penitentiary." Republicans took measures to improve their chances in the South through the use of military intervention. Under the premise of the Reconstruction Enforcement Act, Federal officials arrested Democratic opponents charged with conspiring to prevent blacks from voting. More than 1,000 such arrests took place in North Carolina alone. Despite, or because of, these measures, the Republicans did not fare well in the South, where their base of support rested almost solely with black voters. The black vote was sufficient to swing enough states in the South in favor of Grant, however, who captured 286 of the 352 electoral votes available. Grant received 56 percent of the popular vote, the highest total since 1828. It would not be surpassed until 1904.

Both candidates were physically and mentally exhausted by the time the election was held. Greeley was forced to endure the death of his wife, a few weeks before election day. Greeley himself would die a few weeks after the election. Grant, who had been personally stung by the mudslinging of the campaign, breathed a sigh of relief once it was over. In speaking of his victory, the President stated, "I have been the subject of abuse and slander, scarcely ever equaled in political history, which today I feel that I can afford to disregard, in view of your verdict, which I gratefully accept as my vindication."[2]

In 1876, the nation celebrated its 100th anniversary with all the pomp and ceremony due this milestone of the oldest democracy existing in the world. It somehow seemed proper that the anniversary year would also witness a presidential election. Grant had seemed to be the front-runner for the Republicans, having indicated a desire to serve a third term, if so nominated, in 1875. But the Democrats had gained a majority in Congress, and that body voted a resolution upholding the long-standing tradition of a two-term limit on the presidency, causing Grant to withdraw himself from the race. It was probably well that Grant eliminated himself as a potential candidate given the tumult and scandal of his second term in office. Widespread corruption and patronage had been brought to the attention of the public, involving everything from the Federal funding of the Union Pacific Railroad to corruption in the Treasury Department. Grant seems to have been personally innocent of any wrongdoing in the various scandals that rocked his administration, but he was nonetheless held accountable for the improprieties taking place within his sphere of influence. The scandals of the Grant administration, combined with the fact that Reconstruction had been completed in a majority of Southern states, led to a resurgence of the Democratic Party, which, as previously stated, had gained a majority in the House of Representatives in the 1874 election. All signs pointed to a potential Democratic victory in the 1876 election.

The election of 1876 posed a peculiar problem for the Republican Party in that it offered no distinct issue to bond together the various factions from which it was composed. These divergent components had been banded together in the past over the issues of slavery, secession, maintaining the Union, and Reconstruction. Now, all of these battle cries were sounds of the past, and the party was faced with no central issue with which it could cement an alliance of its various parts.

Both parties held their national conventions in June, with the Republicans meeting in Cincinnati and the Democrats in St. Louis. James G. Blaine of Maine was the leading candidate for the Republican nomination. Blaine was a moderate who had served in the House of Representatives both as Speaker of the House and Minority Leader. Oliver Morton of Indiana, Benjamin Bristow of Kentucky, and Rutherford Hayes of Ohio were Blaine's main competition for the nomination. In the first ballot, Blaine received 285 votes, Morton got 124, Bristow acquired 113, and Hayes lagged far behind with a mere 61. But Hayes's campaign managers had negotiated a deal with the Bristow and Morton camps that if their candidates were unable to secure a nomination in the early ballots, they would shift their support to Hayes. By the time a fifth ballot was taken, it became evident that neither Bristow nor Morton would be able to overtake Blaine on their own, and their delegates began to cast their votes for Hayes. On the seventh ballot Hayes secured the nomination when he received 384 votes to Blaine's 351. Following Hayes's nomination, the convention named Congressman William Wheeler of New York to be the Republican vice-presidential candidate.

The resurgence of the Democratic Party brought with it a new crop of party leaders who had national recognition and seemed viable candidates for the presidency. Chief among these was Samuel Tilden, the reformist governor of New York who had toppled Boss Tweed and the notorious Tammany Hall political machine. Tilden had served as chair of the New York Democratic Party and as national campaign manager for Horatio Seymour in 1868. He easily defeated his closest competitor, Governor Thomas Hendricks of Indiana, receiving 535 votes to Hendricks's 143½. Hendricks was then added to the ticket, however, as Tilden's running mate. The Democratic platform condemned the corruption of the Grant administration, demanded the repeal of the 1875 Specie Act, supported civil service reform, advocated conservation of public lands, denounced Congressional Reconstruction, and supported a tariff for revenue purposes only.

Mudslinging, while not as severe as in the previous election, was the order of the day, as each side did its best to discredit the other. The Democratic-controlled Congress sought to affect the outcome of the election by rushing through a bill for Colorado statehood, convinced that the state would cast its three electoral votes for the Tilden-Hendricks ticket. This ill-fated action actually cost the Democrats the election, as Colorado's electoral votes fell to Hayes in one of the most closely contested elections in history. When the ballots were counted, Tilden had received 51 percent of the popular vote, and had a lead of 184 to 165 in the electoral vote. But 185 electoral votes were necessary to proclaim a victor, and Tilden was one vote short. The three electoral votes that the Democrats had counted on getting from Colorado would have put him over the top and secured the White House for their party. The elections in Oregon, South Carolina, Florida, and Louisiana were being disputed, and their collective twenty electoral votes were still up for grabs. On Wednesday, November 8, the morning after the election, most of the newspapers in the country proclaimed Tilden to be the winner. The *New York Herald* and *Times* were two prominent exceptions. The *Herald* asked, "Who is elected President? As we go to press this question is nearly as much of a mystery as it was Tuesday morning." In their later afternoon edition, the paper stated that their computations projected Hayes to be the winner. Tilden had 184 electoral votes, and the *Herald* credited Hayes with 181 (giving him a premature nod in South Carolina and Louisiana). The paper went on to say that Florida would probably fall to the Republicans, although the Democrats were claiming victory there. If that proved to be the case, then Hayes would win the election by one electoral vote.[3]

As the Constitution did not provide for the circumstance of a disputed election, the government sought to arrive at a solution to the problem that was agreeable to both camps. What was decided on was a commission of fifteen members (five from the Senate, five from the House of Representatives, and five from the Supreme Court), who would be charged with determining the winner in the disputed elections. The Commission Act, as it became known, gained the approval of both parties, and the commission met for the first time on February 2, 1877, nearly three months after the election had been held. It was made up of three Republican and two Democratic Senators, three Democratic and two Republican Congressmen, and two Republican, two Democratic, and one Independent member of the Supreme Court. The Independent juror, David Davis, was elected to the United States Senate from Illinois on January 25, 1877. Tilden's nephew, William Pelton, had pulled strings without Tilden's knowledge to secure the election for Davis, in the hope that he would gratefully cast his vote for the Democrats when the commission decided the disputed elections. The move backfired when Davis resigned from the commission to take his seat in the Senate, opening the way for the appointment of Justice Joseph Bradley, a Republican, to fill the vacant seat.

When the commission rendered its verdict on all the disputed elections, the members voted strictly along partisan party lines, with the eight Republicans voting for Hayes and the seven Democrats voting for Tilden. The disputed elections were decided by a vote of the commission, rather than by a strict accounting of the votes that had actually been cast. Hayes was thus awarded the electoral votes from the disputed elections, and was declared the winner of the election with a total of 185 electoral votes to Tilden's 184. As the editor of the *New York Herald* had predicted, Florida became a crucial state in the election. The returns of the county canvassers gave Tilden a majority of 90, but those were converted to a majority of 925 for Hayes by two of the three members of the Board of State Canvassers, both Republicans, giving Hayes Florida's electoral votes and a winning majority in the electoral college.[4]

Congress did not ratify the decision of the commission until March 2, 1877, three short days before Hayes was inaugurated as president. Among Hayes's first official acts was to order the remaining Federal troops in the South to be removed, ending the period of Reconstruction. It had been alleged that this action was agreed to as a condition for the Democrats in Congress not holding up the ratification of the commission's decision and turning the election into an even more protracted and messy affair then it already had been. The Republicans had won the presidency for a second time despite the fact that a majority of voters in the nation had cast their ballots for the opposing candidate. Civil war had been the result of the first instance. Compromise governed the second.

The election of 1880 promised to be a test case for the two-term limit traditionally placed upon the office of the president, as Ulysses S. Grant announced his openness to receiving his party's nomination for that office. Hayes had run with the promise that he would not seek reelection, and he stood by his word, leaving the nomination available for a large number of Republican hopefuls. Grant attempted to profit from this void in Republican leadership by seeking an unprecedented third term in office. Despite the scandals that had plagued his second term in office, Grant was still a favorite with the voters, due largely to his reputation as a war hero. A strong economy and the lack of any major issues meant that this election would likely come down to a popularity contest between the two parties. Grant's main opposition came from Senator James Blaine, the leader of the moderate portion of the party. When the party met in June for its national convention in Chicago, two-thirds of the delegates were already pledged to either Grant or Blaine. Among the dark-horse candidates was John Sherman, the Treasury Secretary from Ohio. Sherman's campaign manager was James Garfield, a former Union general and congressman from Ohio. When Garfield rose to nominate Sherman for the presidency, he gave an impassioned speech that pleaded for party unity while barely mentioning Sherman. The reason for Garfield's curious omission of mentioning Sherman's name in his nomination speech would become clear during the later proceedings of the convention.

The delegates had a difficult time selecting a candidate, with Grant leading on the first thirty-three ballots cast, while not receiving the number required to secure the nomination. Sherman lagged far behind the front-runners, in part because his campaign manager was conducting a campaign of his own in the background. Garfield had his own campaign manager, Wharton Barker, who was canvassing the delegates in an effort to convince them to throw their support behind Sherman's campaign manager, and not Sherman himself. Barker had convinced a Pennsylvania delegate to do so as early as the second ballot, and he continued to garner a trickle of support through the successive ballots.

By the time the thirty-fourth ballot was taken, Barker's efforts began to bear fruit when the Wisconsin delegation shifted all of its votes in favor of Garfield. On the thirty-fifth ballot Indiana followed Wisconsin's lead and cast their votes for Garfield. When the thirty-sixth ballot was cast, Grant was still maintaining a vote total of over 300, but the delegates of the other various candidates had shifted their support to Garfield, giving that candidate a total of 399 votes, enough to secure the nomination. As one delegate described it:

> Everybody saw that Blaine was now out of the way, and it was a matter of beating Grant, so far as the opposition was concerned. It was evident, too, that it would have to be done with Garfield, and Connecticut led off on this ballot with eleven votes for him. Then most of the Washburne vote of Illinois followed this, and

when Indiana was called, General Harrison cast twenty-nine of her thirty votes for Garfield. The storm at this point broke. The people rose up and gave one tremendous cheer, and hats and handkerchiefs were tossed high, as they had so often been before. The confusion had not fairly subsided when Iowa followed with twenty-two votes for Garfield, and the outburst was renewed and gained in force with every fresh start. A little further down Maine cast her fourteen votes for the Ohio man, and the cheering was greater than ever. The confusion was so great that it was almost impossible to go on with the call. The delegations of Maryland, Massachusetts, Michigan, Minnesota and Mississippi each insisted on an individual roll-call, and the Blaine and Sherman votes nearly all turned up for Garfield.

The other states were called, and the number of votes for Garfield steadily rose. By the time Vermont was called, its delegates were "wildly cheered when the ten Edmunds votes swung around, and Wisconsin's eighteen following shortly after, gave the man from Ohio a majority of the whole number."[6]

With the nomination in hand, Garfield broke precedent by taking an active role in the selection of his running mate. His choice was Levi Morton of New York, but the Congressman declined the nomination, largely because he had been convinced that Garfield would lose in the fall election. The second choice fell to Chester Arthur, a past collector of the Port of New York, and, like Garfield, a former general in the Union army. Arthur was nominated by the delegates on the first ballot by a vote of 468 to 103.

The Democratic national convention was also held in June, in Cincinnati. Samuel Tilden was still a party favorite for the nomination, and he was regarded by many as the legitimate winner of the 1876 election. But Tilden was discouraged from seeking the nomination due to poor health. Several members of the commission that decided the 1876 election sought the nomination in 1880, including Senator Thomas Bayard of Delaware, Senator Allen Thurman of Ohio, Congressman Henry Payne also of Ohio, and Supreme Court Justice Stephen Fields of California. Congressman Samuel J. Randall and General Winfield S. Hancock, both from Pennsylvania, and Thomas Hendricks of Indiana rounded out the list of Democratic hopefuls. Winfield S. Hancock became the leading candidate with the delegates, primarily because he had the least amount of baggage and was acceptable to all of the different factions of the party. Hancock was given the nomination on the second ballot, when his vote total soared from an initial tally of 310 to an overwhelming 705. The delegates moved to make the nomination unanimous before selecting William English, a former congressman from Indiana, as his running mate.

In the campaign, the Republicans avoided any substantive issues and concentrated on appealing to the patriotism of the electorate, continuing with their previous theme of branding the Democrats as being traitors for their role in the Civil War and their implied association with the Confederacy. The voters were reminded of the peace and prosperity the nation had enjoyed under the administration of the Republican Party since the conclusion of the war. Republicans attacked Hancock's lack of political experience, as he had never before held an elected office. They distributed a booklet called "A Record of the Statesmanship and Political Achievements of General Winfield Scott Hancock" which contained nothing but several blank pages. Despite the fact that Hancock was one of the most famous and well-respected of the Union generals who had served in the war, attempts were made to stain his reputation when wild rumors were circulated that he had conspired to overthrow Lincoln during the war, and had engaged in corrupt business endeavors while commanding in Louisiana during Reconstruction. These accusations were wholly unfounded, and were dismissed by the vast majority of voters, but they continued to be spread by a small minority of Republicans for the duration of the campaign.

The Democrats themselves were not above using fabrication in the campaign. A forged letter was circulated that showed Garfield's supposed support of the Burlingame Treaty of 1868, as well as his support of unlimited Chinese immigration. This had a negative effect on the Republican efforts in the far West, where California and Nevada were swayed in support of Hancock because of concerns over unbridled Chinese immigration.

The results of the November elections gave Garfield the victory with a mere one-tenth of a percent margin in the popular vote, garnering 48.3 percent to Hancock's 48.2 percent. In the electoral college he enjoyed a margin of 214 to 155, however, with each candidate winning the electoral majority in nineteen states. Garfield won in several of the most populous states, however, and his victory in New York, Chester Arthur's native state, was largely responsible for putting him over the top in the electoral count. Hancock won in the South, the border states, New Jersey, California, and Nevada. Garfield captured all the states in the North and the remainder of those in the West. The election was the rebirth of the "solid South" as a Democratic force, but proved that the Republicans could win without a strong showing in the old Confederacy. In many ways, the 1880 election mirrored the one that had taken place twenty years before, when Abraham Lincoln failed to carry any of the Southern states. The South was right back to where it had begun in 1860, solidly opposed to Republican policies, but unable to counter that party's control and largely unrepresented in national affairs.

The 1880 election would bear another grim resemblance to the 1860 election in that the winning Republican candidate would become the victim of assassination. In September of 1881, Charles Jules Guiteau, a lawyer and disgruntled office seeker, shot down President Garfield at the Washington railroad station, where he was preparing for a trip to New York.[7] Guiteau had been given a private audience with Garfield for the purpose of seeking an appointment as a United States minister to France, but Garfield had not been impressed with him and failed to support his ambition. Guiteau presumably gunned down the president in retaliation.

The assassination of Garfield did not have the same effect on the political

Drawing of the assassination of President Garfield by Charles Guiteau. Garfield served for less than a year before being shot down by this disgruntled office seeker. (From *The Life of James Abram Garfield: Late President of the United States*, by William Ralston Balch, J.C. McCurdy & Co., Philadelphia, Pa., 1881).

landscape as had the assassination of President Lincoln. Garfield's brief presidency was viewed to be a failure, as his administration was largely blamed for the economic recession that plagued the Northeast during his term of office, and Republicans were unable to affix a martyr's mantle to Garfield, as they had done with Lincoln following his death.

With the South firmly in the hands of the Democrats once more, the Democratic majority that was won in the United States House of Representatives in the 1882 elections signaled a shift in national politics that did not bode well for Republicans in the upcoming presidential contest. Democratic wins in the gubernatorial elections in New York, Massachusetts, Kansas, and Michigan were indeed a foreshadowing of things to come. In 1884, the Republicans nominated Senator James Blaine as their candidate. Blaine had been a major force in Republican politics for two decades, and had been a serious contender for the nomination several times before.

The Democrats nominated Grover Cleveland, the governor of New York, who had won his post in the 1882 elections. Cleveland was known to be a reformer who was strong on civil service laws, and whose views on the tariff were such that they did not alienate voters on either side of the issue. Cleveland had won the support of some reform Republicans when he cut off the patronage of New York's Tammany Hall political machine. Many reform Republicans were estranged by Blaine's nomination and actively supported Cleveland's candidacy. These Republicans were in favor of civil service reform, and Cleveland's policies and actions appealed to them. The defectors were labeled "Mugwumps" by the rest of the Republican Party, and were derided as being political fence-sitters.

Scandals rocked the campaign, as both sides engaged in mudslinging and accusations of wrongdoing. In November, the Republican defectors aided Cleveland in gaining victory in West Virginia, Kentucky, Connecticut, New Jersey, New York, Missouri, Maryland, and Indiana. He was also victorious in all of the Southern states. Blaine carried the rest of the Northern states and all of the West. As with the 1880 election, New York was pivotal in deciding the winner, and Cleveland won his home state by one of the narrowest margins in all political history. New Yorkers cast 4,875,971 votes for Cleveland and 4,852,234 for Blaine, giving Cleveland the victory by a mere .24 percent of the votes cast.

When Grover Cleveland was sworn in as president in 1885, it ushered in a new era of American politics. Republicans had controlled the White House since Abraham Lincoln had been sworn into office in 1861, and the party had subsequently directed the affairs of state for twenty-four years. Democrats had been held in check for more than two decades, but they had now gained sufficient support to once more challenge for control of the national destiny.

The parties themselves would change and adjust to political need in the coming decades, in an effort to keep themselves current and capture the electorate. Republicans would shift from their radical image to eventually assume the conservative label with which they are viewed today. Democrats would lose the conservative ideals that had defined them through most of the 19th century, and would adopt the liberal policies with which they were identified through most of the 20th century. The shifting in political ideologies leads one to question who really won, and who really lost, in the struggle for national dominance that brought about the Civil War. When Ronald Reagan advocated a smaller Federal government, and a states' rights approach national affairs, Republicans were swept into office in 1980 with an overwhelming mandate for political change. Many of the policies he advocated could be traced directly to the platforms of the Democratic Party of the 1800s, and bore little resemblance to the Republican platforms of the same period. In the end, the winners lost, the losers won, and the nation endured. Lincoln and his party, however, had succeeded in expanding the size and scope of the Federal government, and forever changed the landscape of politics in the nation.

Conclusion

I think it is evident to anyone who has read the information contained in this book that the Civil War was not fought to free the slaves. If that had been the case, Lincoln's first inaugural address would not have included guarantees for the perpetuation of the institution, John C. Frémont's proclamation of emancipation in Missouri would have been supported, West Virginia would not have been brought into the Union as a slave state, and the Emancipation Proclamation would have freed all slaves, not just those residing in regions under Confederate control. To be sure, slavery had been a major dividing factor between the two sides for decades, and was a primary reason for the antagonism that grew between the two sides in the years leading up to the Civil War, but it was not the causative factor in touching off the war. The shift in official policy toward slavery took place as a political expedient to facilitate a broader agenda: the ultimate centralization of political power in the Federal government.

To be sure, the abolitionists formed a vocal and important part of the Republican Party, and for that reason, Republican leadership took measures to appease them and keep them in the fold, but they were only a small fraction of the party as a whole. Abolitionists clashed with the Republican majority throughout the course of the war, feeling that the actions of the party leadership were too timid in regard to slavery. The Republican mainstream viewed the abolitionists to be extremists whose fanatical policies would hinder chances for a reunified nation. As war weariness became increasingly evident in the North, many of the mainstream Republicans began to waver in their support of a continuation of the conflict, as was evidenced in the elections of 1862 and 1863, when Democratic candidates made inroads into the control of state and national politics that the Republicans has thus far enjoyed. Abolitionists, however, remained a constant source of unfaltering support for the war effort, and increasingly became the administration's greatest ally in its policy to see the thing through to the end, regardless of the cost. As such, the abolitionists formed an uneasy alliance with Lincoln and his moderate administration that would result in radical control of the government at the time of Lincoln's death, and would set the stage for the punitive period of Reconstruction.

Certainly, there is no concrete evidence available to suggest that Republican leaders acted in unison to destroy the fabric of the Union as it had been before the war, and to recreate it according to their own model. But that does not change the fact that precisely such an event took place. Republican ideology itself dictated such an occurrence if and when the party came to power. The fact that Republicans refused to entertain any offers of compromise, combined with Lincoln's skillful maneuvering to ensure that the Confederacy committed the first hostile act in the crisis, is enough to cause one to question if the administration had the best interests of the country in mind, or if it instead sought to further the agenda of its own party, regardless of the implications. The suspension of the writ of habeas corpus, the attacks on Northern Democratic officers in the army, the suppression of the press, and the tampering with free elections all point to a concerted effort to seize and retain control of the reins of power. The expansion of the influence of the central government into such areas as banking, education, and transportation bore witness to the dominance of the Federal government over the lives of its citizens, fulfilling the hopes of the old Federalist Party, and setting in motion events that have led to the monolithic central government we see today.

To be sure, the freeing of the slaves was one end result of the Civil War. It was not, however, the cause of the conflict, or the main focus of the Republican Party when it came into power. The facts related in the pages of this book serve to refute any such claim. Instead, the war was fought to determine what form of government the citizens of America would live under. Was it to be a loosely bound confederation of individual states, predicated upon the institutions of states' rights and self-determination, or would it be a strong centralized institution, in which the states were subservient to the will of the national government?

Centralization won out in the end, bringing with it a host of positive and negative results. It can reasonably be argued that America could not have passed through the industrial age, and the growth and expansion that saw the nation emerge as a world power, without the strong, guiding hand of a powerful central government. It can be debated whether advances such as desegregation and the enforcement of civil rights acts would not have been possible in the loosely tethered structure of the antebellum era. It can also be argued that the bureaucratic regulations of big government stifle the spirit of individual freedom that is every American's legacy under the Constitution. Hamilton felt that the masses were not competent to conduct their own affairs when it came to politics, and advocated a government comparable to a monarchy, where superior men would decide the issues of the day, unencumbered by mob rule. We certainly do not have the latter form of government, but we are a far cry from the town meetings of old New England, or the states' rights principles of the Old South. The Civil War moved us somewhere toward the middle of the two extremes, possibly the greatest political compromise in all of American history, and the enduring legacy of those four bloody years of conflict.

If the material included in this book has caused the reader to question what he has previously learned, or been told, then the author has accomplished his purpose. History is not exact. There are too many variables. Only through research and reason can we sift through the information available to us to arrive at a clearer understanding of the truth. If you do not merely accept information because it appears in a book, but instead question those parts that seem out of place, or do not make sense, then you have learned the guiding principle of being a historian, and are on the path of the quest for truth.

Chapter Notes

Chapter One

1. Adam Smith, *The Republican Party: A Photographic History of the GOP* (San Diego, Ca.: Thunder Bay Press, 2003), 16–17.

2. John Higham, *Strangers in the Land: Patterns of American Nativism 1860–1925* (New York: Atheneum Books, 1975), 8; *New American Supplement to the New Werner Twentieth Century Edition of the Encyclopedia Britannica* (Akron, Oh.: The Werner Company, 1905), 626–627.

3. J. Clarence Stonebraker, *The Unwritten South: Cause, Progress and Result of the Civil War; Relics of Hidden Truth After Forty Years* (Hagerstown, Md.: Hagerstown Bookbinding and Printing Co., 1903), 42–44.

4. Geoffrey C. Ward, Ric Burns, and Ken Burns, *The Civil War: An Illustrated History* (New York: Alfred A. Knopf, Inc., 1990), 19.

5. Smith, 17.

6. *The Sons of the Sires; A History of the Rise, Progress, and Destiny of the American Party, and Its Probable Influence on the Next Presidential Election* (Philadelphia: Lippincott, Grambo & Co., 1855), IV–V, 25.

7. J.G. Randall and David Herbert Donald, *The Civil War and Reconstruction* (Lexington, Mass.: D.C. Heath and Company, 1969), 100–101.

8. Ibid., 101.

9. Samuel M. Smucker, *The Life of Col. John Charles Frémont, and His Narrative of Explorations and Adventures in Kansas, Nebraska, Oregon, and California* (New York: Miller, Orton & Mulligan, 1856), 3–4.

Chapter Two

1. David Herbert Donald, *Lincoln* (New York: Simon & Schuster Books, 1995), 199.

2. Ibid, 200–201.

3. Ward, 2–4.

4. Ward, 4–5; Ezra J. Warner, *Generals in Gray: Lives of the Confederate Commanders* (Baton Rouge: Louisiana State University Press, 1959), 181.

5. *Harpers Weekly*, November 12, 1859; Boyd B. Stutler, "An Eyewitness Describes the Hanging of John Brown," *American Heritage Magazine* 2 (February 1955); Ward, 7–8.

6. Ward, 5.

7. Philip Van Doren Stern, *Prologue to Sumter: The Beginnings of the Civil War from John Brown's Raid to the Surrender of Fort Sumter* (Greenwich, Ct.: Fawcett Publications, Inc., 1961), 47–52.

8. Robert Selph Henry, *The Story of the Confederacy* (New York: Grosset & Dunlap, Publishers, 1936), 20–21.

9. George Fort Milton, *The Eve of Conflict: Stephen A. Douglas and the Needless War* (New York: Octagon Books, Inc., 1963), 372.

10. Edwin C. Rozwenc, *The Causes of the American Civil War* (Lexington, Mass.: D.C. Heath and Company, 1972), 24–25.

11. Warner, *Generals in Gray*, 34.

12. Harold Holzer, *Lincoln at Cooper Union: The Speech That Made Abraham Lincoln President* (New York: Simon and Schuster, 2004), 154–160

13. Dale Carnegie, *Lincoln the Unknown* (Hauppauge, N.Y.: Dale Carnegie & Associates, Inc., 1959), 113.

14. William and Bruce Catton, *Two Roads to Sumter* (New York: McGraw-Hill Books, 1963), 245.

15. Carnegie, 114.

Chapter Three

1. Victor S. Clark, *History of Manufactures in the United States,* 2 vols. (New York: McGraw-Hill Carnegie Institution, 1929), 2.

2. Clyde N. Wilson, *Calhoun's Economic*

Platform, in Slavery, Secession, and Southern History (Charlottesville: University of Virginia Press), 87–88.

3. Murat Halstead, *Caucuses of 1860: A History of the National Political Conventions* (Columbus, Oh., 1860), 153.

4. Catton, *Two Roads to Sumter*, 255.

5. Alexander Harris, *A Review of the Political Conflict in America from the Commencement of the Anti-Slavery Agitation to the Close of Southern Reconstruction; Comprising Also a Resume of the Career of Thaddeus Stevens: Being a Survey of the Struggles of Parties, Which Destroyed the Republic and Virtually Monarchized Its Government* (New York: T.H. Pollock, Publisher, 1876), 200.

6. Harris, 200–202; *The Congressional Globe, 1860–61* (Washington, D.C.: Government Printing Office, 1861), 1391.

7. James Buchanan, *Mr. Buchanan's Administration on the Eve of the Rebellion* (New York: D. Appleton and Company, 1866), 136–137.

8. *The Congressional Globe*, 237.

9. Harris, 203–204.

10. Delia Ray, *A Nation Torn: The Story of How the Civil War Began* (New York: Lodestar Books, 1990), 1–11.

11. Milton, 515.

12. Harris, 204.

13. Ibid., 206.

14. Stonebraker, 61–62.

15. Henry, 26–27.

16. Ibid., 29–30.

17. Carnegie, 122–123.

18. *New York Tribune*, November 9, 1860.

19. Milton, 520.

20. Ibid., 521.

21. Randall and Donald, 164–165.

22. Catton, 119–120.

23. Ibid., 120–121.

24. W.A. Swanberg, *First Blood: The Story of Fort Sumter* (New York: Charles Scribners' Sons, 1957), 127–128, 146–148.

25. Alonzo Rothschild, *Lincoln, Master of Men: A Study in Character* (Boston: Houghton Mifflin Company, 1906), 139.

26. Henry, 30–33.

27 Randall and Donald, 174.

28 Roy P. Basler, *The Collected Works of Abraham Lincoln*, vol. 4 (New Brunswick, N.J.: Rutgers University Press, 1953–1955), 351.

29 Theodore C. Pease and J.G. Randall, *The Diary of Orville Hickman Browning*, vol. 1 (Springfield, Ill.: Illinois State Historical Society, 1933), 476.

30 Charles W. Ramsdell, "Lincoln and Fort Sumter," *Journal of Southern History* 3 (1937): 259–288.

31. Milton, 521.

32. Ibid, 522.

Chapter Four

1. John S. Bowman, *The Civil War Almanac* (New York: World Almanac Publications, 1983), 51; Swanberg, 328.

2. William C. Davis, *First Blood: Fort Sumter to Bull Run* (Alexandria, Va.: Time-Life Books, 1983), 11, 13.

3. Ibid., 13.

4. Randall and Donald, 181.

5. Carl Sandburg, *Abraham Lincoln: The Prairie Years and the War Years*, 3 vols. (New York: Dell Publishing Company, 1962), 233.

6. Rothschild, 141.

7. Randall and Donald, 182–184.

8. Henry, 36.

9. Elbert J. Benton, *The Movement for Peace Without a Victory in the Civil War* (Cleveland, Oh.: The Western Reserve Historical Society, 1918), 5.

10. Randall and Donald, 195–196.

11. John Bach McMaster, *Our House Divided: A History of the People of the United States During Lincoln's Administration* (New York: Fawcett Publications, Inc., 1961), 169.

12. *The War of the Rebellion: A Compilation of the Official Records of the Union and Confederate Armies,* Series 2, vol. 1 (Washington, D.C., Government Printing Office, 1891), 566–568.

13. McMaster, 170–171; *Official Records*, 586.

14. Mark E. Neely, Jr., "The Lincoln Administration and Arbitrary Arrests: A Reconsideration," *Journal of the Abraham Lincoln Association* 5 (1983): 13.

15. Ibid., 8.

16. David Nevin, *The Road to Shiloh: Early Battles in the West* (Alexandria, Va.: Time-Life Books, 1983), 9–11.

17. Catton, 372; Henry, 38–39 ; Nevin, 13, 17.

18. Henry, 38–39.

19. Marguerite Higgins, *Jessie Benton Fremont* (Boston: Houghton Mifflin Company, 1961), 160–181; Nevin, 29–33.

20. K. Merton Coulter, *The Civil War and Readjustment in Kentucky* (Chapel Hill: University of North Carolina Press, 1926), pgs 1–3.

21. William C. Davis, *The Orphan Brigade: The Kentucky Confederates Who Couldn't Go Home* (New York: Doubleday and Company, Inc., 1980), 4–6.

22. Ibid., 9–12.

23. Davis, *The Orphan Brigade*, 9–12; Bowman, 55.

24. William C. Davis, "John C. Breckinridge: A Personality Profile," *Civil War Times Illustrated* 6, no. 3 (June 1967): 14–15.

25. Harris, 319.

Chapter Five

1. Bowman, 94.
2. Ibid., 114.
3. Robert P. Broadwater, "The Curtin Rises," *State College Magazine* 18, no. 2 (February 2003): 37; J.G. Randall, *Midstream: Lincoln the President* (New York: Dodd, Mead and Company, 1953), 277.
4. Broadwater, 37–38.
5. Geoffrey Perret, *Lincoln's War: The Untold Story of America's Greatest President as Commander in Chief* (New York: Random House, 2004), 213; Abraham Lincoln Papers, vol. 5 (Washington, D.C.: Library of Congress), 501.
6. Broadwater, 38–39.
7. Bowman, 115; Broadwater, 40.
8. Broadwater, 41.
9. Benton, 24.
10. *Democratic Standard*, September 17, 1862.
11. "The Genius of Liberty And Northern War Disillusionment," *Confederate Veteran Magazine* 3 (1998), 32–33.
12. James Ford Rhodes, *History of the United States from the Compromise of 1850 to the Final Restoration of Home Rule at the South in 1877*, vol. 3 (New York: The Macmillan Company, 1910), 555
13. "Francis W. Hughes and the 1862 Pennsylvania Election," *Pennsylvania Magazine of History and Biography* 95 (1971), 3.
14. Bowman, 118–119.
15. Harris, 356.
16. Ibid., 357–358.
17. "The Genius of Liberty And Northern War Disillusionment," 31.
18. Randall, *Midstream*, 277.

Chapter Six

1. Ezra J. Warner, *Generals in Blue: Lives of the Union Commanders* (Baton Rouge: Louisiana University Press, 1964), 603.
2. Warner, *Generals in Blue*, 603; Burke Davis, *The Civil War: Strange and Fascinating Facts* (New York: The Fairfax Press, 1960), 91.
3. Warner, *Generals in Blue*, 61, 281, 446.
4. "Rebels From The Confederate State of Illinois," *Confederate Veteran Magazine* 6 (2000): 14.
5. Warner, *Generals in Blue*, 290–291.
6. T. Harry Williams, *Lincoln and His Generals* (New York: Gramercy Books, 2000), 46–47.
7. Ibid., 50.
8. Allan Pinkerton, *The Spy of the Rebellion: Being a True History of the Spy System of the United States Army During the Late Rebellion, Revealing Many Secrets of the War Hitherto Not Made Public* (New York: G.W. Dillingham Co., Publishers, 1911), 33–150. Pinkerton gives numerous examples through these pages of the close affiliation he had established with Lincoln and the administration, and the almost daily contact he and his operatives had with the president and members of his official family.
9. George B. McClellan, *McClellan's Own Story The War for the Union, the Soldiers Who Fought It, the Civilians Who Directed It, and His Relations to It and to Them* (New York: Charles J. Webster, 1887), 259.
10. Perret, 63.
11. McClellan, 260–269; Perret, 170.
12. Robert Underwood Johnson and Clarence Clough Buel, *Battles and Leaders of the Civil War*, vol. 2 (New York: Castle Books, 1956), 315, 317.
13. Paul M. Angle, *The Lincoln Reader* (New Brunswick, N.J.: Rutgers University Press, 1947), 390–391.
14. John Michael Priest, *Before Antietam: The Battle for South Mountain* (Shippensburg, Pa.: White Mane Publishing Company, Inc., 1992), 4.
15. Hunter Alexander, *Johnny Reb and Billy Yank* (New York: The Neale Publishing Co., 1905), 273–274.
16. McClellan, *McClellan's Own Story*, 655.
17. Ibid., 652.
18. Warner, *Generals in Blue*, 379–380.
19. Ibid., 51–53.
20. Robert P. Broadwater, *The Battle of Perryville: Culmination of the Failed Kentucky Campaign* (Jefferson, N.C.: McFarland Publishing, 2005), 146–147.
21. Nathaniel S. Shaler, "Campaigns in Kentucky and Tennessee, Including the Battle of Chickamauga 1862–1864," *Papers Read to the Military Historical Society of Massachusetts* (Boston: Military Historical Society of Massachusetts, 1905), 289.
22. Warner, *Generals in Blue*, 293.
23. Lloyd Lewis, *Sherman: Fighting Prophet* (New York: Harcourt, Brace and Company, 1932), 255.
24. Warner, *Generals in Blue*, 293.
25. Rod Gragg, *Confederate Goliath: The Battle of Fort Fisher* (New York: Harper Collins Publishers, 1991), 104.
26. Warner, *Generals in Blue*, 61.

Chapter Seven

1. Randall and Donald, 282.
2. Ibid., 283.

3. Ibid., 283–284.

4. Warner, *Generals in Blue*, 480.

5. *Joint Committee on the Conduct of the War Reports*, vol. 2 (Washington, D.C.: Government Printing Office, 1862–1866), 427–429.

6. Howard K. Beale, *The Diary of Edward Bates 1859–1866 Contained in the Annual Report of the American Historical Association, 1930*, vol. 1 (Washington, D.C.: American Historical Association, 1933), 229.

7. Randall and Donald, 282–283; Warner, *Generals in Blue*, 480–481.

8. Carl Sandburg, *Abraham Lincoln: The Prairie Years and the War Years* (New York: Harcourt, Brace & World, Inc., 1954), 273; Perrett, 328.

9. Sandburg, 273.

10. Donald, 327; Sandburg, 274.

11. Perrett, 331; *Congressional Globe*, 324–334.

12. Perrett, 329–330.

13. *Guide to the United States Congress* (Washington, D.C.: Government Printing Office, 1971), 267.

14. Sandburg, 277.

15. Perrett, 330.

16. Bruce Catton, *Terrible Swift Sword* (New York: Doubleday & Company, Inc., 1963), 187.

17. Perrett, 327.

18. Ibid., 330.

19. T. Harry Williams, *Lincoln and the Radicals* (Madison: University of Wisconsin Press, 1960), 366–367.

20. Letter to Letitia Chandler from Zachariah Chandler dated May 20, 1863, Zachariah Chandler Papers, Library of Congress, Washington, D.C.

21. *Harper's Weekly*, August 20, 1861.

22. *Joint Committee on the Conduct of the War Reports*, vol. 1, Government Printing Office, Washington, D.C. 1862–1866, 449.

23. Perrett, 329.

24. Reports of the Proceedings of the 38th Congress, 1st Session, United States Senate, Report Number 18, pages 4–5, Library of Congress, Washington, D.C.

25. McClure, Alexander, *Abraham Lincoln and Men of War Times*, Lippincott Publishing, Philadelphia, Pa. 1892, 259–260.

26. Randall, *Midstream*, 134.

27. Perrett, 331.

Chapter Eight

1. John M. Kelly Diary, in possession of the author.

2. Donald Dale Jackson, *Twenty Million Yankees: The Northern Home Front* (Alexandria, Va.: Time-Life Books, 1985), 98.

3. Ibid.

4. McMaster, 398–399.

5. "Story of the New York City Draft Riots," *Civil War Times Illustrated* 4, no. 5 (August 1965): 6–8.

6. "Story of the New York City Draft Riots," pgs 7–8.

7. Jackson, 103.

8. "Story of the New York City Draft Riots," 8–9.

9. Ibid., 10.

10. Jackson, 106, 108; Peter J. Parish, *The American Civil War* (New York: Holmes & Meier Publishers, Inc., 1975), 501; "Story of the New York City Draft Riots," 10.

11. James M. McPherson, *Battle Cry of Freedom: The Civil War Era* (New York: Ballantine Books, 1988), 610.

12. Jackson, 108.

13. "Story of the New York City Draft Riots," 28.

14. Ibid., 28–29.

15. Jackson, 108.

16. "Story of the New York City Draft Riots," 28–29.

17. McPherson, 610; Jackson, 110.

18. Jackson, 99; Ward, Burns, and Burns, 245; Robert P. Broadwater, *From Beyond the Battlefields: Civil War Side Shows and Little Known Events* (Bellwood, Pa.: Dixie Dreams Press, 2004), 67; Benton, 34–35.

19. Jackson, 95, 99.

20. Kenneth D. Williams, *War Sentiment in Fayette County, Pennsylvania, 1861–1862: A Research Project Submitted to the Faculty of the School of Graduate Studies of California University of Pennsylvania in partial fulfillment of the requirements for the degree of Master of Arts* (unpublished), 11; "The Genius of Liberty and Northern War Disillusionment," 35.

21. Richard T. Hughes, *Bloody Knox: December 13, 1864 — Clearfield County's Resistance to the Civil War and the Bloody Knox Saga* (Clearfield, Pa.: published by the author, 2004), 2, 8, 9, 15, 16.

Chapter Nine

1. "The Great Copperhead Conspiracy," *Civil War Times Illustrated* 4, no. 3 (June 1965): 21.

2. *Cincinnati Commercial*, August 17, 1861.

3. "The Great Copperhead Conspiracy," 22.

4. Ibid.

5. Benton, 35–36; Jennifer L. Weber, *Copperheads: The Rise and Fall of Lincoln's Opponents in the North* (New York: Oxford University Press, 2006), 152.

6. "The Great Copperhead Conspiracy," 22; Weber, 148.

7. Jackson, 149.

8. Weber, 148–149.

9. Benton, 13–14.

10. *Congressional Globe*, pt. 1, 258.

11. Benton, 16–17.

12. Benton, 20–21; *The Old Guard Magazine* 1, no. 2 (1861): 45.

13. Andrew Dickson White, *Copperhead Minstrel: A Choice Collection of Democratic Poems and Songs, for the Usage of Political Clubs and the Social Circle* (Ithaca, N.Y.: Cornell University Library, 2007), 51.

14. Ibid., pg 13.

15. "The Great Copperhead Conspiracy," 22–23.

16. "The Great Copperhead Conspiracy," 23–25; Benton, 36–27.

17. Benton, 37–38.

18. Letter from Braxton Bragg to Samuel Cooper dated May 27, 1863, Braxton Bragg Papers, W.P. Palmer Civil War Collection, Western Reserve Historical Society.

19. *The War of the Rebellion: A Compilation of the Official Records of the Union and Confederate Armies*, Series II, vol. 6 (Washington, D.C.: Government Printing Office, 1886), 23.

20. Benton, 46–47.

21. James L. Vallandigham, *A Life of Clement L. Vallandigham* (Baltimore: Turnbull Brothers, 1872), 318, 321.

22. Benton, 49–50.

Chapter Ten

1. William H. Price, *The Civil War Centennial Handbook* (Arlington, Va.: Prince Lithograph, Inc., 1961), 68.

2. Ibid.

3. J.W. Schuckers, *The Life and Public Services of Salmon Portland Chase* (New York: D. Appleton & Co., 1874), 494.

4. Robert B. Warden, *An Account of the Private Life and Public Services of Salmon Portland Chase* (Cincinnati, Oh.: Wilstach, Baldwin and Company, 1874), 573–574.

5. William Watson Davis, *The Civil War and Reconstruction in Florida* (New York: Columbia University Press, 1913), 274.

6. Ibid., 275.

7. *The War of the Rebellion*, Series I, vol. 35, part 1 (Washington, D.C.: Government Printing Office, 1891), 278.

8. Tyler Dennett, *John Hay: From Poetry to Politics* (New York: Dodd, Mead and Company, 1934), 43.

9. Price, 68.

10. Parish, 533.

11. Randall and Donald, 468.

12. Ibid., 468–469.

13. Randall and Donald, 469; Carnegie, 187.

14. Randall and Donald, 474.

15. Ibid., 475.

16. Ibid., 475.

17. Benjamin Butler, *Butler's Book: Autobiography and Personal Reminiscences of Major-General Benjamin Butler* (Boston: A.M. Thayer and Company, 1892), 754.

18. Ibid., pg 540.

19. Sidney David Brummer, *Political History of New York State During the Period of the Civil War* (New York: Columbia University Press, 1911), 437.

20. Louis Taylor Merrill, "Ben Butler in the Presidential Campaign of 1864," *The Mississippi Historical Review* 33, no. 4 (March 1947): 540, 565.

21. Benjamin P. Thomas and Harold M. Hyman, *Stanton: The Life and Times of Lincoln's Secretary of War* (New York: Alfred A. Knopf, 1962), 331–334.

22. Ibid., 331–334.

23. Lyman Jackson, *History of the Sixth New Hampshire Regiment* (Concord, N.H.: Republican Press Association, 1891), 344–346.

24. Joseph T. Glatthaar, *The March to the Sea and Beyond: Sherman's Troops in the Savannah and Carolina Campaigns* (New York: New York University Press, 1986), 187.

25. Thomas and Hyman, 331–334.

26. "The Genius of Liberty and Northern War Disillusionment," 36.

27. Benjamin P. Thomas, *Abraham Lincoln: A Biography* (New York: Alfred A. Knopf, 1940), 451–452.

28. Johnathan W. White, "Canvassing the Troops: The Federal Government and the Soldiers' Right to Vote," *Civil War History* 50 (2004): 291–317.

29. Thomas, 451.

30. H.G. Pike to Lyman Trumbull, February 6, 1863, Lyman Trumbull Papers, Library of Congress, Washington, D.C.; Union League of Springfield to Abraham Lincoln, March 17, 1863; Union League of York, Pennsylvania, to Abraham Lincoln, December 16, 1863, and February 9, 1864; James Edmunds to Edwin Stanton, March 1, 1864; James Edmunds to Abraham Lincoln, November 1, 2, 1864; all in the Abraham Lincoln Papers, Library of Congress, Washington, D.C.

Chapter Eleven

1. Donald, 567; Basler, *Collected Works of Abraham Lincoln*, vol. 8, 116–117.

2. Michael Burlingame, "New Light on the

Bixby Letter," *Journal of the Abraham Lincoln Association* 16, no. 1 (1995): 59–61; Michael Burlingame, "The Trouble With the Bixby Letter," *American Heritage Magazine* 4 (July/August 1999): 16–17.

3. Burlingame, "New Light on the Bixby Letter," 63–64.

4. Joshua Wolf Shenk, "Uncovering the Real Abe Lincoln," *Time* 166, no. 1 (July 4, 2005): 42–44.

5. William Marvel, "Martyr Under The Microscope," *America's Civil War* 19, no. 5 (November 2006): 42–44.

6. Shenk, 40.

7. Marvel, 47.

8. Shenk, 41.

9. Robert Bray, "The Power to Hurt: Lincoln's Early Use of Satire and Invective," *Journal of the Abraham Lincoln Association* 16, no. 1 (1995): 42.

10. Ibid.

11. Paul M. Angle, *The Complete Lincoln–Douglas Debates of 1858* (Chicago: University of Chicago Press, 1991), 128.

12. David Zarefsky, "Public Sentiment Is Everything: Lincoln's View of Political Persuasion," *Journal of the Abraham Lincoln Association* 15, no. 2 (1994): 23.

13. Basler, *Collected Works of Abraham Lincoln*, vol. 4, 194, 197, 210, 211.

14. Ibid., 266.

15. Joel H. Sibley, "Always a Whig in Politics The Partisan Life of Abraham Lincoln," *Journal of the Abraham Lincoln Association* 8 (1996): 22.

16. Colonel Alexander K. McClure, *Lincoln's Yarns and Stories: A Complete Collection of the Funny and Witty Anecdotes that made Abraham Lincoln Famous as America's Greatest Story Teller* (Chicago: The John C. Winston Company, n.d.), 158–159.

Chapter Twelve

1. Richard Carwardine, *Lincoln: A Life of Purpose and Power* (New York: Alfred A. Knopf, 2006), 238–239.

2. Bowman, 269.

3. Claude G. Bowers, *The Tragic Era: The Revolution After Lincoln* (Cambridge, Mass.: The Literary Guild of America, Incorporated, 1929), 35–36.

4. Ibid., 34–35.

5. Ibid., 31–32.

6. James G. Rhodes, *History of the United States from the Compromise of 1850 to the McKinley–Bryan Campaign of 1896*, vol. 6 (New York: Macmillan Books, 1919), 68.

7. Eric Foner, *Reconstruction: America's Unfinished Revolution, 1863–1877* (New York: Harper Perennial Modern Classics, 2002), 273–276.

8. *New York World*, October 9, 1866.

9. Bowers, 143.

10. Ibid., 165.

11. Rhodes, 199.

12. Randall and Donald, 594.

13. Ibid., 593.

14. Ibid., 593–595.

15. Bowers, 300–301.

Chapter Thirteen

1. Howard N. Meyer, *Let Us Have Peace: The Story of Ulysses S. Grant* (New York: Collier Books, 1966), 168.

2. Ibid., 213.

3. Rhodes, *History of the United States ... 1877*, vol. 7, 227.

4. Ibid., 229–230.

5. William Ralston Balch, *The Life of James Abram Garfield: Late President of the United States* (Philadelphia: J.C. McCurdy & Co., 1881), 373.

6. Ibid., 475–476.

7. Ibid., 593–594.

Bibliography

Primary Sources

Manuscript Collections

Braxton Bragg Papers, W.P. Palmer Civil War Collection, Western Reserve Historical Society.

Simon Cameron Papers, Library of Congress, Washington D.C.

Zachariah Chandler Papers, Library of Congress, Washington, D.C.

John M. Kelly Diary, in possession of the author.

Abraham Lincoln Papers, Library of Congress, Washington, D.C.

Reports of the Proceedings of the 38th Congress, Library of Congress, Washington, D.C.

Lyman Trumbull Papers, Library of Congress, Washington, D.C.

Books

Alexander, Hunter. *Johnny Reb and Billy Yank.* New York: The Neale Publishing Co., 1905.

Allen, Edward Frank. *Lincoln's Stories and Speeches.* New York: Books, Inc. Publishers, n.d.

Angle, Paul M. *The Complete Lincoln–Douglas Debates of 1858.* Chicago: University of Chicago Press, 1991.

_____. *The Lincoln Reader.* New Brunswick, N.J.: Rutgers University Press, 1947.

Appleman, Roy Edgar. *Abraham Lincoln: From His Own Words and Contemporary Accounts.* Washington, D.C.: National Park Service, 1961.

Baker, General La Fayette C. *The United States Secret Service in the Late War: Comprising the Author's Introduction to the Leading Men at Washington, with the Origin and Organization of the United States Secret Service Bureau, and a Graphic History of Rich and Exciting Experiences, North and South.* Philadelphia: World Bible House, 1890.

Balch, William Ralston. *The Life of James Abram Garfield: Late President of the United States.* Philadelphia: J.C. McCurdy & Co., 1881.

Basler, Roy P. *The Collected Works of Abraham Lincoln.* New Brunswick, N.J.: Rutgers University Press, 1953–1955.

Beale, Howard K. *The Diary of Edward Bates 1859–1866 Contained in the Annual Report of the American Historical Association, 1930.* Vols. 1–4. Washington, D.C.: American Historical Association, 1933.

Blaine, James G. *Political Discussions Legislative, Diplomatic, and Popular 1856–1886.* Norwich, Ct.: The Henry Bill Publishing Company, 1887.

Blair, William Allan. *A Politician Goes to War: The Civil War Letters of John White Geary.* University Park, Pa.: The Pennsylvania State University Press, 1995.

225

Bowers, Claude G. *The Tragic Era: The Revolution After Lincoln.* Cambridge, Mass.: The Literary Guild of America, Incorporated, 1929.

Buchanan, James. *Mr. Buchanan's Administration of the Eve of the Rebellion.* New York: D. Appleton and Company, 1866.

Bullard, F. Lauriston. *The Diary of a Public Man and a Page of Political Correspondence Stanton to Buchanan.* New Brunswick, N.J.: Rutgers University Press, 1946.

Butler, Benjamin. *Butler's Book: Autobiography and Personal Reminiscences of Major-General Benjamin Butler.* Boston: A.M. Thayer and Company, 1892.

Caren, Eric C. *Civil War Extra: A Newspaper History of the Civil War.* 2 vols. New York: Castle Books, 1999.

Congressional Globe, 1860–61. Washington, D.C.: Government Printing Office, 1861.

Croly, David. *Seymour and Blair, Their Lives and Services.* New York: Richardson and Company, 1868.

Crosby, Frank. *Life of Abraham Lincoln, Sixteenth President of the United States, Containing His Early History and Political Career; Together with the Speeches, Messages, Proclamations and Other Official Documents Illustrative of His Eventful Administration.* Philadelphia: John E. Potter, 1865.

Ford, Worthington Chauncey. *A Cycle of Adams Letters 1861–1865.* 2 vols. Boston: Houghton Mifflin Company, 1920.

Gerry, Margarita Spalding. *Through Five Administrations: Reminiscences of Colonel William H. Crook, Bodyguard to President Lincoln.* New York: Harper & Brothers Publishers, 1910.

Halstead, Murat. *Caucuses of 1860: A History of the National Political Conventions.* Columbus, Oh.: N.p., 1860.

Harris, Alexander. *A Review of the Political Conflict in America from the Commencement of the Anti-Slavery Agitation to the Close of Southern Reconstruction.* New York: T.H. Pollock, Publisher, 1876.

Haven, E.O. *The Republican Manual of American Progress, A Handy Book of Facts and Figures.* New York: E.B. Treat, 1880.

Horton, Rushmore G. *A Youth's History of the Great Civil War.* New York: Van Evrie, Horton and Company, 1866.

Jackson, Lyman. *History of the Sixth New Hampshire Regiment.* Concord, N.H.: Republican Press Association, 1891.

Johnson, Robert Underwood, and Clarence Clough Buel. *Battles and Leaders of the Civil War.* New York: Castle Books, 1956.

Joint Committee on the Conduct of the War Reports. Washington, D.C.: Government Printing Office, 1862–1866.

Keylin, Arleen, and Douglas John Bowen. *The New York Times Book of the Civil War.* New York: Arno Press, 1980.

Lewin, J.G., and P.J. Huff. *Witness to the Civil War: First-Hand Accounts from Frank Leslie's Illustrated Newspaper.* Irvington, N.Y.: Collins, 2006.

McClellan, George B. *McClellan's Own Story. The War for the Union, the Soldiers Who Fought It, the Civilians Who Directed It, and His Relations to It and to Them.* New York: Charles L. Webster, 1887.

_____. *Report on the Organization and Campaigns of the Army of the Potomac to Which is Added an Account of the Campaign in Western Virginia with Plans of Battle Fields.* New York: Sheldon & Company, Publishers, 1864.

McClure, Colonel Alexander K. *Abraham Lincoln and Men of War Times.* Philadelphia: Lippincott Publishing, 1892.

_____. *Lincoln's Yarns and Stories: A Complete Collection of the Funny and Witty Anecdotes that made Abraham Lincoln Famous as America's Greatest Story Teller.* Chicago: The John C. Winston Company, n.d.

Message of the President of the United States to the Two Houses of Congress at the Commencement of the Third Session of the Thirty-Seventh Congress. Vol. 4. Washington, D.C.: Government Printing Office, 1862.

Pease, Theodore C., and J.G. Randall. *The Diary of Orville Hickman Browning.* Vol. 1. Springfield, Il., Illinois State Historical Society, 1933.

Pinkerton, Allan. *The Spy of the Rebellion; Being a True History of the Spy System of the United States Army During the Late Rebellion, Revealing Many Secrets of the War Hitherto Not Made Public.* New York: G.W. Dillingham Co., Publishers, 1885.

Rhodes, James G. *History of the United States from the Compromise of 1850 to the McKinley–Bryan Campaign of 1896.* New York: Macmillan Books, 1919.

Rozwenc, Edwin C. *The Causes of the American Civil War.* Lexington, Mass.: D.C. Heath and Company, 1972.

Schuckers, J.W. *The Life and Public Services of Salmon Portland Chase.* New York: D. Appleton & Co., 1874.

Shaler, Nathaniel S. "Campaigns in Kentucky and Tennessee. Including the Battle of Chickamauga 1862–1864." *Papers Read to the Military Historical Society of Massachusetts.* Boston: Military Historical Society of Massachusetts, 1905.

Smucker, Samuel M. *The Life of Col. John Charles Frémont, and His Narrative of Explorations and Adventures in Kansas, Nebraska, Oregon, and California.* New York: The Memoir, Miller, Orton & Mulligan, 1856.

The Sons of the Sires; A History of the Rise, Progress, and Destiny of the American Party, and Its Probable Influence on the Next Presidential Election, to Which is Added a Review of the Letter of the Hon. Henry A. Wise Against the Know-Nothings. Philadelphia: Lippincott, Grambo & Co., 1855.

Stern, Philip Van Doren. *Secret Missions of the Civil War: First-hand Accounts by Men and Women Who Risked Their Lives in Underground Activities for the North and South.* Chicago: Rand McNally & Company, 1959.

Stonebraker, J. Clarence. *The Unwritten South: Cause, Progress and Result of the Civil War; Relics of Hidden Truth After Forty Years.* Hagerstown, Md.: Hagerstown Bookbinding and Printing Company, 1903.

Truesdale, John. *The Blue Coats, and How They Lived, Fought and Died for the Union, with Scenes and Incidents in the Great Rebellion.* St. Louis: Jones Brothers & Co., 1867.

Vallandigham, James L. *A Life of Clement L. Vallandigham.* Baltimore: Turnbull Brothers, 1872.

Victor, Orville J. *The History, Civil, Political and Military of the Southern Rebellion.* New York: J.D. Torrey, 1861.

The War of the Rebellion: A Compilation of the Official Records of the Union and Confederate Armies. Washington, D.C.: Government Printing Office, 1891.

Warden, Robert B. *An Account of the Private Life and Public Services of Salmon Portland Chase.* Cincinnati: Wilstach, Baldwin and Company, 1874.

White, Andrew Dickson. *Copperhead Minstrel: A Choice Collection of Democratic Poems and Songs, for the Usage of Political Clubs and the Social Circle.* Ithaca, N.Y.: Cornell University Library, 2007.

Wilson, Clyde N. *Calhoun's Economic Platform, in Slavery, Secession, and Southern History.* Charlottesville, Va.: University of Virginia Press, n.d.

Newspapers and Periodicals

Albany Argus, November 8, 1864.
Cincinnati Commercial, August 17, 1861.
The Daily Delta, April 13, 1861.

Democratic Standard, September 17, 1862.
Harpers Weekly: November 12, 1859; August 20, 1861.
Journal of Southern History 3 (1937): "Lincoln and Fort Sumter."
New York Illustrated News, April 20, 1861.
New York Tribune, November 9, 1860.
New York World, October 9–27, 1866.
The Old Guard Magazine 1, no. 2 (1861).

Secondary Sources
Books
Adams, James Truslow. *The March of Democracy: A History of the United States.* New York: Charles Scribner's Sons, 1965.
Belz, Herman. *Emancipation and Equal Rights: Politics and Constitutionalism in the Civil War Era.* New York: W.W. Norton, 1978.
_____. *Lincoln and the Constitution: The Dictatorship Question Reconsidered.* Fort Wayne, In.: Louis A. Warren Lincoln Library and Museum, 1984.
Benedict, Michael Les. *A Compromise of Principle: Congressional Republicanism and Reconstruction, 1863–1869.* New York: W.W. Norton, 1975.
Benson, Godfrey Rathbone. *Abraham Lincoln.* New York: Pocket Books, 1945.
Benton, Elbert J. *The Movement for Peace Without a Victory During the Civil War.* Cleveland, Oh.: The Western Reserve Historical Society, 1918.
Blair, William Alan. *A Politician Goes to War: The Civil War Letters of John White Geary.* University Park, Pa.: The Pennsylvania State University Press, 1995.
Bowman, John S. *The Civil War Almanac.* New York: World Almanac Publications, 1983.
Brandt, Nat. *The Man Who Tried to Burn New York.* New York: Berkley Books, 1990.
Broadwater, Robert P. *The Battle of Perryville: Culmination of the Failed Kentucky Campaign.* Jefferson, N.C.: McFarland, 2005.
_____. *From Beyond the Battlefields: Civil War Side Shows and Little Known Events.* Bellwood, Pa.: Dixie Dreams Press, 2004.
Brummer, Sidney David. *Political History of New York State During the Period of the Civil War.* New York: Columbia University Press, 1911.
Carnegie, Dale. *Lincoln the Unknown.* Hauppauge, N.Y.: Dale Carnegie & Associates, Inc., 1959.
Carwardine, Richard. *Lincoln: A Life of Purpose and Power.* New York: Alfred A. Knopf, 2003.
Catton, Bruce. *The Coming Fury.* Garden City, N.Y.: Doubleday & Company, Inc., 1961.
_____. *Terrible Swift Sword.* New York: Doubleday & Company, Inc., 1963.
Catton, William, and Bruce Catton. *Two Roads to Sumter.* New York: McGraw-Hill Book Company, 1971.
Clark, Victor S. *History of Manufactures in the United States.* 2 vols. New York: McGraw-Hill Carnegie Institution, 1929.
Coolidge, Olivia. *The Apprenticeship of Abraham Lincoln.* New York: Charles Scribner's Sons, 1974.
Coulter, K. Merton. *The Civil War and Readjustment in Kentucky.* Chapel Hill: University of North Carolina Press, 1926.
Cozzens, Peter, and Robert I. Girardi. *The Military Memoirs of General John Pope.* Chapel Hill: University of North Carolina Press, 1998.
Craven, Avery O. *Edmund Ruffin, Southerner: A Study in Secession.* Baton Rouge: Louisiana State University Press, 1966.
Crosby, Frank. *Life of Abraham Lincoln, Sixteenth President of the United States.* Philadelphia: John E. Potter, 1865.

Dabney, Robert L. *Defense of Virginia, and Through Her, of the South in Recent Pending Contests Against the Sectional Party.* New York: Negro Universities Press, 1969.

Davis, Burke. *The Civil War: Strange and Fascinating Facts.* New York: The Fairfax Press, 1960.

Davis, William C. *Brother Against Brother: The War Begins.* Alexandria, Va.: Time-Life Books, 1983.

_____. *First Blood: Fort Sumter to Bull Run.* Alexandria, Va.: Time-Life Books, 1983.

_____. *Look Away! A History of the Confederate States of America.* Old Tappan, N.J.: The Free Press, 2002.

_____ *The Orphan Brigade: The Kentucky Confederates Who Couldn't Go Home.* New York: Doubleday and Company, Inc., 1980.

Davis, William Watson. *The Civil War and Reconstruction in Florida.* New York: Columbia University Press, 1913.

Dennett, Tyler. *John Hay: From Poetry to Politics.* New York: Dodd, Mead & Company, 1934.

Denney, Robert E. *The Civil War Years: A Day-by-Day Chronicle.* New York: Gramercy Books, 1992.

Donald, David Herbert. *Inside Lincoln's Cabinet: The Civil War Diaries of Salmon P. Chase.* New York: Longmans, Green, 1954.

_____. *Liberty and Union: The Crisis of Popular Government 1830–1890.* Boston: Little, Brown & Company, 1978.

_____. *Lincoln.* New York: Simon & Schuster Books, 1995.

Filler, Louis. *The Crusade Against Slavery: 1830–1860.* New York: Harper & Row, Publishers, 1960.

Foner, Eric: *Free Soil, Free Labor, Free Men: The Ideology of the Republican Party Before the Civil War.* New York: Oxford University Press, 1970.

_____. *Reconstruction: America's Unfinished Revolution, 1863–1877.* New York: Harper Perennial Modern Classics, 2002.

Fried, Albert. *John Brown's Journey: Notes and Reflections on His America and Mine.* New York: Anchor Press/ Doubleday, 1978.

Glatthaar, Joseph T. *The March to the Sea and Beyond: Sherman's Troops in the Savannah and Carolina Campaigns.* New York: New York University Press, 1986.

Gragg, Rod. *Confederate Goliath: The Battle of Fort Fisher.* New York: Harper Collins Publishers, 1991.

Guide to the United States Congress. Washington, D.C.: Government Printing Office, 1971.

Halsey, Ashley, Jr. *Who Fired the First Shot?* New York: Fawcett Publications, Inc., 1963.

Hamilton, Holman: *Prologue to Conflict: The Crisis and Compromise of 1850.* New York: W.W. Norton & Company, 1964.

Hancock, Harold Bell. *Delaware During the Civil War: A Political History.* Wilmington, Del.: Historical Society of Delaware, 1961.

Handlin, Oscar. *Truth in History.* Cambridge, Mass.: Harvard University Press, 1979.

Hart, Charles Spencer. *General Washington's Son of Israel and Other Forgotten Stories of History.* Philadelphia: J.B. Lippincott Company, 1937.

Henry, Robert Selph. *The Story of the Confederacy.* New York: Grosset & Dunlap Publishers, 1936.

Higgins, Marguerite. *Jessie Benton Fremont.* Boston: Houghton Mifflin Company, 1962.

Higham, John. *Strangers in the Land: Patterns of American Nativism 1860–1925.* New York: Atheneum Books, 1975.

Hinsdale, Mary L. *A History of the President's Cabinet.* Ann Arbor, Mich.: George Wahr, 1911.

Holzer, Harold. *Lincoln at Cooper Union: The Speech That Made Abraham Lincoln President.* New York: Simon & Schuster, 2004.

Hughes, Richard T. *Bloody Knox , December 13, 1864: Clearfield County's Resistance to the Civil War and the Bloody Knox Saga.* Clearfield, Pa.: published by the author, 2004.

Hyman, Harold M. *A More Perfect Union: The Impact of the Civil War and Reconstruction on the Constitution.* New York: Oxford University Press, 1973.

_____. *Lincoln's Reconstruction: Neither Failure of Vision Nor Vision of Failure.* Fort Wayne, In.: Louis A. Warren Lincoln Library and Museum, 1954.

Jackson, Donald Dale. *Twenty Million Yankees: The Northern Home Front.* Alexandria, Va.: Time-Life Books, 1985.

Keller, Allan. *Thunder at Harper's Ferry: A Stirring Hour-by-Hour Account of John Brown's Raid.* New York: Ace Books, Inc., 1958.

Kelly, Alfred H., Winfred A. Harbison, and Herman Belz. *The American Constitution: A History.* New York: W.W. Norton, 1983.

Knoles, George Harmon. *The Crisis of the Union: 1860–1861.* Baton Rouge, La.: Louisiana State University Press, 1965.

Leech, Margaret. *Reveille in Washington: 1860–1865.* New York: Grosset & Dunlap, 1941.

Lewis, Lloyd. *Sherman: Fighting Prophet.* New York: Harcourt, Brace and Company, 1932.

Lobrano, Gustav S. *Samuel Jones Tilden: A Study in Political Sagacity.* Fort Washington, N.Y.: Kennikat Press, 1939.

Long, David E. *Jewel of Liberty: Abraham Lincoln's Re-Election and the End of Slavery.* New York: DaCapo Publishing, 1997.

Lorant, Stefan. *Lincoln: A Picture Story of His Life.* New York: Harper & Brothers, 1952.

Lynd, Staughton. *Reconstruction.* New York: Harper & Row, Publishers, 1967.

Madison, Lucy Foster. *Lincoln.* New York: The Hampton Publishing Company, 1928.

Martis, Kenneth C. *The Historical Atlas of the Congress of the Confederate States of America: 1861–1865.* New York: Simon & Schuster, 1994.

McKay, Ernest. *Henry Wilson: Practical Radical, a Portrait of a Politician.* Fort Washington, N.Y.: Kennikat Press, 1905.

McMaster, John Bach. *Our House Divided: A History of the People of the United States During Lincoln's Administration.* New York: Fawcett Publications, 1961.

McPherson, James M. *Battle Cry of Freedom: The Civil War Years.* New York: Ballantine Books, 1988.

Meyer, Howard N. *Let Us Have Peace: The Story of Ulysses S. Grant.* New York: Collier Books, 1966.

Miers, Earl Schenck. *Abraham Lincoln in Peace and War.* New York: American Heritage Publishing Company, 1964.

Milton, George Fort. *The Eve of Conflict: Stephen A. Douglas and the Needless War.* New York: Octagon Books, 1963.

Neely, Mark E., Jr. *The Fate of Liberty: Abraham Lincoln and Civil Liberties.* New York: Oxford University Press, 1991.

Nevin, David. *The Road to Shiloh: Early Battles in the West.* Alexandria, Va.: Time-Life Books, 1983.

New American Supplement to the New Werner Twentieth Century Edition of the Encyclopedia Britannica. Akron, Oh.: The Werner Company, 1905.

Newland, Samuel J. *The Pennsylvania Militia: Defending the Commonwealth and the Nation 1669–1870.* Anneville, Pa.: Commonwealth of Pennsylvania Department of Military and Veterans Affairs, 2002.

Parish, Peter J. *The American Civil War.* New York: Holmes & Meier Publishers, Inc., 1975.

Perret, Geoffrey. *Lincoln's War: The Untold Story of America's Greatest President as Commander in Chief.* New York: Random House, 2004.

Phillips, Ulrich B. *American Negro Slavery*. Baton Rouge, La.: Louisiana State University Press, 1969.

Potter, David M., *Lincoln and His Party in the Secession Crisis*. New Haven, Ct.: Yale University Press, 1942.

_____. *The South and the Sectional Conflict*. Baton Rouge: Louisiana State University Press, 1968.

Potter, John Mason. *13 Desperate Days: The Incredible Story of the Unsuccessful Assassination Attempt on the Life of President Abraham Lincoln in 1861*. New York: Ivan Oblensky, Inc., 1964.

Price, William H. *The Civil War Centennial Handbook*. Arlington, Va.: Prince Lithograph, Inc., 1961.

Priest, John Michael. *Before Antietam: The Battle for South Mountain*. Shippensburg, Pa.: White Mane Publishing Company, Inc., 1992.

Quarles, Benjamin. *Black Abolitionists*. New York: Oxford University Press, 1969.

Randall, J.G. *Midstream: Lincoln the President*. New York: Dodd, Mead and Company, 1953.

_____, and David Herbert Donald. *The Civil War and Reconstruction*. Lexington, Mass.: D.C. Heath and Company, 1969.

Randall, Ruth Painter. *Mary Lincoln: Biography of a Marriage*. Boston: Little, Brown and Company, 1953.

Ray, Delia. *A Nation Torn: The Story of How the Civil War Began*. New York: Lodestar Books, 1990.

Ray, Leonard M. *The Loyal War Governors' Conference at Altoona, Pennsylvania*. Altoona, Pa.: Blair County Historical Society, 1962.

Remini, Robert V. *Henry Clay: Statesman for the Union*. New York: W.W. Norton & Company, 1991.

Rhodes, James Ford. *History of the United States from the Compromise of 1850 to the Final Restoration of Home Rule at the South in 1877*. New York: The Macmillan Company, 1910.

Rothschild, Alonzo. *Lincoln, Master of Men: A Study in Character*. Boston: Houghton Mifflin Company, 1906.

Rowland, Thomas J. *In the Shadow of Grant and Sherman: George B. McClellan and Civil War History*. Kent, Ohio: The Kent State University Press, 1998.

Sandburg, Carl. *Abraham Lincoln: The Prairie Years and the War Years*. New York: Harcourt, Brace & World, Inc., 1954.

_____. *Abraham Lincoln: The Prairie Years and the War Years*. 3 vols. New York: Dell Publishing Company, 1962.

Schauffler, Robert Haven. *Lincoln's Birthday: A Comprehensive View of Lincoln as Given in the Most Noteworthy Essays, Orations and Poems, in Fiction and in Lincoln's Own Writings*. New York: Moffat, Tard and Company, 1909.

Shankman, Arnold M. *The Pennsylvania Antiwar Movement, 1861–1865*. Rutherford, N.J.: Fairleigh Dickinson University Press, 1980.

Simon, John Y. *General Grant by Matthew Arnold*. Carbondale, Ill.: Southern Illinois University Press, 1966.

Smith, Adam. *The Republican Party: A Photographic History of the GOP*. San Diego: Thunder Bay Press, 2003.

Sowell, Thomas. *A Conflict of Principles*. New York: William Morrow, 1987.

Stampp, Kenneth M. *The Era of Reconstruction: 1865–1877*. New York: Vintage Books, 1965.

Stern, Phillip Van Doren. *Prologue to Sumter: The Beginnings of the Civil War from the John Brown Raid to the Surrender of Fort Sumter*. Greenwich, Ct.: Fawcett Publications, 1961.

Swanberg, W.A. *First Blood: The Story of Fort Sumter.* New York: Charles Scribner's Sons, 1957.

Thomas, Benjamin P. *Abraham Lincoln: A Biography.* New York: Alfred A. Knopf, 1954.

_____, and Harold M. Hyman. *Stanton: The Life and Times of Lincoln's Secretary of War.* New York: Alfred A. Knopf, 1962.

Tyler, Alice Felt. *Freedom's Ferment: Phases of American Social History to 1860.* Minneapolis: The University of Minnesota Press, 1944.

Ward, Geoffrey C., Ric Burns, and Ken Burns. *The Civil War: An Illustrated History.* New York: Alfred A. Knopf, Inc., 1990.

Warner, Ezra J. *Generals in Blue: Lives of the Union Commanders.* Baton Rouge: Louisiana State University Press, 1964.

_____. *Generals in Gray: Lives of the Confederate Commanders.* Baton Rouge: Louisiana State University Press, 1959.

Weber, Jennifer L. *Copperheads: The Rise and Fall of Lincoln's Opponents in the North.* New York: Oxford University Press, 2006.

Williams, Kenneth D. *War Sentiment in Fayette County, Pennsylvania 1861–1865: A Research Project Submitted to the Faculty of the School of Graduate Study of California University of Pennsylvania in partial fulfillment of the requirements for the degree of Master of Arts.* Unpublished.

Williams, T. Harry. *Lincoln and His Generals.* New York: Gramercy Books, 2000.

_____. *Lincoln and the Radicals.* Madison: University of Wisconsin Press, 1960.

Willis, Garry. *Lincoln at Gettysburg: The Words That Remade America.* New York: Simon & Schuster, 1992.

Woldman, Albert A. *Lincoln and the Russians.* Cleveland: The World Publishing Company, 1952.

Woodward, C. Vann. *Reunion and Reaction.* New York: Doubleday Anchor Books, 1956.

Magazines and Periodicals

"America's Little Giant: Stephen A. Douglas." *Civil War Times Illustrated* 13, no. 1 (April 1974).

"The Anti-Lincoln Tradition." *Journal of the Abraham Lincoln Association* 4 (1982).

"Baltimore Street Riot, April 1861." *Civil War Times* 3, no.1.

Bray, Robert. "The Power to Hurt: Lincoln's Early Use of Satire and Invective." *Journal of the Abraham Lincoln Association* 16, no. 1 (1995).

Broadwater, Robert P. "The Curtin Rises." *State College Magazine* 18, no. 2 (February 2003).

Burlingame, Michael. "New Light on the Bixby Letter." *Journal of the Abraham Lincoln Association* 16, no. 1 (1995).

_____. "The Trouble With the Bixby Letter." *American Heritage Magazine* no. 4 (July/August 1999).

"Charles P. Stone and the Crime of Unlucky Generals." *Civil War Times Illustrated* 13, no. 7 (November 1974).

"The Civil War as a Constitutional Crisis." *American Historical Review* no. 69 (1964).

"The Civil War Need Not Have Taken Place." *Civil War Times Illustrated* 3, no. 10 (February 1965).

"The Court Martial of Fitz-John Porter." *Columbiad Journal* 2, no. 4 (Winter 1998).

Davis, William C. "John C. Breckinridge: A Personality Profile." *Civil War Times Illustrated* 6, no. 3 (June 1967).

"The Destruction of The Crisis." *Civil War Times Illustrated* 9, no. 8 (December 1970).

"The Election of 1864." *The Mississippi Historical Review* 18, no. 4 (March 1932).

"A Few Appropriate Remarks." *American History Illustrated* 23, no. 7 (November 1988).

"40 Acres and a Mule." *Civil War Times Illustrated* 40, no. 2.

"Francis W. Hughes and the 1862 Political Election." *Pennsylvania Magazine of History and Biography* 95 (1971).

"The Genius of Liberty and Northern War Disillusionment." *Confederate Veteran Magazine* 3 (1998).

"George B. McClellan: Little Mac." *Civil War Times Illustrated* 13, no. 2 (May 1974).

"The Great Copperhead Conspiracy of 1864." *Civil War Times Illustrated* 4, no. 3 (June 1965).

"Lincoln and War Powers. Commentary on papers by Prof. E. Berwanger and Dr. M. Neely, 10th annual Lincoln Symposium Feb. 12, 1983." *Journal of the Abraham Lincoln Association* 5 (1983).

"Lincoln as the Uncommon Common Man." *Civil War Times Illustrated* 1, no. 10 (February 1963).

"Lincoln in Crisis." *Civil War Times Illustrated* 39, no. 7 (February 2001).

"Lincoln's Construction of the Executive Power in the Secession Crisis." *Journal of the Abraham Lincoln Association* 27, no. 1 (2006).

"Lincoln's Special Session." *Civil War Times Illustrated* 10, no. 3 (June 1971).

Marvel, William. "Martyr Under the Microscope." *America's Civil War* 19, no. 5 (November 2006).

"Master Fraud of the Century." *American History Illustrated* 23, no. 7 (November 1988).

"The McClellan–Lincoln Controversy." *Civil War Times Illustrated* 5, no. 7 (November 1966).

Merrill, Louis Taylor. "Ben Butler in the Presidential Campaign of 1864." *The Mississippi Historical Review* 33, no. 4 (March 1947).

Neely Jr., Mark E. "The Lincoln Administration and Arbitrary Arrests: A Reconsideration." *Journal of the Abraham Lincoln Association* 5 (1983).

"The Problem of Lincoln's Political Thought." *Journal of the Abraham Lincoln Association* 10, no. 1 (1988–89).

Ramsdell, Charles W. "Lincoln and Fort Sumter." *Journal of Southern History* 3 (1937).

"Rebels From The Confederate State of Illinois." *Confederate Veteran Magazine* 6 (2000).

"Review Essay." *Journal of the Abraham Lincoln Association* 17, no. 2 (1996).

"The St. Louis Riots." *Civil War Times Illustrated* 2, no. 3 (June 1963).

Shenk, Joshua Wolf. "Uncovering the Real Abe Lincoln." *Time* 166, no. 1 (July 4, 2005).

Sibley, Joel H. "Always a Whig in Politics: The Partisan Life of Abraham Lincoln." *Journal of the Abraham Lincoln Association* 8 (1986).

"Story of the New York Draft Riots." *Civil War Times Illustrated* 4, no. 5 (August 1965).

Stutler, Boyd B. "An Eyewitness Describes the Hanging of John Brown." *American Heritage Magazine* no. 2 (February 1955).

"Two Generals Can Not Command This Army." *Columbiad Journal* 2, no. 1 (Spring 1998).

"The U.S. Supreme Court in the Civil War." *Civil War Times Illustrated* 1, no.10 (February 1963).

"We Cannot Have Free Government Without Elections: Abraham Lincoln and the Election of 1864." *Journal of the Illinois State Historical Society* (Summer 2001).

White, Johnathan W. "Canvassing the Troops: The Federal Government and the Soldiers' Right to Vote." *Civil War History* 50 (2004).

"Zachariah Chandler: I Have Done My Share." *Civil War Times Illustrated* 9, no. 3 (May 1970).

Zarefsky, David. "Public Sentiment Is Everything: Lincoln's View of Political Persuasion." *Journal of the Abraham Lincoln Association* 15, no. 2 (1994).

Index